OPEN SOURCE COOKING
THE NEW ERA OF COLLABORATION AND CONNECTIVITY

OPEN SOURCE COOKING
THE NEW ERA OF COLLABORATION AND CONNECTIVITY

EVOLUTION GAME CHANGER BAR ADMIRE INFLUENCES DRINK INSPIRATIONAL TRAVEL TRAINING CLARITY UNEXPECTED TRIBUTE MODERN PHOTO EXPERIMENTING PHILOSOPHY PASSION PERSPECTIVE TEACH COLLABORATE KNOWLEDGE REVELATION CUISINE INDUSTRY MENTOR STUDYING TRADITION CONNECTION PROCESSES FUNDAMENTALS FARM COCKTAIL LEARNING CHALLENGE IDEAS VALUES CONNECT EDUCATION TALENTS STAGE EXCITEMENT CHEF PERSONAL FRESH AMERICAN OUTLET LISTEN RESONATE STORY SPIRIT FLAVORS GROW IMPROVED RECIPE THIRSTY HUNGRY ASIA MENU WINE GENERATIONS REGIONAL SPAIN PROGRESSION

HOSTS

10 Years of ICC Photo Captions | Columns, left to right: Audrey Saunders and Dale DeGroff (2013); Masaharu Morimoto (2008); Cándido López, Antoinette Bruno, Joan Roca, and Will Blunt (2008); Antoinette Bruno, Elizabeth Falkner, and Gabrielle Hamilton (2010); Daniel Boulud (2011); George Mendes (2014); Alex Talbot, Nathan Myhrvold, and Johhny Iuzzini (2009); Will Blunt, José Andrés, and Antoinette Bruno; Jordan Khan, Grant Achatz, Wylie Dufresne, and Alex Stupak (2007); Susan Spicer and John Besh (2012); Dan Barber (2010); Paco Torreblanca, John Sconzo, and Juan Mari Arzak (2009)

CONGRESS BOOK
Caroline Hatchett
Editor
Irene Khan
Designer
Antoinette Bruno, Will Blunt, Sean Kenniff, Lisa Elbert, Korakot Suriya-arporn, Emily Bell
Contributing Editors
Megan Swann
Photography Editor
Elizaveta Ivanova
Illustrator

CONGRESS EVENT
Wilson Chung
Congress Director
Ebony Hurwitz
Events Manager
Rebecca Heisler
Presenter Coordinator
Sarah Lee
Event Coordinator
Martin Graves
Production Manager
Paul Repetti
Executive Chef
Phil Bey
Main Stage Executive Chef
Susanna Ok
Catering Kitchen Manager
Mark Diebus
Inventory Manager
Jessica Wurst
Evening Events Coordinator
Leigh Michelle Power
EAT@ICC Coordinator
Claire Bertin-Lang
MIX@ICC Director
Sara Moll
Crush@ICC Director
Sara Deljoo & Francesca Imgrüth
Trade Show Floor Coordinators
Lauren Danecek
Volunteer Coordinator
Rob Plonskier
Production Assistant

CONGRESS ADVISORY BOARD
José Andrés, Daniel Boulud, Josh DeChellis, Iacopo Falai, Traci Des Jardin, Wylie Dufresne, Elizabeth Falkner, Todd Gray, Johnny Iuzzini, Mourad Lahlou, Paul Liebrandt, Rick Moonen, Ken Oringer, Lex Poulos, Marcus Samuelsson, Audrey Saunders, Norman Van Aken, Jean-Georges Vongerichten

STARCHEFS
Antoinette Bruno, **CEO and Editor-in-Chief;** Will Blunt, **Managing Editor;** Evan Leventhal, **Director of Marketing;** Leah Hammerman, **Marketing Associate;** Maria Espina, **Marketing Associate;** Caroline Hatchett, **Editor;** Sean Kenniff, **Features Writer;** Lisa Elbert, **Editorial Assistant;** Wilson Chung, **Events Director;** Ebony Hurwitz, **Events Manager;** Megan Swann, **Photo Editor;** Irene Khan, **Designer;** Mary Choi, **JobFinder Account Executive;** Julia Abanavas, **Culinary Liaison;** Kerry Jepsen, Jessica Yoon, **Interns;** Bruno, **Canine Mascot**

PUBLISHED BY STARCHEFS
COPYRIGHT © 2015

All rights reserved, including the right to reproduce the book or portions thereof in any form whatsoever.

For information:
StarChefs
217 Havemeyer Street, 3rd floor
Brooklyn, NY 11211
212.966.3775

ISBN: 978-0-9846661-4-0

5

LETTER FROM THE EDITORS

In the beginning, it was "Yes, Chef!" But sometime around when Google, cell phones, and El Bulli really took off, a culture of closely held secrets and competition cracked wide open. In its place, grew global kitchen community. StarChefs first witnessed the change back in 2002, when we tagged along with José Andrés to Spain to attend Lo Mejor de la Gastronomía in San Sebastián.

Here we are more than a decade later, at the 10th Annual StarChefs International Chefs Congress, exploring the evolution of that camaraderie and its commitment to sharing with Open Source Cooking. If you've ever followed a great chef on Instagram, worked with someone on a pop-up, or taken menu inspiration from a line cook, you've taken part in The New Era of Collaboration and Connectivity.

"One of the best pieces of advice I've received was from Albert Adrià during a demo," says Main Stage Presenter and Pastry Chef William Werner. "I used to stress out that I had to own every recipe that I developed or conceptualized, but Albert credited his team—the ones who evolved them, perfected them, and put them into service."

In that very spirit, StarChefs singles out Spain—this year's host country—for its contributions to modern cuisine and for its chefs who have helped shape an industry, many from the ICC Main Stage. More than 15,000 of you have attended ICC in the past decade, making it the most important and anticipated industry event (and party) of the food year. Since 2006, John Sconzo and his team have tirelessly documented the spontaneous, the historic, and the lightening-strike moments that have happened at ICC. We share his photographs and StarChefs' favorite memories on pages 8 and 9.

Our hearts are full as we thank all of you for your constant, invaluable support. Together we're forging the future of the industry. This also wouldn't be possible without the unwavering support of our sponsors, including our founding sponsors, The Trade Commission of Spain, Vitamix, and Winston Industries. It's with their support that we can share **Open Source Cooking: The New Era of Collaboration and Connectivity**.

Antoinette Bruno
Editor-in-Chief

Will Blunt
Managing Editor

Smooth, Vibrant, Bold, Magnificent.

Spain, the number one producer of olive oil, offers the largest variety of unique oils that are as distinctive and diverse as nature itself. Explore them all and discover which ones are your favorites. Visit: www.oliveoilfromspain.com or e-mail: newyork@mcx.es

Homaro Cantu
In Memoriam: 1976 to 2015

The son of an engineer, Homaro Cantu was a scientist at heart. As a child, his innate curiosity drove him to repeatedly dismantle his father's lawnmower and chomp on $20 bills (an early experiment with edible paper, perhaps?). Like a scientist, Cantu wanted to know what made stuff work from the inside-out. His forum was food.

Cantu grew up in Portland, Oregon, and graduated from Le Cordon Bleu. He worked his way up the ranks in nearly 50 kitchens on the West Coast before moving to Chicago to work at Charlie Trotter's. Cantu spent four years in the iconic kitchen before finally leaving to open Moto, where he really began to play. With tasting menus longer than 20 courses, meals at Moto were more like epic journeys in taste. The menus themselves were printed on edible paper, ending up as garnishes for risotto or alphabet soup. Earning monikers like "Techno Chef," Cantu considered himself a cook at his core—one with nitrogen, helium, an ion gun, a polymer box (one of his many patented ideas), and even a class IV laser in his toolbox. "Gastronomy has to catch up to the evolution in technology, and I'm just helping that process along," he said. Cantu's aim was to shatter the rules of the dining table by introducing new technologies and enticing diners to embrace unimaginable edible creations.

He also dreamed of using fortified edible paper and the miracle berry (which makes unpalatable foods edible) to fight world hunger. It was a cause close to his heart, having been homeless for some years as a child. In 2014, after the death of his mentor Charlie Trotter, Cantu was instrumental in setting up the Trotter Project, a nonprofit culinary mentorship program for at-risk youth. Cantu had many other projects in the works, including a miracle berry café, a Cantu-style brewery, and a second cookbook. Tragically, Cantu died in April 2015. He is survived by his wife Katie McGowan and their two daughters. Gone too soon, Cantu transformed the notion of what a chef can be in the 21st century. His legacy endures through the countless men and women who trained and cooked in his visionary kitchens.

Photos provided by Alexander Plotkin, Jennifer M. Roberts-Rindskopf, John Sconzo, Mike Silberman, Mike Liu, Jeff Kraus, Lee Wolen, Eric WIlley, Giuseppe Tentori

Josh Ozersky

In Memoriam: 1967 to 2015

Josh Ozersky, aka Mr. Cutlets, was known in the restaurant community as a lover of all things meat, especially the hamburger. So who better than Mr. Cutlets himself to ghost write the biography of the hamburger? The Hamburger: A History was published in April 2009, cementing the author as a meat-lover's culinary historian.

Beyond his zestful carnivorousness, Ozersky was a prolific commentator. He wrote frequently about the vernacular of American cookery, and his culinary opinions, expositions, and exaltations ranged from food trucks to fine dining. The James Beard Award-winning food writer was the former restaurant critic for *Newsday*, national editor for Citysearch, founding editor of Grubstreet, and editor-at-large for *Esquire*. Ozersky also wrote for many other publications, including *The New York Times*, *The New York Post*, *Saveur*, *Time*, and *Details*. His books include Meat Me in Manhattan: A Carnivore's Guide to New York and Archie Bunker's America: TV in an Era of Changing Times.

Ozersky TV, the writer's eponymous food site, launched in 2009 and was home to an increasing array of short, zippy food-related videos about anything and everything—from the specific dynamics of a successful kitchen to the inimitable excellence of a well made roast beef sandwich. When he wasn't commenting on the state of cuisine, Ozersky worked on expanding the literary canon of American food iconography, whether hamburger or human. Ozersky's contribution to the culinary and literary worlds was cut short when he died in May 2014. He was just 47. Ozersky is survived by his wife Danit Lidor and all the chefs and meat lovers his work touched, and through whom his memory will live on.

Photos provided by The Cecil, Patrick McKee, Lee Kowarski, Bruce Bronster, Lee Kowarski,
Kristina Franziska Haas, Judiaann Woo/Travel Oregon, Sarah Abell, Veronica Rogov

Sasha Petraske

In Memoriam: 1973 to 2015

Sasha Petraske was a passionate speakeasy proselytizer back in the 1990s, way before the concept went mainstream. In 1999, with the founding of his landmark bar, Milk & Honey, on the Lower East Side, Petraske opened the doors to the new aesthetic and opened eyes to skillfully made pre-prohibition cocktails. At the time, he was still in his 20s, already influencing a generation of bartenders and drinkers by his sheer love of classic cocktails and historical sensibility. But Petraske was more than a businessman, leader, and beverage industry luminary. He was a husband, brother, son, and beloved member of the cocktail community—and since August of this year, deeply missed by many. Petraske died at just 42 years of age.

Petraske will be remembered for his wonderfully persnickety speakeasy concept: rules of conduct, a general reverent hush, limited membership thanks to a constantly changing phone number, and, oh yes, a list of beautifully, adeptly mixed cocktails. As it turns out, the "speakeasy trend" Milk & Honey inspired was not Petraske's intention. Those rules, and even the secret entrance, were in part in deference to the neighborhood. But the word of mouth turned into a roar and then a revolution as Petraske expanded the Milk & Honey concept to London; opened Little Branch, Middle Branch, and Attaboy in Manhattan; Dutch Kills in Queens.

Teaching was always an important part of Petraske's identity as a bartender. He founded the San Antonio Cocktail Conference, bringing a sophisticated cocktail conversation to a region that absolutely deserved (and thrived on) it. And while it's likely impossible to trace all of Petraske's influence—it grows like a massive family tree through the bartenders who've worked in his establishments—it's worthwhile to try. Whether you're drinking a Penicillin or simply enjoying a craft cocktail in a bar that takes itself seriously (but not too seriously), there's a solid chance you owe that liquid happiness to a man who changed the way we all gather and drink. To contribute to the causes that mattered most to Petraske, visit www.youcaring.com/sashapetraske.

Photos (left to right) provided by Sammy Ross, Audrey Saunders and Robert Hess, Jill and Dale DeGroff, Gabi Porter, Georgette Petraske, Gabi Porter, Georgette Petraske, Cervantes Ramirez, Sebastián Pinzón Silva courtesy of Eben Freeman

PHOTO: ALIZA ELIAZAROV

Jamie Bissonnette

Toro | New York, NY

Even as a child, Jamie Bissonnette was drawn to the kitchen, eschewing cartoons for cooking shows on the Discovery Channel. An early bloomer, Bissonnette earned his culinary arts degree from The Art Institute of Fort Lauderdale by 19 and spent his early 20s cooking and eating his way through Paris, San Francisco, and New York.

Road-tested and hungry to work, Bissonnette settled in Boston and began working in some of the city's most notable kitchens, including Peking Tom's, Pigalle, Andy Husband's Tremont 647, and Kenmore Square behemoth Eastern Standard. But it was Bissonnette's innate ease and curiosity with international cooking styles that made him a key player for Ken Oringer, who asked Bissonnette to head the kitchen at KO Prime at the Nine Zero Hotel in 2007. For his work, the *Improper Bostonian* named Bissonnette "Rising Star Chef" and KO Prime "Best New Restaurant."

After a successful two-year turn at KO, Oringer asked Bissonnette to open Spanish small plates restaurant Toro, where he earned a 2009 StarChefs Boston Rising Stars Award. Striking while the iron was very hot, the duo opened another small, neighborhood-style spot, Coppa, this time with Italian small plates, house-made pasta, and wood-oven pizza. In 2013, Oringer and Bissonnette ventured southward, opening a second iteration of Toro in the Chelsea neighborhood of New York City.

Bissonnette has been featured in *The Boston Globe*, *The Wall Street Journal*, *Bon Appétit*, *Edible Boston*, and on Instagram, sitting on the toilet reading his book, <u>The New Charcuterie Cookbook: Exceptional Cured Meats to Make and Serve at Home</u> (2014). In 2011, he was awarded *Food & Wines*'s first-ever "People's Choice Best New Chef," and in 2014, with his third nomination, Bissonnette took home the James Beard Award for "Best Chef, Northeast."

 JAMIEBISS

COOLEST TECHNIQUE YOU'VE LEARNED FROM ANOTHER CHEF: Louis DiBiccari of Tavern Road in Boston showed me his method for cooking octopus six years ago, and it blew my mind.

A DISH YOU MAKE THAT'S INSPIRED BY ANOTHER RESTAURANT: The seppia risotto at Toro NYC. We had a seppia risotto with orzo and cheese at Cucharo San Telmo in San Sebastián, Spain. Ours is a bit different, and I think theirs may be better, but I was never sober enough by the time I got there to remember exactly.

IF YOU COULD EAT AT ANY RESTAURANT IN THE WORLD TONIGHT, IT WOULD BE: Asador Etxebarri

FAVORITE INDUSTRY INSTAGRAM ACCOUNT: Definitely @chefjacqueslamerde

FAVORITE COOKBOOK: <u>La Technique: An Illustrated Guide to the Fundamental Techniques of Cooking</u> by Jacques Pépin

CHEF WITH WHOM YOU'D MOST LIKE TO COLLABORATE: Easy. Ken Oringer. We always have the most fun, and break rules. If I couldn't work with him, I've always wanted to cook with Matt Lambert of the Musket Room.

Richard Blais

Juniper & Ivy | San Diego, CA

Most chefs begin their cooking careers at humble establishments. Richard Blais is no exception. His first position in the kitchen was the fish station at McDonald's. Instead of holding him back, his fast food beginnings fast-forwarded him full-blast into a highly successful path as a chef. Blais studied at the Culinary Institute of America and worked between semesters at none other than The French Laundry, where he absorbed the meticulousness of a veritable culinary temple, alongside guys like Grant Achatz and Eric Ziebold. Graduating from the CIA in 1998, Blais went to work for the master of refined, modernized tradition, Daniel Boulud at his flagship Daniel.

Seasoned with tradition and technique, Blais went to Spain for a stage under Ferran Adrià at El Bulli. The technique-fueled fantasia of El Bulli bolstered Blais' hunger for something different, and ideally something his own. Heading to Atlanta in 2000, Blais briefly oversaw a local seafood concept before opening restaurant BLAIS and, eventually, restaurant consultancy group Trail Blais, the culinary think tank behind some of the city's most exciting concepts. Appearances on Bravo's "Top Chef"—and a victory on "Top Chef: All Stars"—as well as regular stops on the Food Network and his recently published Try This At Home cookbook, have kept Blais and his off-kilter imagination very much in the public eye. Currently, his restaurant repertoire includes multiple outposts of Flip Burger Boutique and The Spence in Atlanta, as well as Juniper & Ivy on the opposite coast in San Diego, California.

PHOTO: HEIDI GELDHAUSER

 **RICHARDBLAIS**

COOLEST TECHNIQUE YOU'VE LEARNED FROM ANOTHER CHEF: My pastry chef Brad has taught me how to make Cheez-Its in the microwave. Does that count?

A DISH YOU MAKE THAT'S INSPIRED BY ANOTHER RESTAURANT, CHEF, OR CULTURE: We have a burger that is inspired by In-N-Out. We always have an "homage" dish floating around. We also do a cold remixed version of Thomas Keller's Oysters and Pearls.

IF YOU COULD EAT AT ANY RESTAURANT IN THE WORLD TONIGHT, IT WOULD BE: Can I time travel? If so, I'd like to eat a meal from Escoffier. Maybe Fernand Point? Maybe Harvey's from Marco Pierre White, yeah the last one for sure.

FAVORITE INDUSTRY INSTAGRAM ACCOUNT: @chefjacqueslamerde, no question, brah.

CHEF WITH WHOM YOU'D MOST LIKE TO COLLABORATE: Jon Shook and Vinny Dotolo

José Andrés

minibar by josé andrés | Washington, D.C.

José Andrés has the career of most chefs' dreams —the kind that starts with a strong creative vision that somehow super-nova explodes into an empire of restaurants (17 concepts with an ever-growing number of locations), cookbooks, television appearances, and worldwide influence. The latest addition to his Think Food Group is vegetable-focused Beefsteak, the flagship of which opened spring 2015 in the Foggy Bottom neighborhood of Washington, D.C. But it all began in Mieres, Spain, where Andrés began cooking at an early age— baking with his mother at 8, composing dishes by 12, excelling in culinary school at 16, and apprenticing at El Bulli with Ferran Adrià.

Andrés moved to New York in 1990, decamped for D.C. not long after, and became chef and partner at Jaleo—the foundation of a partnership that became Think Food Group, a pioneer in high-concept, tradition-rich cuisine. From Café Atlántico and Zaytinya to minibar, TFG is prolific. The group has expanded to Puerto Rico, Miami, Las Vegas, and Los Angeles, where it opened the first SLS Hotel in Beverly Hills, and The Bazaar by José Andrés, which quickly earned the only four-star review from *The Los Angeles Times*.

Between a burgeoning restaurant empire and his own creative output, Andrés shines impossibly bright in the culinary world, and respect has been paid. He was named "Outstanding Chef" by the James Beard Foundation in 2011, and one of the 100 most influential people in the world by *Time*. Dean of the Spanish Studies program at the International Culinary Center in New York, Andrés makes frequent trips home to Spain to reconnect with family and food. Andrés also takes time to work with organizations like D.C. Central Kitchen and L.A. Kitchen on issues including hunger and food waste.

FROM MINIBAR TO BEEFSTEAK

Superstar Chef José Andrés returns to the ICC Main Stage to present the latest techniques and concepts from Think Food Group, a family of restaurants that spans the country and gamut of cuisine. From his modern flagship minibar to the group's new, vegetable-focused Beefsteak, the "what's next" of the industry begins and flourishes under the direction of Andrés.

Presented by Vitamix

 **CHEFJOSEANDRES**

MOST INFLUENTIAL MENTOR WITH WHOM YOU'VE WORKED: Ferran Adrià. He was always so generous with his knowledge. If he were the CEO of a pharmaceutical company, there would be no diseases in the world.

COOLEST TECHNIQUE YOU'VE LEARNED FROM ANOTHER CHEF: To never stop asking "why?" That's how progress is made.

A DISH YOU MAKE THAT'S INSPIRED BY ANOTHER RESTAURANT, CHEF, OR CULTURE: Last year my team and I collaborated with the Los Angeles Philharmonic and their Artistic Director Gustavo Dudamel to create a dish we call "Manhattan on Ice," inspired by the Leonard Bernstein suite from "On the Waterfront." It was to draw the beautiful connection between great food and great music. Inspired by American pop culture, our Philly Cheesesteak is another one where we took from outside influences. We transformed the popular meat and cheese sandwich into something whimsical and elegant, yet still worthy of America's attention. And last but not least, my liquid olives. Not inspired by another chef or restaurant—they are a pure copy of Ferran's from El Bulli, and proud of it!

IF YOU COULD EAT AT ANY RESTAURANT IN THE WORLD TONIGHT, IT WOULD BE: Casa Gerardo in Prendes, Asturias

FAVORITE INDUSTRY INSTAGRAM ACCOUNT: I love keeping up with friends like Anthony Bourdain, @anthonybourdain; Mario Batali, @mariobatali; and Andrew Zimmern, @chefaz on Instagram. It's also a great outlet for us to share our ideas and inspiration with each other.

FAVORITE COOKBOOK: I'll never stop loving the Oishinbo series, the comics about the epic search for the ultimate Japanese meal. Another book that has been very influential to me throughout my career is my first edition copy of The Philosophy of Taste by Brillat-Savarin, published in 1825. Brillat-Savarin was a visionary of his time when he wrote this, because back then philosophers didn't write a lot about food. His quote, "tell me what you eat and I will tell you what you are," is something I think of every single day. The Virginia Housewife by Mary Randolph is always a favorite because it is a tribute to my home, Spain. Originally published in 1824, its gazpacho recipe is living proof of just how far back the relationship goes between Spain and America.

CHEF WITH WHOM YOU'D MOST LIKE TO COLLABORATE: Albert Adrià. He is a genius. He is my brother, my teacher, my inspiration. The most important thing to remember when collaborating with someone is that you want to being doing it with people you love and admire, but you also have to be laughing while doing so. Friends like Ming Tsai and Ken Oringer taught me that.

PUMPKIN SEED OIL AND MANDARIN TART

Chef José Andrés of minibar by josé andrés | Washington, D.C.
Adapted by StarChefs
Yield: 24 servings

INGREDIENTS

Mandarin Reduction: (Yield: 1 cup)
500 grams mandarin orange purée
100 grams glucose syrup

Pumpkin Seed Oil: (Yield: 265 grams)
35 grams cocoa butter
230 grams pure Syrian pumpkin
   seed oil

Tart Shells:
Liquid nitrogen

To Assemble and Serve:
Liquid nitrogen
Maldon sea salt

METHOD

For the Mandarin Reduction:
In a pot, warm the mandarin purée and glucose syrup with just enough heat to dissolve the glucose. Decrease heat and gently reduce until it is the consistency of honey. Cool, cover, and refrigerate.

For the Pumpkin Seed Oil:
In 2 small saucepans, separately warm cocoa butter and pumpkin seed oil. When butter melts and oil reaches 35°C, remove pans from heat. Combine butter and oil in a shallow half hotel pan. Slide hotel pan into vacuum bag and seal, removing as much air as possible. Set aside at room temperature.

For the Tart Shells:
Place 2 tablespoons Mandarin Reduction into a small piping bag; refrigerate. In a small saucepan, warm Pumpkin Seed Oil to 40°C. Fill a 4-ounce cup with the Pumpkin Seed Oil, to just below the rim. Place a folded side-towel in a shallow half hotel pan, so that it covers the bottom. In a second half hotel pan, cover the bottom with a folded, flattened napkin. Into a bowl of liquid nitrogen, slide a small flower mold with a long narrow handle. Splash a little liquid nitrogen onto the side-towel and napkin to freeze, and place the second hotel pan (with the napkin) on top of the pan with the towel. Set an empty pint container next to the bowl of liquid nitrogen. Dip an offset spatula in the liquid nitrogen to freeze. Remove flower mold from bowl and gently blow on it to create a frost. Completely submerge mold in Pumpkin Seed Oil. Quickly remove, allowing excess to drip off. Use the offset spatula to push the tart out of the mold onto the frozen napkin. Repeat. When all the Pumpkin Seed Oil has been used, transfer pans with flower-shaped oil shells to the bottom of a freezer.

To Assemble and Serve:
Remove pan with Tart Shells from freezer. Cover a large service tray with cloth napkins, smoothing to flatten napkins. Arrange small, flat service spatulas on the tray. (This preparation may be done tableside.) Hit the tray with liquid nitrogen, freezing the napkin and spatulas. Using a dropper, carefully squeeze a large drop of Mandarin Reduction into center of each Tart Shell, and add a few flakes of sea salt. With a frozen spatula, transfer tarts to frozen napkin. Serve immediately.

Michel Bras

Restaurant Bras | Laguiole, France

Chef Michel Bras' resume is deceptively short and for one good reason: the master of "la cuisine du terroir" never left his territory. Unlike so many other chefs of his generation and caliber, Bras never found a good enough reason to leave his beloved Aubrac, France. There are no apprenticeships, no stages, no other restaurants to list under his name.

He was born in 1946 to a blacksmith father and chef mother, whose pots he helped tend at the family's hotel restaurant, Lou Mazuc. Though he never left the Lou Mazuc kitchen to train elsewhere, he studied culinary literature, philosophy, and photography with zeal. He cooked and created with intuition, as he does to this day. When Bras was 33, he inherited the inn from his parents. His innovative cooking caught the attention of famed French restaurant guide Gault et Millau, and Lou Mazuc was awarded two Michelin stars.

Bras' mission—"to create a restaurant in the middle of nature"—led him to open hotel restaurant Michel Bras in 1992. The modern structure of nearly all glass with slate and granite, sits on a plateau overlooking Aubrac. In 1999, Bras earned three Michelin stars for his work at his eponymous restaurant. In 2003, with his son beside him, restaurant Michel Bras became Bras Michel & Sébastien.

Bras is the author of several books, including the seminal 2002 cookbook Essential Cuisine, for which he took all the photos. Bras was the subject of the series "Inventing Cuisine: Michel Bras" by Paul Lacoste. He opened a second eponymous restaurant in the Windsor Hotel Toya in Hokkaido, Japan in 2002, and a brasserie within Musée Soulages in Rodez, France, just 20 miles from where he was born.

ESSENTIAL CUISINE ON THE HUDSON

This fall, the terroir of the Hudson Valley will have a new champion: Michel Bras, who'll bring his legendary (and for one day only, Hudson-inspired) Gargouillou salad to the ICC Main Stage. Witness first-hand as the father of naturalist cooking expounds on his legendary career and presents one of the world's most iconic dishes.

MOST INFLUENTIAL CHEF WITH WHOM YOU'VE WORKED: I am an autodidact. I never left my territory, my home. Tables (aka "restaurants") awoke the kitchen spirit within me. [Alain] Chapel for his approach to vegetables, and [Frédy] Girardet for his philosophy.

COOLEST TECHNIQUE YOU'VE LEARNED FROM ANOTHER CHEF: Nothing really. I trained only by myself by creating techniques that are personal.

A DISH YOU MAKE THAT'S INSPIRED BY ANOTHER CULTURE: I love the vegetables they cook in India. Yes, it is rather fatty, but it has a real spirit to it: There, the vegetable has always had its rightful place in the kitchen, far before our contemporary kitchen took over.

FAVORITE COOKBOOK: I don't have a favorite book, if not the last one I'm reading. I find inspiration in everyday life.

CHEF WITH WHOM YOU'D MOST LIKE TO COLLABORATE: Olivier Roellinger because he cooks the Sea, and I cook the Earth. Also, he is a very good friend, with whom I share the same human values.

GARGOUILLOU OF YOUNG VEGETABLES
Chef Michel Bras of Restaurant Bras | Laguiole, France
Adapted by StarChefs

Each season the garden, the market, and nature offer us lots of vegetables, herbs, leaves, and seeds. The gargouillou is a liberated marriage of different shapes, colors, and tastes. Choose according to what is available among perennial vegetables, root vegetables, fruits—the list is endless. Let your inspiration be your guide to make a Gargouillou that suits your taste.

INGREDIENTS AND METHOD

PERENNIAL VEGETABLES
asparagus, fiddleheads, hops, bryony ...
Remove the base of any stalks, as necessary, breaking them off or simply scraping them. Some of these vegetables are cooked in boiling salted water, others blanched. Refresh vegetables in cold water.

artichoke, cardoon ...
Remove all the leaves of the artichoke, retaining only the bottom. Remove the strings of the cardoons and cut into sections. Cook in a broth flavored with coriander seeds, orange zest, shallots, and a few drops of aromatic oil.

LEAFY VEGETABLES WITH FLOWERS
wild beet, blond and red orach, spinach, malabar spinach, new zealand spinach, good king henry spinach, lamb's quarter, comfrey, parsley ...
Remove the stems from most of these; when necessary remove the hard central stalk. Cook most of these leaves directly in butter or in oil. You can also cook them in boiling salted water.

cabbage, chinese cabbage, bok choy, french oxheart cabbage, brussels sprouts, mustard greens ...
Proceed in the same manner as above.

swiss chard, borage, pascal celery ...
Separate the greens from the stalks. Remove the strings from the stalks with a knife. Cook everything in boiling salted water. You can finish the cooking in some of the leftover roast juice.

buccos (a type of cabbage), broccoli rabe, cabbage shoot ...
Tie in little bunches. Cook in a large quantity of boiling salted water.

broccoli, cauliflower ...
Separate the florets from the stalks. Select the tender stalks, peel them, and cut into fine slices. Cook the tops and the stalks separately in boiling salted water. Refresh.

watercress, clover, geslu (a type of salad greens), ice plant, chickweed, salad of all colors and tastes ...
Remove the stems. These greens are usually eaten raw but some of them may be cooked.

BULBS
garlic, bear's garlic, rocambole garlic, shallots, small onions ...
Peel and blanch. Cook in boiling salted water or, better yet, in a broth flavored with coriander seeds, orange zest, wild thyme, and bay leaf with a few drops of aromatic oil. Or roast them in their skins.

chives, scallions, leeks, white onion ...
Sort and wash. Separate the white parts from the green. For better results, cook the two parts separately in water.

PHOTO: MICHEL BRAS

fennel ...
Remove the stalks, fronds, and membrane. You can use the bulb raw, cook it in water, or slowly in a little fat.

onions from cévennes, onions from lézignan ...
Peel. Oven-roasting the onions wrapped in aluminum foil is a very good way to cook these sweet onions.

ROOT VEGETABLES
carrots, turnips, turnip-root chervil, water parsnips, wild parsnips, parsley root, pink radishes, celeriac, jerusalem artichoke ...
Peel with a knife, leaving a short length of the tops on the smaller vegetables. Cut lengthwise with a knife or a mandolin, about ⅛ inch thick. Cook in boiling salted water. Then the parsley root and turnip-root chervil can be prepared in a purée.

beets, crapaudine ...
Even though these vegetables are usually eaten cooked, you can also eat them raw, either grated or sliced in a julienne.

black radishes, long or round; daikon ...
Rub with a brush to clean, and cut into very fine slices, ⅛ inch thick with a mandolin. You can cook them in butter.

celeriac, salsify, black salsify ...
Peel and cook in boiling salted water to which you have added a few drops of oil to prevent oxidization.

crosne, conopode ...
Clean by rubbing against one another with rock salt. Pan fry the crosne and use the conopode raw.

burdock, bellflowers, rampion
Scrape and use raw or cooked.

VEGETABLES WITH PODS
green beans, saint fiacre green beans, snow peas, snap peas ...
Snap off the stems, remove the strings, and cook in a large quantity of boiling salted water.

fava beans ...
Shell and cook in salted boiling water. Refresh. Peel the individual beans.

shell beans, flageolets, lentils, chickpeas, okra, soy beans ...
These vegetables are better if cooked slowly and for a long time with aromatic vegetables and herbs.

FRUITS
chayote, pattypan squash, summer squash, zucchini ...
Slice in very thin slices, ⅛ inch thick, and cook in boiling salted water or pan fry in a little oil.

cucumber ...
Clean and place in a drainer with salt for a few hours to release some of the water. Rinse and prepare with butter or aromatic oil.

red or yellow tomatoes ...
Blanch in boiling water and remove the skins. Remove the seeds and use raw or cooked.

green tomatoes ...
Peel with a knife, remove the seeds, and cook into a marmalade.

red, yellow, or green bell peppers
Oil the skin lightly and roast in a very hot oven. Remove the charred skin and preserve in oil.

pumpkin, hard squash ...
Peel the thick skin and prepare a purée.

FLAVORED PEARLS AND TOUCHES
cèpes
8 ounces cèpes
½ cup oil
¼ cup water
2 cloves garlic
10 coriander seeds
5 peppercorns
4 sprigs wild thyme
bay leaf
parsley
salt
juice of 1 lemon
This method can be used to prepare any kind of small, firm mushroom. Using a knife, scrape the stems of the mushrooms. Wipe the stems and the caps with a wet cloth. Plunge in boiling water for 30 seconds. Drain and refresh. Combine the oil, water, garlic, coriander, peppercorns, thyme, bay leaf, and parsley in a frying pan. Season with salt and simmer for 5 minutes. Add the mushrooms and simmer for 5 minutes more. Season with lemon juice and adjust the seasoning.

parsley oil
1 ounce parsley
¼ cup grapeseed oil
salt
To make things easier, make a bigger quantity and keep some of the oil for later use. Oil can also be prepared with chives, scallions, lovage, and other herbs. Wash the parsley, removing the longest stems. Mix the leaves with grapeseed oil and a pinch of salt. Macerate for 3 to 4 hours. Drain in a colander. This oil can be kept for a few days in a cool place.

COUNTRY HERBS
burnet, yarrow, and other plants ...
Flowers, and roots that can be picked in nature.

SPROUTS
A large quantity of seeds can be used for sprouting: cereal, cruciferous, leguminous, mucilaginous, oleaginous, umbelliferae—for example, alfafa, wheat, fenugreek, green soy beans, lentils, chickpeas. Sprouting has two phases: soaking and the actual sprouting. You can buy a seed tray, but you will also get good results using jars. The soaking time varies according to the type of seeds. For wheat and fenugreek, you need 10 to 12 hours; for green soybeans, lentils, and chickpeas, 12 to 24 hours. Place the seeds in jars and cover them with a good quantity of water. Place a square of netting over the jar opening and secure it with a rubber band.

After soaking, pour the water out and rinse the seeds. Tilt the jar 45 degrees, so that the opening is below the base. Cover the jar with a dark cloth. Rinse twice a day. The sprouts will be ready to eat in a few days. To get good germination, it is important to meet four conditions: The seeds must always be wet, warm, aerated, and in the dark. They can keep in a cool place, if they are rinsed regularly. Certain varieties of seeds can germinate in the light.

CRYSTAL LEAVES
herbs from the garden
vegetable leaves
aromatic oil
coarse grey sea salt
Wash the leaves in a large quantity of water, being careful not to crush them. It is preferable to blanch the vegetable leaves. Pat dry. Brush a drop of aromatic oil on each one and sprinkle with salt. Place on a tray lined with parchment paper. Slide into the oven. The leaves must be shiny, and as brittle as glass, with no change of color.

TO FINISH
country ham, vegetable broth, butter, cooked vegetables, raw vegetables, garden herbs, country herbs, sprouts, flavored pearls, and touches
Fry slices of country ham in a deep frying pan. Skim off the fat and deglaze with vegetable broth. Add a pat of butter; it will blend into the ham juice. Toss the vegetables to heat them. Place the vegetables on the plate, arranging them to give an impression of motion. Decorate with chopped garden herbs, country herbs, and sprouts. Play with flavored pearls and touches.

SPAIN ————————————

As the last century turned, so did the culinary world—toward Spain, unquestionably the new home of modern, open source cooking. Chefs such as Ferran Adrià, Juan Mari Arzak, Joan Roca, and Quique Dacosta forged an inventive post-modern cuisine. And they shared it, welcoming the world into the new era of collaboration and connectivity. At the 10th Annual ICC, StarChefs welcomes Spain as our honored host country with support from the Trade Commission of Spain and Tourist Office of Spain with the regions of Madrid and Valencia.

Discover OUR *gastronomy*

Mediterranean diet:
Intangible Cultural
Heritage of Humanity

Photo: Socarrat d'arròs a banda-Quique Dacosta

       regionofvalencia.com

January 23rd
February 7th
2016

Gastronomy for the Five Senses

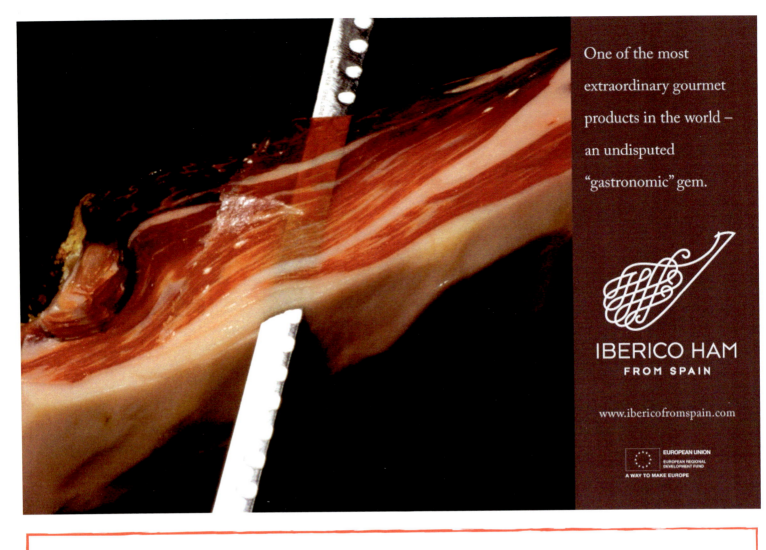

One of the most extraordinary gourmet products in the world – an undisputed "gastronomic" gem.

IBERICO HAM
FROM SPAIN

www.ibericofromspain.com

EUROPEAN UNION
EUROPEAN REGIONAL
DEVELOPMENT FUND
A WAY TO MAKE EUROPE

SPAIN, LAND OF 100 CHEESES

CHEESE ™
FROM SPAIN

FOODS FROM SPAIN | TRADE COMMISSION OF SPAIN
405 Lexington Ave. 44th fl. New York NY 10174-4499 Tel: 1.212.6614959 E-mail: newyork@mcx.es cheesefromspain.com

Quique Dacosta

Quique Dacosta | Dénia, Spain

Quique Dacosta was born in Jarandilla de la Vera, Extremadura, Spain. At 14, he was just a kid working in a pizzeria with a growing penchant for food. Reading cookbooks, mostly French, helped stoke his interest in cuisine. By 18, Dacosta was visiting some of Spain's best restaurants, unwittingly treading the ground that would become his professional home. Eventually, he began working in the restaurant that would later become his own, El Poblet in Dénia (today known as Quique Dacosta Restaurante). There, on the southeastern coast of Spain, near Valencia, he cooked regional cuisine that began to evolve into something more local and maritime. As Dacosta came to the fore of the restaurant, its outlook changed from casual-local to hyper, poetically local, forging a new era for Valencian cuisine in the late 80s and early 90s. He officially took over the restaurant in 1999 and changed its name in 2008.

In form and content, Dacosta's progressive food emphasizes nature, and has been called a kind of "plant cuisine" that reflects the fleeting flora and fauna of his environment. But the perspective that guides it is global, modern, and comprehensive. No surprise, it's garnered Dacosta (man and restaurant) years of recognition, from a 2004 "Chef of the Year" award from Lo Mejor de la Gastronomía and the Cándido Foundation's Creativity Prize for Dacosta's techno-poetic culinary style to regular placement on San Pellegrino's "50 Best" list and a 2009 induction into the Cookbook Hall of Fame by the Gourmand World Cookbook Awards (essentially the "Oscars" of cookbooks) for his third, eponymous, cookbook. He earned a third Michelin star in 2012.

MOODS. QUIQUE DACOSTA.

Valencian Chef Quique Dacosta is a flag-bearer for the modern, molecular, multi-sensory dining that put Spanish cuisine on the map. In his return to the ICC Main Stage, Dacosta will demonstrate his techno-emotional cooking with a focus on the fleeting flora and fauna of Valencia.

Presented by Trade Commission of Spain and Tourist Office of Spain with the region of Valencia

PHOTO: SUSANA MARTINEZ

 QIQEDACOSTA

CLASSIC VALENCIAN DISH CHEFS MUST TRY WHEN THEY VISIT THE REGION: Authentic paella. When cuisines travel, dishes tend to become distorted. Getting to know the universe of rice in Valencia is highly interesting.

VALENCIAN PRODUCT MOST ESSENTIAL TO YOUR COOKING: Vegetables. Seventy percent of them are grown within 80 kilometers of the restaurant—from the sea, mountains, natural parks, and one of the most important agricultural regions in Europe.

VALENCIAN PRODUCT CHEFS MAY NOT KNOW ABOUT: Flamed, semi-dry octopus; mujol roe; and tonyina de sorra (a tuna dish). Plants such as cat's claw are exclusive. In my opinion, the red shrimp in Dénia's Mediterranean Sea are the best in the world.

ESSENTIAL VALENCIAN RESTAURANTS TO VISIT: In the rice tradition: Casa Carmela and Casa Salvador. In Alicante: Casa Elías, next to Paco Gandia. For creative cuisine: La Finca, in Elche. Camarena in Valencia, next to Poblet. And in Dénia, obviously, Quique Dacosta Restaurante. Today, with these rices, you can understand the past, present, and future of this region.

EGG IN ASHES

Chef Quique Dacosta of Quique Dacosta | Dénia, Spain
Adapted by StarChefs
Yield: 12 servings, 45°C

INGREDIENTS

Egg Shell Molds:
12 large eggs

Gelatinous Chicken Broth:
1 kilogram smoked bacon from
    acorn-fed hogs in Extremadura,
    thinly sliced
665 grams mirepoix
200 grams thinly sliced red onion
200 grams sliced leek, white part only
2 cloves Pedroñeras red garlic,
    crushed and peeled
2 kilograms chicken scraps from
    free-roaming chickens
50 grams Cognac
50 grams dry white wine
3 liters mineral water
500 grams poultry broth
4 sheets gelatin, bloomed

"Egg Shell" and "Asparagus Egg":
500 grams cooked white asparagus,
    puréed, warmed to 70°C
2.5 grams agar agar
Mineral water
Sunflower oil, chilled

Solidified Truffle Juice:
500 grams black truffle juice
8 grams agar agar

Crunchy Truffle Rice Powder:
1½ liters mild chicken broth
100 grams dried black trumpet
    mushrooms, rehydrated in water
275 grams Senia rice
100 grams finely chopped black truffle
200 grams black truffle juice
Sunflower oil
Powdered salt

Truffle Juice Rocks:
150 grams mineral water
60 grams tapioca flour
350 grams black truffle juice
33 grams egg white powder

Smoked Maltodextrin:
Orange peels
50 grams maltodextrin
50 grams of chamomile-infused
    extra virgin olive oil
25 grams toasted rice bran
Salt

PHOTO: PELUT I PELAT

Fried Quinoa:
500 grams chicken broth
75 grams quinoa
1 liter sunflower seed oil

Kadayif Strands:
120 grams raw kadayif pastry dough strands
1 gram sel gris

To Assemble and Serve:
Zest of 1 orange

METHOD

For the Egg Shell Molds:
Using circular scissors, cut eggs open and drain, reserving yolks and setting aside whites for another purpose. Thoroughly rinse shells and set aside to dry.

For the Gelatinous Chicken Broth:
Prepare a blonde chicken stock. Strain and reduce to half its volume. Cool overnight and discard fat from the surface. Warm and add bloomed gelatin, and cool to pouring consistency. Place Egg Shell Molds on a stable base. Pour Gelatinous Chicken Broth broth into empty shells, until two-thirds full. Add a reserved yolk to center of broth, gently jiggling the shell so the yolk rises to surface of the broth. Completely cover the yolk with more broth. Repeat with remaining shells. Refrigerate at least 2 hours, until broth gels and "eggs" reach 4°C.

For the "Egg Shell" and "Asparagus Egg":
To a blender, add hot asparagus purée. Blend while slowly adding agar agar. When agar has dissolved and combined with asparagus, transfer to a container at least 3 inches deep; let mixture come to room temperature. Under gently running cold water, peel Egg Shell Molds from gelled Gelatinous Chicken Broth. Submerge peeled "eggs" in asparagus mixture. Move eggs slightly every 3 minutes, so they don't stick to the bottom of the container, for 12 total minutes. The juices from the gelatinous asparagus purée will uniformly gel on the eggs, creating a new, edible shell. Carefully remove eggs from asparagus bath and rinse excess asparagus juice from the new shell with mineral water. Gently pat dry. Set eggs aside in cold sunflower oil; keep cool.

For the Solidified Truffle Juice:
In a small saucepan, combine half the truffle juice and agar agar and bring to a simmer. Remove from heat and shear the gelled mixture in the pan. Add remaining truffle juice, stirring thoroughly to combine. Pour into a compact mold and allow to set at room temperature.

For the Crunchy Truffle Rice Powder:
In a saucepan, combine broth and drained mushrooms. Bring to a boil, add rice, reduce heat to medium, and cook, stirring constantly, until rice is overcooked and becomes a paste. Remove from heat, add truffle and juice, and transfer to blender; purée. Line a sheet tray with wax paper, and spread mixture as thinly as possible. Dry at 46°C for 6 hours. Break dried rice sheet into pieces, and place in blender. Pulse to a coarse powder. Spread back onto tray. Allow to set at room temperature, uncovered, for at least one night. In a deep fryer, heat sunflower oil to 186°C. Using a fine strainer or fry-basket, fry powder. Drain on paper towels. Season with powdered salt. Keep hot, uncovered.

For the Truffle Juice Rocks:
In a saucepan, combine water and tapioca. Bring to a boil, stirring constantly until paste forms. Transfer pan to ice bath, add truffle juice and egg white powder, and stir to combine. When chilled, cover and refrigerate 6 hours. Heat oven to 120°C. Transfer mixture to bowl of stand mixer fitted with whisk, and whip to consistency of meringue. Transfer to a piping bag. Line a sheet tray with wax paper. Pipe small balls of mixture onto paper. Bake 1 hour. Reduce heat to 60°C and bake 4 hours more. Keep hot, uncovered.

For the Smoked Maltodextrin:
Prepare smoker with orange peels. Into a bowl with the maltodextrin, slowly whisk oil in a steady stream. The mixture should be loose and powdery. Whisk in bran and salt. Cold smoke mixture to desired depth of flavor. Let sit at room temperature, uncovered.

For the Fried Quinoa:
In a saucepan, combine broth and quinoa. Heat until just about to boil, reduce heat, and simmer rapidly for 45 minutes; drain. Heat oven to 65°C. Spread quinoa onto sheet tray and dry in oven. In a separate saucepan, heat sunflower oil to 180°C. Fry dried quinoa until crisp. Drain on absorbent paper; let cool. Transfer to bowl with half the Smoked Maltodextrin and toss to combine; reserve.

For the Kadayif Strands:
Heat oven to 120°C. On a sheet tray, spread kadayif and bake 20 minutes; let cool. Sprinkle remaining Smoked Maltodextrin over Kadayif Strands. Season with salt.

To Assemble and Serve:
Prepare a smoking gun with orange zest. Bring Asparagus Eggs to room temperature. In a serving box, make a nest of Crunchy Truffle Rice Powder, Truffle Juice Rocks, and Fried Quinoa. Heat the water bath of an immersion circulator to 62°C; warm egg in bath for 12 minutes. Remove egg from bath, dry thoroughly, and place in middle of the nest. With a microplane, grate solidified Truffle Juice over top, and garnish with additional Fried Quinoa. Place Kadayif Strands around the egg. Cover box, leaving lid slightly askew. Fill box with smoke, secure lid, and serve.

Mario Sandoval

Coque | Madrid, Spain

Sense, memory, landscape, and reinvention define Spanish Chef Mario Sandoval's cuisine. Sandoval was born in 1977, but the restaurant that he would eventually helm and usher into prominence, Coque, was birthed by his grandparents more than 20 years before.

Sandoval grew up steeped in food tradition. He studied cooking at the Superior School of Restaurant and Kitchen Management of Madrid, and staged around Spain and France. He took over the reins of Coque from his father in 1999, and began taking the establishment in a more avant-garde direction through intense research, experimentation, and the mining of local foodways. Coque's wood-fire oven, gardens, and farmland, and Sandoval's progressive tasting menus are all contributing factors to the restaurant's rapidly rising profile. Today, meals at Coque—guided by Sandoval brothers Diego (manager) and Rafael (head sommelier)—begin in the wine cellar with cocktails and snacks, then move through the kitchen for apéritifs, progressing to the dining room, and come to a finale in the dessert lounge.

In 2004, the restaurant received its first Michelin star, and the Sandovals opened event space, La Romaneé, and bakery, Dulcemanía. Since then, Dream Food and Food Concept catering companies have been added to the family business, as well as El Bistró de Sandoval.

Sandoval has written five cookbooks, and is the originator of the field of study "Gastrogenómica," which aims to recover nearly lost species of fruits and vegetables native to the province of Madrid by studying their DNA. He also is the founder of Dream Food Innovación y Gastronomía, focused on food research and the development of restaurant infrastructures. In 2013, Sandoval was elected president of the Spanish Chefs and Pastry Chefs Federation, and was nominated for "Best Chef" by the Spanish Royal Academy of Gastronomy.

MADRID, UPDATED

Mario Sandoval is forging a new identity for cuisine in Madrid, and he's celebrating it on the ICC Main Stage. At 26, Sandoval (a student of Gallego, Arzak, and Adrià) was the youngest chef ever to receive a Michelin star for his cooking at Coque, just outside of Spain's capital. In the years since, he has pushed to develop a style that is wholly indebted to its home region, one that's rooted in tradition and terroir.

Presented by Tourist Office of Spain and the region of Madrid

 CHEFSANDOVAL CHEFMSANDOVAL

CLASSIC DISHES CHEFS MUST TRY WHEN VISITING MADRID: Callos and cocido (chickpea stews with tripe and pork, respectively), partridge escabeche, soldadito de Pavía (battered and fried cod snacks), suckling pig, rosquillas (donuts), and barquillos (cigarette cookies)

REGIONAL PRODUCTS CHEFS MAY NOT KNOW ABOUT: Changlot Real de la Vega Carabaña extra virgin olive oil; veal from Sierra de Guadarrama; Sierra de Madrid rosemary honey; blue foot mushrooms, Villaconejos melons, and asparagus and strawberries from Aranjuez

ESSENTIAL RESTAURANTS TO VISIT IN MADRID:
Paco Roncero's La Terraza del Casino, David Muñoz's DiverXO, Sergi Arola's Gastro, Ramón Freixa's eponymous Ramón Freixa, and Diego Guerrero's DSTAgE

HOW MADRID'S RESTAURANT SCENE EVOLVED SINCE YOU STARTED COOKING: It has radically changed thanks to Madrid Fusión and with the new values of innovators, who are making food that is more modern and versatile for the public.

TOSTA DE IBÉRICOS

Chef Mario Sandoval of Coque | Madrid, Spain
Adapted by StarChefs
Yield: 4 servings

INGREDIENTS

Bread:
50 grams milk
10 grams sugar
100 grams flour, plus additional for dusting
20 grams eggs, beaten
10 grams butter, softened
Thyme leaves
Oregano
Ground cinnamon

Caramelized Onions:
30 grams extra virgin olive oil
100 grams julienned onion
20 grams sugar
40 milliliters red wine

Steak Tartare:
200 grams veal sirloin, finely chopped
10 grams Spanish extra virgin olive oil
30 grams pasteurized egg yolk
Salt
Black pepper
Worcestershire sauce
Tabasco
Maille whole grain mustard

Pluma Ibérian Ham:
250 grams Pluma Ibérian pork
Salt
Pepper
Spanish extra virgin olive oil

To Assemble and Serve:
Maldon sea salt
Baby shoots

METHOD

For the Bread:
In the bowl of a stand mixer fitted with a spiral hook, combine milk, sugar, flour, egg, and butter. Mix until dough comes together. Let rest 24 hours. Heat oven to 200°C. On a floured work surface, roll out dough to ⅛-inch thick. Sprinkle with herbs and ground cinnamon to taste. Cut with an oval biscuit cutter and bake on a parchment lined sheet pan for 10 minutes. Cool on a rack.

For the Caramelized Onions:
In a sauté pan over medium-low flame, heat olive oil. Add onion and slowly cook until browned. Add sugar and red wine, and cook to a syrupy consistency. Remove from heat and set aside.

For the Steak Tartare:
In a bowl, combine veal, olive oil, and egg yolk, and season with the rest of the ingredients. Cover and set aside.

For the Pluma Ibérian Ham:
Season pork with salt, pepper, and a drizzle of olive oil. Heat olive oil in a sauté pan over medium-high flame. Sear pork until browned on all sides. Remove from heat and rest. Trim pork until it resembles the shape of the Bread, and then thinly slice.

To Assemble and Serve:
Spread a layer of Steak Tartare onto a piece of Bread. Cover with Caramelized Onions and top with sliced Pluma Ibérian Ham. Season with sea salt and garnish with baby shoots.

Featured Ingredients: Spanish extra virgin olive oil and
Fermin pluma Ibérica bellota
Featured Equipment: Hobart mixer

VINAGRE DE JEREZ,
THE AUTHENTIC
SHERRY VINEGAR FROM SPAIN

VINAGRE DE JEREZ
DENOMINACIÓN DE
ORIGEN PROTEGIDA

www.vinagredejerez.org

Larry Forgione

Conservatory for American Food Studies | St. Helena, CA

Born on Long Island in 1952, Chef Larry Forgione, "Godfather of American Cuisine" graduated from the Culinary Institute of America in 1974. Beginning his career under Chef Michel Bourdin at the Connaught Hotel in London, England, he became the first American chef to be awarded a "Mention of Honor from Prix Pierre Tattinger" in Paris. He was also a silver medalist in the British Culinary Olympics. An extremely promising start fueled Forgione as he returned to the United States in 1977 and turned his focus to American cuisine. Forgione worked as executive chef at New York's El Morocco, Regine's, and The River Café. In 1982, well before "farm-to-table" had any caché, Forgione and Justin Ruskin founded American Spoon Foods in Petosky, Michigan, to grow fresh produce for Forgione's menu.

In 1983, Forgione opened An American Place in New York City, which was not only featured heavily in the influential "Great Chefs" series, but earned Forgione the James Beard Foundation's "America's Best Chef" Award and the CIA's "Chef of the Year" title, all in 1993. And his An American Place Cookbook was awarded the James Beard Award for "Best American Cookbook. Forgione is a founding trustee of the James Beard Foundation, helped start the CIA's externship program, and is a founder of the Fresh Start program, as well as Citymeals-on-Wheels' Cheftopia, an annual fundraiser and tribute to James Beard.

Most recently, and appropriately, the "Godfather" finds himself at the helm of the CIA's Conservatory for American Food Studies and its Farm-to-Table Cooking curriculum. Forgione is both co-founder and culinary director of the Conservatory, leading students through their farm-to-table studies and guiding their hands-on experience at The Conservatory at Greystone, the student-led restaurant open to the public.

MOST INFLUENTIAL MENTOR WITH WHOM YOU'VE WORKED: Michel Bourdin as someone I worked with, but James Beard is the person I call my mentor and friend. They were both incredibly generous with their time, knowledge, and believing in me.

A DISH YOU MAKE THAT'S INSPIRED BY ANOTHER RESTAURANT, CHEF, OR CULTURE: Over the years, there have been so many inspirations from our own culinary history: cedar planked salmon, original Native American "polenta," crisp soft belly clams, cod cheeks, whitebait, etc. They're all are fairly common, but not so until I popularized them in the late 70s and early 80s.

IF YOU COULD EAT AT ANY RESTAURANT IN THE WORLD TONIGHT, IT WOULD BE: Toss up between one of Marc's or Bryan's restaurants

FAVORITE INDUSTRY INSTAGRAM ACCOUNT: What is Instagram?

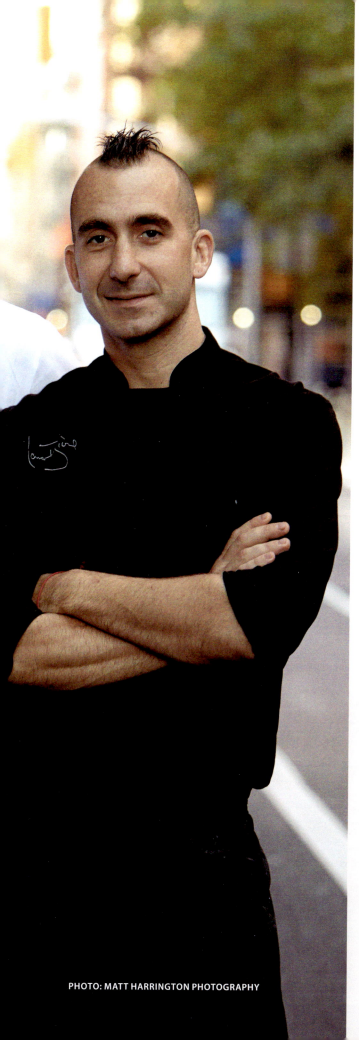

Marc Forgione
Marc Forgione | New York, NY

When Marc Forgione began asking his famous father for money as a teenager, dad insisted he work for it. So the kitchens where Forgione used to toddle around as a youngster, including the iconic An American Place, became the testing grounds of his young adulthood. Forgione (the younger) spent college summers working the line, and after earning a degree in hotel and restaurant management, he returned to work briefly for his father before going to work for Patricia Yeo at AZ, Pino Maffo at Pazo, and Laurent Tourondel at BLT Steak.

Forgione then sent himself to France. With posts in three of Michel Guérard's top restaurants, Forgione got more than a lesson in French discipline, he came away with a deeper relationship with the ingredients and a sense of humility in the kitchen that still informs his perspective today. After working again for Tourondel, who entrusted him to oversee the opening of many BLT outlets as corporate chef, Forgione finally opened his own place, Marc Forgione.

The restaurant earned many accolades, including a Michelin star in its first year and a second in 2011, and Forgione was named a StarChefs Rising Star in 2010. With his victory in season three of "The Next Iron Chef" and the opening of his steakhouse, American Cut, Forgione has solidified his own place as an independent force in American cuisine. In summer 2013, Forgione opened his third New York restaurant, the Southeast Asian-inspired Khe-Yo in Tribeca.

FATHER-SON OPEN SOURCE

Together on the ICC Main Stage, Chefs Larry Forgione and Marc Forgione will explore the roots and future of farm-to-table cooking in America. They'll present side-by-side venison dishes that chronicle the evolution of the American palate through a single bloodline.

Presented by Front of the House

 MARCFORGIONE MARCFORGIONE

COOLEST TECHNIQUE YOU'VE LEARNED FROM ANOTHER CHEF: I don't know who the first chef was to use "meat glue," but it's certainly become a cool way to keep shapes and sizes together in different types of meats. So, to whoever that is, thank you.

A DISH YOU MAKE THAT'S INSPIRED BY ANOTHER CULTURE: My chili lobster is my interpretation of Singapore's famous chili crab.

IF YOU COULD EAT AT ANY RESTAURANT IN THE WORLD TONIGHT, IT WOULD BE: I'm dying to try Mugaritz.

FAVORITE COOKBOOK: Essential Cuisine by Michel Bras was my first favorite cookbook.

CHEF WITH WHOM YOU'D MOST LIKE TO COLLABORATE: I'd love to light a fire and cook something outside with Francis Mallman.

CURED VENISON, WILD MUSHROOM TEA, FERMENTED CABBAGE, AND PICKLED MUSTARD SEEDS

Chef Marc Forgione of Marc Forgione | New York, NY
Adapted by StarChefs
Yield: 4 servings

INGREDIENTS

Fermented Cabbage:
2½ pounds cabbage, finely chopped
1½ tablespoons sea salt
8 ounces grated horseradish

Cured Venison:
1 tablespoon wild juniper berries
1 teaspoon coriander seeds
1 teaspoon cinnamon
Peel of 1 orange
1 teaspoon pink salt
2 tablespoons kosher salt
1 tablespoon brown sugar
One 5-ounce venison loin, trimmed

Mushroom Tea:
3 cups water
2 sprigs thyme
1 bay leaf
Sea salt
Black pepper
1 pound hen of the woods mushrooms, cut into 1-inch pieces
2 tablespoons extra virgin olive oil
4 ounces matsutake mushroom scraps
1 tablespoon low-sodium soy sauce

Pickled Mustard Seeds:
¾ cup water
1½ cups white wine vinegar

2½ tablespoons sugar
1 teaspoon turmeric
1½ tablespoons kosher salt
1 cup mustard seeds

To Assemble and Serve:
1 tablespoon wild juniper berries
1 teaspoon coriander seeds
1 orange peel
1 teaspoon-size piece of a cinnamon stick
Small wild juniper branches
Smoked olive oil
4 matsutake mushrooms, cleaned, trimmed, stems peeled, sliced thinly on a mandolin

METHOD

For the Fermented Cabbage:
In a large bowl, combine cabbage and salt. Add horseradish and mix well. Transfer to a cambro, cover with plates, and weigh down with a brick or heavy can. Cover with a clean towel. Press down periodically to force out the water from the cabbage, until the brine rises above the plates, about 24 hours total. Store the container in a dry, cool area. A little mold may appear on the surface. If this happens, skim off as much as you can. The cabbage will be done after about a week of fermentation.

For the Cured Venison:
In a bowl, combine juniper, coriander, orange, salts, and sugar. Season venison with the mixture and seal in a vacuum bag. Refrigerate overnight. Remove venison from bag and rinse under cold water. Pat dry with paper towels. With a meat slicer, cut venison into ⅛-inch thick slices.

For the Mushroom Tea:
In a medium saucepan with an insert for steaming, combine water, thyme, bay leaf, and 1 pinch salt. Top with insert and place mushrooms inside. Bring to a boil, cover, and steam mushrooms for 10 minutes. Remove steamer from heat. Discard mushroom pieces. Using a chinois, strain liquid into a saucepan and simmer until reduced by half. Place the liquid into a nonreactive container and add the matsutake scraps and soy sauce, and "make it rain" for 25 minutes. Line a chinois with a coffee filter. Strain liquid and discard solids.

For the Pickled Mustard Seeds:
In a saucepot, combine water, vinegar, sugar, turmeric, and salt. Bring to a boil. Pour into nonreactive container with mustard seeds. Let stand at room temperature for at least 3 hours.

To Assemble and Serve:
In a percolator, infuse hot Mushroom Tea with juniper berries, coriander, orange, and cinnamon. When infused, pour liquid into a small pot. Heat a piece of Japanese charcoal and place in a small bowl that will fit the pot. Surround with wild juniper branches. Place the pot over the charcoal and branches. Mound a little Fermented Cabbage on a plate, arrange 5 slices Cured Venison over the cabbage. Finish with smoked olive oil, Pickled Mustard Seeds, and matsutake mushrooms. Instruct guests to dip venison slices into the tea.

Featured Ingredient: Fossil Farms venison

PAN-ROASTED VENISON, WILD MUSHROOMS, AND BRUSSELS SPROUTS

Chef Larry Forgione of the Conservatory for American Food Studies | St. Helena, CA
Adapted by StarChefs
Yield: 4 servings

PHOTO: MEGAN SWANN

INGREDIENTS

Venison:
1 tablespoon olive oil
Four 6-ounce venison loin steaks, fat and sinew
    trimmed
Salt
Black pepper
2 tablespoons salted butter
One 2-inch sprig wild juniper, berries attached

Sauce:
1 tablespoon finely chopped shallots
¼ cup dry vermouth
2 tablespoons whole grain mustard
1½ cups brown poultry stock
1 teaspoon cornstarch, mixed with ½ cup heavy cream
    to make a slurry
2 tablespoons finely chopped parsley
Salt
Black pepper

Mushrooms and Brussels Sprouts:
1 ounce salted butter
1 cup thinly sliced wild mushrooms (cèpes,
    chanterelles, and morels)
12 ounces small Brussels sprouts, blanched, cooled,
    and thinly sliced
Salt
Black pepper

METHOD

For the Venison:
In a large pan over medium flame, heat oil until very hot. Season venison with salt and pepper and sear 1 to 2 minutes on each side. Add butter and cook until slightly browned. Add juniper and baste 30 seconds. Transfer to a sizzle platter and keep warm. Pour off excess oil from pan and let pan cool slightly.

For the Sauce:
Set the same pan used to sear venison over medium heat. Add shallots, vermouth, and 1 tablespoon mustard, scraping the bottom of the pan to dislodge any brown bits. Add stock, increase heat to medium-high, and bring to a boil. Cook 6 to 8 minutes, until liquid reduces by one-third. Stir slurry into sauce. Return to a boil, lower the heat, and simmer 3 to 4 minutes, until thickened. Strain through a chinois into a saucepot. Add parsley and the remaining mustard. Season with salt and pepper. Keep warm.

For the Mushrooms and Brussels Sprouts:
In a large sauté pan, heat butter until it foams and begins to brown. Add mushrooms and Brussels sprouts and sauté 3 to 5 minutes, until lightly colored. Season with salt and pepper.

To Assemble and Serve:
Spoon Mushrooms and Brussels Sprouts into the center of serving plates. Place Venison on top and spoon Sauce over.

Featured Ingredient: Fossil Farms venison

designs you love
quality you deserve
delivery you expect
in-stock

FRONT OF THE HOUSE®

305.757.7940
frontofthehouse.com
@FOHinc

Gavin Kaysen

Spoon and Stable | Minneapolis, MN

Gavin Kaysen is kind of like the chef version of the kid sitting on a stoop when some suit walks by and discovers him—he's got it. Except, for Kaysen it wasn't a stoop but a fast food restaurant kitchen where he was spotted by another restaurant manager and recruited into the world of serious food service. Swept into the industry, he hasn't looked back.

After attending the New England Culinary Institute in Montpelier, Vermont, Kaysen rapidly rose through the ranks, cooking at Domaine Chandon in Yountville, California; L'Auberge de Lavaux in Lausanne, Switzerland; and L'Escargot in London, under Marco Pierre White. Back in the States, Kaysen earned a spot on *Food & Wine*'s "Best New Chefs" list in 2007 as executive chef of El Bizcocho in San Diego. The next year, his work at Café Boulud earned a Michelin star for the restaurant and a James Beard "Rising Star Award" for Kaysen, as well as a StarChefs Rising Stars Award.

No stranger to competition or prestige, Kaysen represented the United States in the 2007 Bocuse d'Or, and helped found the Bocuse d'Or USA Foundation. Thomas Keller and Daniel Boulud selected him to serve as head coach of the Bocuse d'Or USA team in 2013 and 2015. Kaysen's successes (and appearances on Bravo's "Top Chef" and "The Today Show" on NBC) continue to make him a household name, and they gave him the confidence to decamp New York for Minneapolis to open Spoon and Stable, where he brings the kind of casual culinary elegance only a truly (carefully) trained hand can deliver.

COLLABORATION KITCHEN

Learn how to build a crew to be reckoned with. Gavin Kaysen's Minneapolis restaurant, Spoon and Stable, runs on the creative fuel of collaboration. On the ICC Main Stage, Kaysen and a sous chef will take you behind the scenes of their well oiled kitchen and demonstrate how to foster leadership through station ownership, dish conception, menu development.

Presented by Steelite International

PHOTO: WILL BLUNT

 GAVINKAYSEN SPOONANDSTABLE

MOST INFLUENTIAL MENTOR WITH WHOM YOU'VE WORKED: Daniel Boulud. He gave me a PhD in all things hospitality.

COOLEST TECHNIQUE YOU'VE LEARNED FROM ANOTHER CHEF: Taste your food.

A DISH YOU MAKE THAT'S INSPIRED BY ANOTHER CULTURE: Scallop crudo with charred scallion vinaigrette and compressed apples. It is inspired by the local Hmong culture.

IF YOU COULD EAT AT ANY RESTAURANT IN THE WORLD TONIGHT, IT WOULD BE: L'Arpège

FAVORITE INDUSTRY INSTAGRAM ACCOUNT: @grahamelliot

FAVORITE COOKBOOK: The French Laundry Cookbook by Thomas Keller

CHEF WITH WHOM YOU'D MOST LIKE TO COLLABORATE: Magnus Nilsson for the amount of time he spends reflecting on his dishes and getting to know his guests.

PHOTO: WILL BLUNT

ROASTED DUCK BREAST, WHEATBERRIES, RHUBARB, RAMPS, TASSO HAM, AND BURNT HONEY JUS

Chef Gavin Kaysen of Spoon and Stable | Minneapolis, MN
Adapted by StarChefs
Yield: 8 servings

INGREDIENTS

Red Fife Porridge:
Olive oil
1 shallot, finely diced
2 cups Red Fife berries, crushed
1 cup white wine
6 cups chicken stock
2 bay leaves
Salt
Black pepper

Rhubarb:
4 stalks rhubarb
500 grams honey
2 cups water
1 tablespoon dried allspice berries
2 tablespoons pink peppercorns
1 teaspoon salt
4 bay leaves
1 tablespoon Sherry
¼ cup pomegranate juice

Duck Tasso:
450 grams kosher salt
75 grams pink salt
425 grams dextrose
4 duck thighs
250 grams paprika
100 grams cayenne
125 grams ground ancho chile
75 grams white peppercorns, toasted and ground
75 grams red chile flakes, toasted and ground
75 grams green onion powder
25 grams dried allspice berries, toasted and ground
25 grams celery seeds

To Assemble and Serve:
Olive oil
4 duck breasts, skin scored
Salt
Pepper
Duck stock
Burnt honey
Young ramp bulb and leaves, finely chopped
Fava beans, shucked and blanched
Tarragon, finely chopped
Fiddlehead ferns, sautéed
Lemon thyme

METHOD

For the Red Fife Porridge:
In a rondeau over medium flame, heat oil and sweat shallot until translucent. Add Red Fife berries and lightly toast. Deglaze with wine. Add stock and bay leaves. Season with salt and pepper. Simmer 20 to 30 minutes, until tender.

For the Rhubarb:
Trim rhubarb, cut into 6-inch segments, and reserve segments and scraps separately. In a saucepot, combine remaining ingredients and bring to a boil. Remove from heat and cool to room temperature. Heat the water bath of an immersion circulator to 61°C. In a vacuum bag, combine cooled liquid and rhubarb and seal. Cook sous vide 15 minutes. Shock in an ice bath. When cold, cut rhubarb into desired shape and store in liquid. In a Vitamix, purée rhubarb scraps, adding cooled cooking liquid until mixture is smooth.

For the Duck Tasso:
In a shallow hotel pan, combine salts and dextrose. Dredge duck thighs in salt mixture and cure 1 hour. Rinse duck thighs and pat dry with paper towels. In a mixing bowl, combine remaining ingredients. Dredge the flesh side of the duck in the spice mix. Transfer to a hotel pan and refrigerate overnight. Prepare and heat a smoker to 245°F. Smoke duck thighs 3 hours, let cool, remove meat from bones, and dice small.

To Assemble and Serve:
In a sauté pan, heat olive oil. Season duck breasts with salt and pepper and sauté, skin side down, until crisp and cooked to desired doneness. Remove duck from pan and rest. Deglaze pan with stock and honey. Reduce pan jus until thick and syrupy. In a saucepan, heat Red Fife Porridge, diced Duck Tasso, ramps, fava beans, and tarragon. Season with salt and pepper. When hot, spoon mixture onto serving plate. Cut duck lengthwise into thick slices and arrange on top of porridge. Garnish with fiddleheads, Rhubarb segments, Rhubarb purée, and lemon thyme. Finish with drizzle of honey pan jus.

Featured Equipment: Vitamix blender, Mercer Culinary plating tools
Featured Plateware: Steelite Crucial Detail Plateau

STARCHEFS.COM
RISING STARS
2016 CITIES

San Francisco
June

Cleveland-Pittsburgh
December

New Orleans
February

South Florida
December

To nominate a Rising Star Chef, Pastry Chef, Sommelier, Bartender, or Artisan, go to www.starchefs.com/nominate.
Go to www.starchefs.com/risingstars *or call* 212.966.7575 *for more information and tickets.*

STARCHEFS
moving the industry forward

PHOTOS: ANTOINETTE BRUNO

Melissa Kelly

Primo | Rockland, ME

Melissa Kelly grew up on Long Island and spent countless hours in her Italian grandmother's kitchen. After studying business at the State University of New York and University of Maine, Kelly's kitchen inclinations and curiosity led her to the Culinary Institute of America, where she graduated with honors. Kelly continued her training at The Greenbrier in White Sulphur Springs, West Virginia.

Eventually Kelly returned to New York to work for iconic Chef Larry Forgione at An American Place. Becoming a trusted colleague of Forgione, she earned the executive chef position at Beekman 1766 Tavern and later was placed in charge of opening An American Place Waterside in Miami. She also was called upon to assist in the opening of An American Place Japan.

But it was when Kelly made the move out West to work at Chez Panisse that she truly came into her own. Working with Alice Waters, she realized that simplicity, seasonality, and freshness were what mattered to her most. Kelly took this mentality and applied it to her career and travels from Denver to Barbados and the south of France.

Back in New York, Kelly earned her first James Beard Award in 1999, running the kitchen at Old Chatham Sheepherding Company Inn in the Hudson Valley. In 2000, Kelly opened Primo on a 4½-acre farm in Rockland, Maine. More than a decade later, the accolades and the guests are still coming in droves. In 2013, Kelly was the first two-time recipient of James Beard's "Best Chef, Northeast" Award.

 CHEFMELISSAK CHEFMK

FULL CIRCLE KITCHEN

Melissa Kelly is living the genuine, farm-to-table dream. She and her team raise animals, keep bees, and grow most of the produce for her James Beard Award-winning restaurant, Primo, in Rockland, Maine. On the Main Stage, Kelly will break down a heritage hog and pair the cuts with Italian pantry items that she uses to supplement the flora of Maine.

Presented by Italian Trade Commission and Hobart

MOST INFLUENTIAL MENTORS WITH WHOM YOU'VE WORKED: André Soltner for work ethic, Daniel Boulud for style and technique.

COOLEST TECHNIQUE YOU'VE LEARNED FROM ANOTHER CHEF: Hmm, I'm old school. Alice Waters inspires me a bunch, with simplicity and quality.

IF YOU COULD EAT AT ANY RESTAURANT IN THE WORLD TONIGHT, IT WOULD BE: Emilio Vitolo in NYC. Great, simple Italian.

FAVORITE INDUSTRY INSTAGRAM ACCOUNT: @mariobatali

FAVORITE COOKBOOK: I love River Cottage Books, Rose Levy Berenbaum, and Giorgio Locatelli.

CHEF WITH WHOM YOU'D MOST LIKE TO COLLABORATE: I would love to collaborate with Mario Batali. He's smart, funny, passionate, amazing: my style.

COTECHINO

Chef Melissa Kelly of Primo | Rockland, ME
Inspired by Paul Bertolli and Adapted by StarChefs
Yield: 11 pounds sausage

INGREDIENTS

5 pounds de-fatted pork skin, preferably from the belly, cut into 2-inch pieces
5 pounds lean pork shoulder, cut into 1-inch cubes, chilled
1 pound plus 11 ounces fatback, cut into 1-inch cubes, chilled
80 grams salt
7 grams Insta Cure No. 1
9 grams finely ground black pepper
1 gram ground coriander seeds
1 gram ground clove
1 gram cayenne
1 gram ground cinnamon
18 grams dextrose powder
1 scant teaspoon mace
⅛ teaspoon freshly ground nutmeg
Hog middles or beef wide middles casing

METHOD

To a pot, add pork skin and cover with water. Bring to a boil, skimming off any white froth that rises to the surface. Reduce heat and simmer 40 minutes to 1 hour, until skin is very tender; drain. Scrape away any fat adhering to the underside of the skins. Lay skins out on a sheet tray and chill. Through a meat grinder set with a 3/16-inch die, grind skin. In a bowl, combine pork, fatback, and ground skin. Fit the grinder with a 3/8-inch die, and pass mixture through the grinder into a bowl. Add salt, Insta Cure, black pepper, coriander, clove, cayenne, cinnamon, dextrose, mace, and nutmeg. Using a heavy duty spatula, mix until filling is slightly stiff and sticky to the touch. Stuff filling in casing and tie tightly. Heat a water bath to 170°F and poach sausage 1 hour.

Featured Equipment: Hobart mixer with grinder attachment

Peruvian Cacao

The flavor and fragance of land like no other.

peru.info

Perú

PHOTO: GUSTAVO VIVANCO

 VIRGILIOCENTRAL

COOLEST TECHNIQUE YOU'VE LEARNED FROM ANOTHER CHEF:
The simplicity and wisdom of perfectly sharpening a knife

IF YOU COULD EAT AT ANY RESTAURANT IN THE WORLD TONIGHT, IT WOULD BE:
Mugaritz

FAVORITE INDUSTRY INSTAGRAM ACCOUNT:
@BoBech

FAVORITE COOKBOOK:
White Heat by Marco Pierre White

CHEF WITH WHOM YOU'D MOST LIKE TO COLLABORATE:
Albert Adrià. His career and technique are just one of the best!

MOST IMPORTANT PLACE TO INVEST MONEY IN YOUR BUSINESS: Research and travel

Virgilio Martínez
Central | Lima, Peru

Early in life, Virgilio Martínez was confused about his identity, and that fact alone makes him perfectly Peruvian. Growing up, Martínez made it a rule that each Sunday his family would eat Chinese food, but he was also interested in Japanese and Italian cuisines—all three of which have had significant influence on Peru's culinary melting pot. Growing up in Lima, with a burning desire to cook and no culinary school to attend, Martínez decided (after getting his law degree) to travel.

BUILDING ON TRADITION: "SUDADO" AND THE CORN OF PERU

Modern Peruvian cuisine is built on an ancient foundation, and its practitioners are stewards to a deep and shared heritage. On the ICC Main Stage, two of Peru's most esteemed chefs, Virgilio Martínez and Hector Solis, will mine the potential of their heritage—specifically native corn and sudado, a traditional fish stew. Solis will tackle a full-flavored, traditional version of sudado, and Martínez will go hyper-modern, applying his philosophy of altitude-based cuisine to the humble dish.

Presented by PROMPerú

When he ended up in Canada, Martínez got a cooking job. He loved the experience so much that he enrolled in Le Cordon Bleu in London, graduated in 1998, and then worked his way around much of the world. He explored the cuisines of France, Italy, London, Southeast Asia (Martínez traveled and worked in Singapore), and New York (where he worked at Lutèce). After 10 years, Martínez returned home to helm Gastón Acurio's Astrid y Gastón, eventually exporting the restaurant and the flavors of Peru to Madrid and Bogotá.

Martínez opened his own restaurant, Central, in Lima's trendy Miraflores neighborhood in 2010, offering market-driven cuisine inspired by the Pacific Ocean and the Peruvian Andes. The following year, he set his sights on London, opening Lima in July 2012. Lima focuses on traditional Peruvian dishes with modern approaches. Martínez's food continues to garner worldwide attention, and Central was ranked fourth on this year's San Pellegrino "50 Best Restaurants" list.

SUDADO
Chef Virgilio Martínez of Central | Lima, Peru
Adapted by StarChefs
Yield: 64 servings

PHOTO: GREG DE VILLIERS

INGREDIENTS

Octopus:
Twelve 2-kilogram octopuses, heads
    removed
Salt
1 kilogram leeks, coarsely chopped
1 kilogram carrots, coarsely chopped
1 kilogram onion, coarsely chopped
200 grams garlic, coarsely chopped

Sudado Sachet:
500 grams red onion brunoise
1 kilogram tomatoes, peeled,
    seeded, and cut into brunoise
300 grams cilantro, leaves picked,
    stems set aside for Tiger's Milk Base
100 grams garlic brunoise
200 grams ají amarillo, seeded and
    coarsely chopped

Tiger's Milk Base:
100 grams celery, coarsely chopped
100 grams onion, coarsely chopped
2 cloves garlic, peeled
One 3-centimeter knob ginger,
    peeled and sliced
2 tablespoons salt
1 teaspoon sugar

Sudado Broth:
6 liters mussel broth
150 grams white rocoto paste

150 grams yellow rocoto paste
200 milliliters lemon juice
2 tablespoons ají limo chile paste
Salt
Xanthan gum

Corn Tiger's Milk:
Juice from 1 kilogram limes
40 grams white fish fillet
200 grams ice cubes
30 grams salt
1 teaspoon finely chopped ají limo

Airampo "Painted" Fish:
2 liters water
300 grams airampo seeds (from the
    prickly pear cactus)
600 grams salt
200 grams sugar
510 grams fish fillets, cut into 2-inch
    pieces

For the Black Rice Crisps:
2 cups overcooked rice, chilled
Squid ink
Salt

Gray Rocks:
Egg whites, whipped to soft peaks
Squid ink

Loche Squash Purée and Crisps:
3 kilograms loche squash,
    peeled, seeded, and diced into
    5-centimeter cubes
6 grams salt
100 grams butter, diced

Yellow Corn Cake:
4 liters corn stock
80 milliliters honey
1 kilogram Ajaleado corn kernels
1 kilogram Sarco corn kernels
500 grams Granada corn kernels
500 grams Uchiquilla corn kernels
15 milliliters corn oil
1 white onion, coarsely chopped
5 cloves garlic, coarsely chopped
250 grams ají amarillo paste
5 grams coarsely chopped cilantro
15 grams salt

Corn Skin Ring:
50 grams dried Chullpi corn kernels
Salt
900 grams Sarco corn purée
100 grams ají amarillo paste
200 grams cassava (yucca) flour

Corn Silk:
Corn oil
100 grams corn silk

METHOD

For the Octopus:
In a large container, place octopus arms, and coat with salt. After 30 minutes, rinse octopus and pat dry. Cover and freeze octopus for 24 hours. Let octopus defrost. Tenderize with mallet to break down fibers. Transfer octopus to a large pot, add remaining ingredients, and cover with water. Heat pot until mixture starts to boil. Reduce heat and simmer 45 minutes. Chill octopus in cooking liquid. When cold, drain and cut octopus into 3-centimeter segments.

For the Sudado Sachet:
Set a dehydrator to 55°C. On separate trays, dry onion, tomato, cilantro, garlic, and ají amarillo for 1 hour. By weight, make a mixture of 23 percent red onion, 48 percent tomato, 14 percent cilantro, 5 percent garlic, and 10 percent ají amarillo. Divide mixture into sachets. Set aside in a dry place.

For the Tiger's Milk Base:
In a blender, combine celery, onion, garlic, ginger, salt, and sugar; purée. Transfer to a third pan, add 100 grams cilantro stems reserved from Sudado Sachet, and marinate 1 hour. Discard stems, cover, and refrigerate.

For the Sudado Broth:
In a pot, bring mussel broth to a boil. Add rocoto pastes, lemon juice, chile paste, and 100 grams Tiger's Milk Base. Season with salt. Reduce 10 minutes, until 1 liter remains. Remove from heat, pour into a blender, and shear in xanthan gum until mixture thickens. Pour through a chinois into a storage container. Add Sudado Sachet, let cool, cover, and refrigerate.

For the Yellow Corn Cake:
Heat oven to 180°C. In a pot, bring 1 liter corn stock and 20 milliliters honey to a boil. Add Ajaleado corn kernels and cook 1 hour. Drain corn and keep warm. Repeat process with remaining corns. In a rondeau, heat oil until shimmering. Sauté onion and garlic until fragrant. Add cooked corn, ají amarillo, and cilantro. Cook 5 minutes. Transfer to a blender, purée, and pass through a chinois into a bowl. Season with salt. Reserve 50 grams corn mixture for Corn Tiger's Milk. Spread the remaining mixture on a parchment-lined sheet tray. Bake 45 minutes. Using a small, circular mold, cut cakes into rounds.

For the Corn Tiger's Milk:
In a blender, combine lime juice, ¼ cup Tiger's Milk Base, 50 grams reserved Yellow Corn Cake batter, fish, and ice. Blend 1 minute. Strain through a chinois into storage container. Season with salt and stir in ají limo. Cover and refrigerate.

For the Airampo "Painted" Fish:
In a pot, bring water to boil. Add airampo seeds and boil 5 minutes. Strain into a shallow container, discarding seeds. Add salt and sugar, stir to combine, and let cool completely. Submerge fish in liquid. Refrigerate 1 hour and then drain dyed fish. Set a dehydrator to 65°C and dry fish for 4 hours.

For the Black Rice Crisps:
In a bowl, combine rice and ink, as when incorporating dye into a dough. Season with salt. Roll into long, thin log. Cover and chill. Heat oven to 175°C. Slice log as thinly as possible into chips. Line a sheet tray with a silicone mat. Arrange slice in layer on the mat. Bake 15 minutes, until crisp.

For the Gray Rocks:
In a bowl, combine whipped egg whites with enough squid ink to turn them gray. Form gray whites into small balls and place on parchment-lined sheet tray. Set a dehydrator to 65°C, and dehydrate balls 3 hours, until completely dry, like rocks.

For the Loche Squash Purée and Crisps:
In a large pot of boiling water, cook squash until tender; drain. Working in batches, transfer squash to blender and purée. Season with salt. Transfer one-third of the squash purée to a silicone mat and spread into a thin, even layer. Add butter to remaining squash purée and blend until combined; cover and keep warm. Set a dehydrator to 70°C. Dry squash on silicone mat for 1½ hours; let cool completely. Break dried squash into crisps and store in a cool, dry place.

For the Corn Skin Ring:
Heat oven to 120°C. In a sauté pan over medium heat, toast Chullpi corn, stirring constantly, until golden brown. Season with salt and let cool completely. Transfer to a spice grinder and pulverize to fine powder. In a separate pan over medium heat, combine remaining ingredients and season with salt. Cook 30 minutes, stirring constantly. Place a sheet of circular stencils on a silicone mat. Spread corn mixture over stencils and sprinkle with Chullpi corn powder; bake 30 minutes. Store Corn Skin Rings in a cool, dry place.

For the Corn Silk:
Heat oil in deep fryer to 175°C. Working in batches, fry corn silk for 2 seconds. Drain on paper towels.

To Assemble and Serve:
Prepare and heat grill. Quickly char Octopus. Warm and plate a Yellow Corn Cake and top with Octopus. Pour a small amount of Corn Tiger's Milk and Loche Squash Purée around cake. Finish with Black Rice and Loche Squash Crisps, Gray Rocks, and pieces of Airampo "Painted" Fish. Garnish with Corn Skin Rings and Corn Silk. Warm Sudado Broth and ladle onto dish tableside.

Featured Ingredients: Peruvian corn and ají amarillo

PHOTO: ANTOINETTE BRUNO

 HECTORSFIESTA

MOST INFLUENTIAL MENTOR WITH WHOM YOU'VE WORKED: My mother, because she taught me all that I know. She is my instructor, teacher, inspiration, and mentor.

COOLEST TECHNIQUE YOU'VE LEARNED FROM ANOTHER CHEF: Choose the freshest ingredients, as in fish, seafood, or vegetables. I have a team in the fishing ports of Peru's coast so I can get the freshest products.

A DISH YOU MAKE THAT'S INSPIRED BY ANOTHER CULTURE: The hot ceviche that is cooked on the grill. The original dish is "panquitas de life," a dish of the pre-Inca Moche culture.

IF YOU COULD EAT AT ANY RESTAURANT IN THE WORLD TONIGHT, IT WOULD BE: Sacha, by my friend Sacha [Hormaechea] in Madrid

CHEF WITH WHOM YOU'D MOST LIKE TO COLLABORATE: Victor Arguinzoniz of Asador Etxebarri

Hector Solis

Fiesta | Lima, Peru

Chef Hector Solis was born in Lambayeque, a small city in northern Peru. The people of the region are descendants of the Mochina tribe, a group who was and still is dedicated to living the good life by keeping alive the time-honored customs of their traditional cuisine. In Lambayeque, a devotion to cooking begins at birth, and for Solis, it was a birthright. From a young age, he learned to cook from his mother and grandparents. He's also a third generation entrepreneur and restaurateur. Solis' father, Don Alberto, opened the original, groundbreaking Fiesta restaurant in Chiclayo, the capital of Lambayeque, in 1996.

After receiving a degree in economics and studying hospitality management at Le Cordon Bleu in Lima, Solis joined the family business with a vision for the future of Fiesta and Peruvian food. In 2002, he opened Fiesta Tacna followed by Fiesta Trujillo in 2007. Today there are five such fine-dining establishments throughout Peru, plus Solis's most recent addition, the more casual La Picantería. Carrying on the family tradition of progressive Peruvian cuisine while remaining true to his roots, Solis has shepherded the food of his culture into the modern era of global cuisine.

Solis pushes the boundaries of Peruvian cooking while relying heavily on high-quality indigenous ingredients like native chiles, heirloom potatoes, chicha de jora (Peruvian corn beer), and most famously, his warm, fragrant, barely cooked ceviches (a great contribution to the culinary world in itself). Many ingredients are sourced directly from his own farm or the local markets near his establishments. In addition to cooking and overseeing the Fiesta empire, Solis writes cookbooks, travels to important gastronomic events around the world, and mentors potential protégés—all while spreading the wealth of his culinary inheritance and becoming one of Peru's greatest cultural exports.

SUDADO

Chef Hector Solis of Fiesta | Lima, Peru
Adapted by StarChefs
Yield: 5 servings

INGREDIENTS

Pepian:
Vegetable oil
9 ounces corn kernels, puréed
½ white onion, finely chopped
3 tablespoons finely chopped garlic
½ ají amarillo
Salt

Sudado:
3 tablespoons vegetable oil
5 tablespoons finely chopped garlic
1 tablespoon ají amarillo paste
4 tomatoes, seeded and diced
2 red onions, thinly sliced
Five 6-ounce sea bass steaks
Juice of 3 lemons
1 tablespoon finely chopped cilantro

To Assemble and Serve:
1 tomato, peeled and cut into small
    wedges
1 red onion, cut into petals and
    blanched
Seaweed

METHOD

For the Pepian:
In a large saucepan over medium-low flame, heat oil and sauté onion and garlic until soft and fragrant. Add ají amarillo and corn. Stir constantly until mixture thickens. Season with salt. Cover and keep warm.

For the Sudado:
In a saucepan over medium-low flame, heat oil and sauté garlic until soft and fragrant. Add ají amarillo, tomatoes, onions, sea bass, and a splash of water. Cover and cook 10 minutes. Remove from heat and stir in lemon juice and cilantro.

To Assemble and Serve:
Spoon Pepian into a bowl and top with sea bass. Spoon stew around fish and garnish with tomatoes, onion petals, and seaweed.

Featured Ingredients: Peruvian ají amarillo and corn

PHOTO: MEGAN SWANN

José Ramírez-Ruiz & Pam Yung

Semilla | Brooklyn, NY

After cutting their teeth at top New York City restaurants, such as Per Se, Brooklyn Fare, and Isa, Chef José Ramírez-Ruiz and Pastry Chef Pam Yung decided it was time to sink their teeth into a venture all their own. In 2012, the two opened veggie-forward, BYOB pop-up Chez José in Williamsburg. Although a big success, Chez José was in a small space and could only accommodate four to eight guests in a given seating. When nearby restaurant Lake Trout closed, Ramírez-Ruiz and Yung jumped at the chance to take over the (slightly) larger venue, and planted the seeds for Semilla.

Solidifying a partnership with Lake Trout's owner Joe Carroll (also responsible for neighborhood fave Fette Sau), the chef-duo started renovations in 2013. The ground floor location on Havemeyer Street was built out and finished entirely by Ramírez-Ruiz and Yung. With enough space to come into their own, they forged ahead and opened Semilla in 2014 with Ramírez-Ruiz's artful, almost-all-vegetable prefixe menu; Yung's desserts and soon-to-be sought-after breads; and an intriguing wine and beer list. Much like a Friday night on their lively, still-just-a-bit-gritty block in Williamsburg, people started making noise about Semilla.

By early 2015 *The New York Times* awarded it two stars. The ever-transforming menu is complex, yet simmering in simplicity and charm. A four-star review from Eater's Bill Addison called Semilla "New York's Next Great Restaurant," and *Bon Appétit* named it one of America's top 10 new restaurants of 2015. Sabering off quite a year for Ramírez-Ruiz and Yung, Semilla received a Michelin star in September.

 SEMILLABK

MOST INFLUENTIAL MENTORS WITH WHOM YOU'VE WORKED:
José: Jonathan Benno of Lincoln and Oriol Rovira of Els Casals in Barcelona
Pam: Will Goldfarb. It was my first cooking job and definitely a nontraditional start.

COOLEST TECHNIQUE YOU'VE LEARNED FROM ANOTHER CHEF:
José: Oriol Rovira taught me how to cook rice. It sounds simple, but it's hard to understand. Most American chefs make risotto, not rice. Spaniards cook rice, like sloppier risotto made on an open flame without constant stirring. In the countryside, they take chicken pieces, roast them in the pot, add garlic, onion, rice, and water. It's more rustic and has more flavor, and it's the way we cook rice at Semilla.
Pam: Taste and season everything—savory and sweet. Lots of pastry chefs follow recipes without adjusting the seasoning. It's all about the balance of salt, acid, and bitterness.

IF YOU COULD EAT AT ANY RESTAURANT IN THE WORLD TONIGHT, IT WOULD BE:
José: Joe Beef in Montreal
Pam: Not a particular restaurant, just a simple, casual, comfortable place in the company of friends with good bread and butter, wine, and simply prepared, just-caught seafood.

FAVORITE COOKBOOKS:
José: Sugar Shack Au Pied de Cochon by Martin Picard. Ma Gastronomie by Fernand Point is so classic and inspiring. Charlie Trotter's Raw—he was so far ahead of everyone else.
Pam: The endlessly inspiring Bar Tartine by Nicholaus Balla and Cortney Burns

CHEF WITH WHOM YOU'D MOST LIKE TO COLLABORATE:
José: Marc-Olivier Frappier, the chef at Le Vin Papillon and Joe Beef in Montreal. He's 27 and a badass. He knows a whole different type of cuisine, Québécois. It's delicious and beautiful.
Pam: Agata Felluga, a young Roman chef who lived in Paris for 10 years. She was sous chef at Chateaubriand and L'Astrance before that. She's now at Jour de Fête in Strasbourg. She is an incredibly strong woman. We've done demos together, but I would love to be able to cook with her.

PHOTO: MEGAN SWANN

CHESTNUT FRITTER AND RAMP DRESSING

Chef José Ramírez-Ruiz of Semilla | Brooklyn, NY
Adapted by StarChefs
Yield: 30 fritters

INGREDIENTS

Ramp Dressing:
100 grams Kewpie mayonnaise
25 grams fermented ramps
15 grams pickled ramp bulbs
Salt

Chestnut Purée:
150 grams chestnuts (in husk)
50 grams heavy cream

Potato Purée:
Salt
350 grams peeled russet potato
150 grams heavy cream
40 grams thinly sliced garlic
20 grams thyme sprigs
4 grams black pepper
3 grams northern bay leaf
50 grams butter

Chestnut Fritter:
Whole nutmeg
Cinnamon stick
Salt
Sugar
Cornstarch
Beaten eggs
Sourdough bread crumbs

To Assemble and Serve:
Oil for frying

METHOD

For the Ramp Dressing:
To a food processor, add mayonnaise, ramps, and bulbs. Process until smooth. Season with salt.

For the Chestnut Purée:
Heat oven to 575°F. Score chestnut husk. Roast 5 minutes. Using a pairing knife, peel off husk, reserving husk and fur for presentation. In a medium saucepot with boiling water, blanch chestnuts until soft. Drain, cool, and peel away skins, reserving for plating. In a food processor, process chestnuts until smooth, adding cream as necessary. Pass mixture through a tamis.

For the Potato Purée:
In a large pot of simmering salted water, cook potatoes until soft. Drain and set aside in a bowl. In a pan, warm cream with garlic, thyme, pepper, and bay leaf. Add butter and warmed cream mixture to potatoes. Pass through a tamis. Season with salt and pepper.

For the Chestnut Fritter:
In a mixing bowl, combine Potato and Chestnut Purées. Using a microplane for grating, season mixture with nutmeg and cinnamon; season with salt and sugar. Portion mixture in 25-gram spheres. Prepare a breading station with cornstarch, eggs, and breadcrumbs. Bread spheres.

To Assemble and Serve:
In a pot, heat oil to 375°F. Fry the breaded spheres until Chestnut Fritters are golden brown; drain. On a plate, arrange 2 reserved chestnut husks and scatter skins around. Place 1 Chestnut Fritter inside each husk. Serve with Ramp Dressing.

PORCINI MUSHROOM SOUP AND GARLIC CHANTILLY

Chef José Ramírez-Ruiz of Semilla | Brooklyn, NY
Adapted by StarChefs
Yield: 2 servings

PHOTO: MEGAN SWANN

INGREDIENTS

Garlic Chantilly:
20 grams butter
40 grams coarsely chopped garlic
1 quart heavy cream
Salt
Sugar

Dashi:
20 grams bonito flakes
20 grams dried shiitake mushrooms
60 grams kombu, rinsed with filtered water
2 quarts water

Soup:
20 grams butter
10 grams thinly sliced garlic
80 grams finely chopped shallot
75 grams Oloroso Sherry
145 grams heavy cream
132 grams porcini mushrooms
7 grams thyme sprigs
2 grams northern bay leaf
Salt
Black pepper
Tabasco

To Assemble and Serve:
Apple balsamic vinegar in a squeeze bottle

METHOD

For the Garlic Chantilly:
In a pan, melt butter and sauté garlic until golden brown. Deglaze with cream. Slowly simmer for 15 minutes. Transfer to a blender and purée, lightly seasoning with salt and sugar. Transfer mixture to a siphon and charge twice; refrigerate.

For the Dashi:
In a pot, combine kombu, mushrooms, and half the water. Heat to 167.7°F and cook for 10 minutes. Add bonito and cook 10 minutes more. Strain through a chinois, reserving solids and liquids separately. In a separate pot, combine reserved solids and remaining water. Heat to 167.7°F and cook for 10 minutes. Strain and combine with first Dashi.

For the Soup:
In a pan, heat butter and sweat garlic and shallot until translucent. Add Sherry and simmer until pan is almost dry. Add cream, mushrooms, thyme, bay leaf, and 145 grams Dashi. Slowly simmer 10 minutes, until mushrooms are tender. Set aside a few mushroom caps for plating. Transfer Soup to blender and purée. Season with salt, pepper, Tabasco, and more Dashi, as needed.

To Assemble and Serve:
Thinly slice reserved porcini mushroom caps. In a pan, warm Soup. Pour into serving cups. Top with mushroom. Squeeze 5 dots of vinegar on surface of soup. Tableside, discharge a tablespoon-size portion of Garlic Chantilly onto soup.

Barton Seaver

**Healthy and Sustainable Food Program |
South Freeport, ME**

Chef, author, and National Geographic Fellow Barton Seaver is on a mission to help restore relationships between people, ecosystems, and the cultures of our world—through dinner. After graduating from the Culinary Institute of America, Seaver traveled to Essaouira, Morocco, a seaside village where survival is directly linked to the ocean. The experience made a lasting impression on Seaver. Returning to his native Washington, D.C., in 2005, he began his career as a chef, first with José Andrés at Jaleo, then as executive chef of Cafe Saint-Ex, and later at its sister restaurant Bar Pilar.

In 2007, Seaver became chef-owner of the sustainable seafood restaurant Hook in Georgetown, which made *Bon Appétit*'s "Top 10 Eco-Friendly Restaurants" list. In a single year, the restaurant served 78 species of seafood, and Seaver's devotion to sustainability led to national media attention, both for his cooking and his cause. Meanwhile, he was honored as a "Seafood Champion" by the Seafood Choices Alliance, a "Legend & Leader" in ocean conservation by Blue Vision, and was recognized by the Blue Ocean Institute for his sustainability efforts.

Seaver has opened seven restaurants as an executive chef, but he realized he could do more outside the kitchen, leaving the restaurant industry to accept a Fellowship with the Explorer Program at the National Geographic Society, through which he travels the world to investigate the failures and successes of human interaction with nature from a culinary perspective. He's also written four books, joined ranks with Harvard's T.H. Chan School of Public Health as Director of the Healthy and Sustainable Food Program at the Center for Health and Global Environment, was named the first Sustainability Fellow in Residence at The New England Aquarium, is a regular participant at the Aspen Institute, and delivered a highly influential TED talk. Seaver was named to the U.S. Culinary Ambassador Corp in 2012 by Secretary of State Hillary Clinton.

THE CASE FOR AMERICAN SEAFOOD

Which fish are safe? What are the most sustainable species? Who are the right fishermen and fisheries to source from? Would it be easier to just serve pork than wade through the madness? Chef, author, and sustainability advocate Barton Seaver and Gulf seafood guru Tory McPhail have (at least some of) the answers, and they begin with American seafood. Join Seaver and McPhail on the Main Stage as they make the case for putting more seafood on the table.

Presented by Alaska Seafood Marketing Institute, Wild American Shrimp, Louisiana Seafood, Mississippi Seafood, and Front of the House

---

 BARTONSEAVER

MOST INFLUENTIAL MENTOR/COOK WITH WHOM YOU'VE WORKED: Robert Egger, founder of D.C. Central Kitchen and L.A. Kitchen. He taught me that a chef is more than the sum of ingredients we put on a plate, but that we are members of our communities.

IF YOU COULD EAT AT ANY RESTAURANT IN THE WORLD TONIGHT, IT WOULD BE: Cook's Lobster Pound in Maine

FAVORITE CHEF INSTAGRAM ACCOUNT: David Varley, @dwvarley

FAVORITE COOKBOOK: Jeremiah Tower Cooks by Jeremiah Tower

CHEF WITH WHOM YOU'D MOST LIKE TO COLLABORATE: Suzanne Goin

SMOKY ALASKA SABLEFISH AND AUTUMN FLAVORS
Chef Barton Seaver of Healthy and Sustainable Food Program | South Freeport, ME
Adapted by StarChefs
Yield: 4 servings

INGREDIENTS

Autumn Squash Purée:
1½ pound red kuri squash, halved and
    seeded
4 ounces butter
Salt

Smoky Sablefish:
2 cups water, 1 cup chilled
1 slice ginger
1 small stick cinnamon
2 tablespoons red wine vinegar
1 tablespoon salt
½ tablespoon sugar
1¼ pounds Alaska sablefish, deboned,
    skinned, cut into 4-ounce portions
1 tablespoon olive oil

Pistachio Picada:
1 small clove garlic, grated with
    microplane
Grated zest of 1 orange
Salt
2 tablespoons olive oil
½ cup roasted pistachios, hot,
    coarsely chopped

Roasted Grapes:
60 red seedless grapes

Herb Salad:
Leaves form 5 sprigs mint, coarsely
    chopped
Leaves from 5 sprigs chervil
2 small shallots, thinly sliced

METHOD

For the Autumn Squash Purée:
Heat oven to 375°F. Place squash in a baking dish, cut side down, along with a small amount of water. Bake for 45 minutes, until tender. Scoop out flesh into a blender, add butter, and purée. Season with salt.

For the Smoky Sablefish:
In a pot, combine 1 cup water, ginger, cinnamon, vinegar, salt, and sugar. Bring to a boil to dissolve salt and sugar. Remove from heat and add 1 cup cold water. Cool completely and submerge fish in brine for 15 minutes. Heat oven at 275°F. Remove fish from brine and pat dry. Prepare a smoking gun. Gently smoke fish for 5 to 10 minutes. Lightly oil fish and cook in oven for 10 minutes, until it begins to flake.

For the Pistachio Picada:
In a bowl, combine garlic, zest, and olive oil. Season with salt. Stir and let rest. Add pistachios. Mix well to coat nuts evenly in oil. Season with salt.

For the Roasted Grapes:
Heat oven to 400°F. Place grapes on a sheet tray and roast for 10 to 15 minutes, until skins blister and juices begin to caramelize.

For the Herb Salad:
In a small bowl, combine all ingredients.

To Assemble and Serve:
Spread Autumn Squash Purée on a serving plate. Place Smoked Sablefish on top. Arrange Roasted Grapes and Herb Salad next to fish. Top with Pistachio Picada.

Featured Ingredient: Alaska sablefish (black cod)
Featured Plateware: Front of the House Kiln

PHOTO: SARA ESSEX BRADLEY

 **TORYMCPHAIL**

Tory McPhail
Commander's Palace | New Orleans, LA

Hailing from Ferndale, Washington, a small town near the Canadian border, Tory McPhail learned to appreciate the local goods and the comfortable gathering space of his parents' kitchen. After high school, McPhail attended Seattle Community College and received a degree in culinary science. Compelled by New Orleans' history, soul, and Mardi Gras celebrations, he moved to the Crescent City at 19 and was soon hired by Commander's Palace Executive Chef Jamie Shannon. Working diligently through all 12 stations of the kitchen, he honed his craft.

McPhail later completed a series of stints at properties including the Breakers Hotel in Palm Beach; the Michelin-starred L'Escargot in London and its sister restaurant, the Picasso Room; and the Mongoose Restaurant in the U.S. Virgin Islands. In 2000, McPhail returned to the Commander's family as executive sous chef at Commander's Palace Las Vegas. But in 2002, Shannon would need him back in the Big Easy to serve as executive chef of the original Palace. All these years later, McPhail continues to lead the storied kitchen and create strong relationships with local purveyors.

McPhail has made a number of TV appearances, including Bravo's "Top Chef," NBC's "Today," CBS's "Early Show," "After Hours With Daniel Boulud," and numerous Food Network programs. A James Beard "Rising Star Chef" and "Best Chef, South" winner, he was named one of the best chefs in the country by The Daily Meal in 2013 and one of *Saveur*'s inaugural "Tastemaker Chefs" in 2012. He won the Great American Seafood CookOff in 2009, co-authored Commander's Wild Side, served on the Nutrition Advisory Board for *Cooking Light* magazine, and has been a spokesperson for Wild American Shrimp and Old Bay seasoning.

COOLEST TECHNIQUE YOU'VE LEARNED FROM ANOTHER CHEF: Studying the history of cuisine and understanding every aspect of its origins will allow you to crawl inside someone's head. A great dish isn't just a collection of ingredients, it's a living snapshot in time, meant to be eaten and returned to as living history of the region.

A DISH YOU MAKE THAT'S INSPIRED BY ANOTHER RESTAURANT: Foie Gras Du Monde. Its a riff on coffee and beignets made famous at the refreshment stand on Decatur street in the French Quarter. It's foie gras done five ways, with raw foies puréed into hot coffee, giving you the illusion you're drinking a rich hot chocolate.

IF YOU COULD EAT AT ANY RESTAURANT IN THE WORLD TONIGHT, IT WOULD BE: La Tapa in Cruz Bay, St. John. I used to live there and loved the smells of toasted garlic and grilled Caribbean lobsters wafting from the open air island kitchen.

FAVORITE COOKBOOK: This week I'm most excited to read Norman Van Aken's latest cookbook, My Key West Kitchen. It just arrived from Amazon.

SHRIMP AND TASSO HENICAN
Chef Tory McPhail of Commander's Palace | New Orleans, LA
Adapted by StarChefs
Yield: 8 servings

INGREDIENTS

Five Pepper Jelly:
1½ cups light corn syrup
1¼ cups white vinegar
½ teaspoon red pepper flakes
Kosher salt
Black pepper
3 large bell peppers (1 each red, yellow, green), finely diced
4 jalapeños, finely diced

Crystal Hot Sauce Beurre Blanc:
⅓ cup Crystal hot sauce
2 tablespoons minced shallots
6 medium cloves garlic, minced
¼ cup heavy cream
3 ounces unsalted butter, diced, softened
Kosher salt

Gulf Shrimp:
24 jumbo Gulf shrimp, peeled and deveined
2 ounces tasso ham, cut into twenty-four 1-inch strips
½ cup all-purpose flour
Creole seafood seasoning
½ cup vegetable oil

To Assemble and Serve:
12 pieces pickled okra, sliced in half lengthwise

METHOD

For the Five Pepper Jelly:
In a small saucepan over medium-low heat, combine corn syrup, vinegar, red pepper flakes, salt, and black pepper. Simmer until reduced by two-thirds. Transfer to storage container and chill. In a dry skillet over medium heat, cook bell peppers and jalapeños until tender and their color has brightened, about 30 seconds. Using a slotted spoon, transfer bell peppers and jalapeños to container with chilled jelly and stir well to thoroughly combine.

For the Crystal Hot Sauce Beurre Blanc:
In a small saucepan over medium heat, combine hot sauce, shallots, garlic, and cream. Simmer until reduced by half, stirring frequently. Remove from heat and slowly whisk in pieces of butter. Strain through a chinois and keep warm.

For the Gulf Shrimp:
Cut a ¼-inch incision down the back of each shrimp where it has been deveined. Place a tasso strip in each incision. Secure with a toothpick. In a bowl, combine flour with Creole seasoning and lightly dredge each shrimp. In a large skillet over medium flame, heat vegetable oil. Fry shrimp for about 30 seconds on each side. Shrimp should be firm with a red-brown color. Drain on paper towels and toss shrimp in bowl with Crystal Hot Sauce Beurre Blanc, coating thoroughly. Remove the toothpicks.

To Assemble and Serve:
Pool enough Five-Pepper Jelly onto center of serving plate to coat the bottom. Arrange 3 Gulf Shrimp on each plate, alternating with 3 pieces of pickled okra. Serve immediately.

Featured Ingredient: Gulf shrimp

PHOTO ANTOINETTE BRUNO

Bryan Voltaggio

VOLT | Frederick, MD

 BRYANVOLTAGGIO

Chef Bryan Voltaggio grew up eating meals that included hand-picked produce from the family garden in his native Frederick, Maryland. Voltaggio followed his nascent passion for cuisine from its roots in a simple garden plot to the hotel kitchens, where he worked as a sous chef and eventually executive chef—all by the age of 20.

Voltaggio attended the Culinary Institute of America, and through a stage at Charlie Palmer's Aureole in New York City, he met his mentor and future boss. After hiring him as a sous chef at Aureole, Palmer sent the young chef to hone his skills at Maison Pic in Valence, France. Upon returning the the States, Voltaggio continued working for Palmer for several years as executive chef at Charlie Palmer Steak in Washington, D.C., before he finally opened his own restaurant, VOLT, back in his hometown in partnership with then budding restaurateur Hilda Staples. At VOLT, Voltaggio presents a menu that celebrates locality and seasonality through meticulous, innovative techniques. For his cuisine there, he earned a 2010 StarChefs Rising Stars Award.

In 2009, Voltaggio caught the nation's attention as a finalist on both the sixth season of "Top Chef," competing alongside brother Michael, and on the fifth season of "Top Chef Masters" four years later. He was a nominated for "Best Chef, Mid-Atlantic" by the James Beard Foundation in 2010, and was a semifinalist for the same award in 2012. Voltaggio authored Home: Recipes to Cook with Family and Friends in 2014. Beyond VOLT, he has expanded his family of restaurants in the greater D.C. area with Lunchbox, Family Meal (now with four locations), RANGE, and AGGIO.

THE RANGE AND VOLT OF CREATIVE SYNERGY

Three's company, a crowd. It's also a collaboration. When Mid-Atlantic restaurant maven Bryan Voltaggio and his point men Mattie McGhee and Graeme Ritchie get in the chef huddle, great things happen. They've learned how to harness the power of synergy to create some of the most exciting food in the country. Join the huddle on the ICC Main Stage.

Presented by MTucker and Fresh Origins

PHOTO: ANTOINETTE BRUNO

Graeme Ritchie

VOLT | Frederick, MD

Graeme Ritchie was born into the restaurant business. As a 14 year old, he picked up an odds-and-ends shift at the restaurant his mother managed in Rochester, New York—doing everything from laundry to washing dishes. Not a fan of scrubbing pots, Ritchie buddied up to the restaurant's Italian owner, who taught him basic prep skills and instilled in him a strong work ethic and love for cooking. At 16, he graduated to a cook's position, taking a job at his grandfather's country club. But his parents didn't approve of his desires to attend culinary school, and so the passionate Ritchie applied to the Culinary Institute of America in Hyde Park without them knowing.

After graduating from culinary school, Ritchie moved to New York City to work at David Burke & Donatella, followed by a tenure as executive sous chef at Charlie Palmer Steak in Washington, D.C. In 2008, he joined Bryan Voltaggio to open VOLT as executive sous chef and right hand man. After eight years as a Voltaggio veteran, Ritchie assumed the honor of its chef de cuisine post and earned a 2014 StarChefs Rising Stars Award. At VOLT, he strives to give guests a new appreciation for local products, classic flavor profiles, and traditional pairings, presenting ideas that are familiar and yet completely unexpected.

 **GRAEMERITCHIE**

MOST INFLUENTIAL MENTOR WITH WHOM YOU'VE WORKED: Bryan Voltaggio. He's made me who I am as a chef.

COOLEST TECHNIQUE YOU'VE LEARNED FROM ANOTHER CHEF: Alternative sodium use. Seasoning something doesn't always mean using salt. Soy sauces, tamari, shiro, Worcestershire,or any high-sodium additive makes a great substitute for salt and usually adds a new dynamic to the dish.

A DISH YOU MAKE THAT'S INSPIRED BY ANOTHER CULTURE: Slow-cooked chicken wings, seared crisp with kimchi bucatini, mushroom brodo, cilantro, and Thai basil. The dish hits a lot of cultures but truly delivers great flavors that are powerful and refreshing.

CHEF WITH WHOM YOU'D MOST LIKE TO COLLABORATE: My mother. She's always been a huge inspiration to me, but she's never let me cook in her kitchen because I make too much of a mess. For that, I'd love the chance to cook with her, without criticism ...

PHOTO: ANTOINETTE BRUNO

WAGYU SHORT RIB, SALSIFY, MALT, AND LEEK

Chef Graeme Ritchie of Volt | Frederick, MD
Adapted by StarChefs
Yield: 4 portions

INGREDIENTS

Wagyu Short Rib:
1 wagyu boneless short rib (1.812
   kilograms), trimmed, silver skin
   removed
36 grams shio koji rice malt

Salsify Purée:
8 salsify roots, unpeeled
   1 quart milk
½ cup brewer's malt
   Salt

Leeks:
2 leeks, trimmed and peeled

To Assemble and Serve:
Salt
Ground black pepper
   Edible flowers
Fresh origins micro greens

METHOD

For the Wagyu Beef Short Rib:
Rub rib with rice malt, seal in airtight container, and cure in refrigerator for 48 hours. Heat bath of an immersion circulator to 58˚C. Quarter short rib, place each portion in a vacuum bag, and seal. Cook rib portions sous vide for 3 hours. Let bath cool to below 40˚C; hold for service.

For the Salsify Purée:
Under hot binchōtan coals, bury salsify and cook 7 to 8 minutes, allowing them to char. Remove from coals and cool. In a pot, combine milk and malt and bring to a light simmer. Cover, remove from heat, and infuse 1 hour, while the malt leaches out of the grain. Strain and reserve liquid. Place cooled salsify in a separate pot and cover with water. Boil 10 minutes, to soften the charred skins. Remove from water and gently peel away skin. In another pot, combine malted milk and salsify and heat over low flame until salsify is tender. Transfer salsify to a blender and purèe. Season with salt and reserve warm.

For the Leeks:
Prepare and heat grill with binchōtan hardwood charcoal, leave leeks on grill until they steam themselves soft. Immediately transfer to a container with a locking top. When cool, cut leeks into ¼-inch rings.

To Assemble and Serve:
Prepare and heat grill with binchōtan hardwood charcoal. Remove the Wagyu Beef Short Rib portions from bags and reheat on grill, along with Leeks; season Leeks with salt and pepper. Slice meat from bones, 4 strips per portion. Plate Salsify Purée first, top with Wagyu Beef Short Rib and Leeks. Garnish with flowers and micro greens.

Refine your craft with professional chocolate, pastry and dessert courses from Valrhona.

Walk into our state-of-the-art kitchen and learn from masters in the field in small, intimate classes of 8-12 Chef-students. In this vibrant and welcoming venue, perfect your techniques, exchange ideas, and discover emerging trends alongside your professional contemporaries. We invite you to enter the world of L'École Valrhona.

VALRHONA
Expertise & Experience

BROOKLYN, NEW YORK

Information and Registration:
718-522-7001 (ext.110) | www.valrhonaprofessionals.com
ecolebrooklyn@valrhona.com | #ecolebrooklyn

@ValrhonaUSA

PHOTO: ELLE WILDHAGEN

 CRAFTSMANWOLVES

COOLEST TECHNIQUE YOU'VE LEARNED FROM ANOTHER CHEF: It's not so much a technique, but one of the best pieces of advice I've received was from Albert Adrià. I used to stress out that I had to own every recipe that I developed or conceptualized, but Albert credited his team for being the ones to evolve them, perfect them, and put them into service.

A DISH INSPIRED BY ANOTHER CULTURE: Our horchata cake is inspired by the neighborhood we're in—the Mission in San Francisco.

IF YOU COULD EAT AT ANY RESTAURANT IN THE WORLD TONIGHT, IT WOULD BE: My house with good friends and family and a couple amazing bottles of wine.

CHEF WITH WHOM YOU'D MOST LIKE TO COLLABORATE: Chef Andoni Luis Aduriz of Mugaritz

William Werner

Craftsman and Wolves | San Francisco, CA

Florida native William Werner spent his early years the way any reasonably ambitious local might: working as a lifeguard, planning a career in medicine, and surfing. But when some elder lifeguards showed him the basics of cooking, he fell hard for cuisine, and the camaraderie that comes with it.

THOUGHTS, NOTES, AND RECIPES FROM A CHEF-DRIVEN PASTRY SHOP

Pastry Chef William Werner is pushing to expand his brand of modern, chef-driven pastry on the West Coast. What's the secret sauce behind Craftsman and Wolves? Find out on the ICC Main Stage as Werner presents the desserts and philosophies behind one of America's most exciting pastry shops.

Presented by Valrhona

Unable to afford culinary school, Werner looked for hands-on training at a vegetarian restaurant. The chef, a Chez Panisse and French Laundry alum, became a mentor, imparting the standards of those iconic restaurants to young Werner. When a pastry chef position opened, Werner found the cerebral aspects of the sweet station appealing. Since transitioning to pastry, he has worked for myriad places from Ritz-Carlton Hotels to San Francisco's Quince, developing a distinct and inventive outlook.

In 2011, he opened the pop-up concept Tell Tale Preserve Company and began selling an array of pastries at farmers markets and coffee shops. In summer 2012, Werner opened Craftsman and Wolves, a contemporary pâtisserie in San Francisco's Mission district. In 2013, Werner was nominated for the James Beard Foundation's "Outstanding Pastry Chef" Award and earned a StarChefs Rising Stars Award. He also serves as a Valrhona Pastry Chef Consultant. Later this year, Werner will open a Southern California outpost of Craftsman and Wolves in Culver City's newly developed Platform space. A second, highly anticipated San Francisco location also will soon open in Russian Hill.

BLOND CHOCOLATE, HORCHATA, AND HAZELNUT

Pastry Chef William Werner of Craftsman and Wolves | San Francisco, CA
Adapted by StarChefs
Yield: 60 squares

INGREDIENTS

Praline Cake:
5 grams lemon zest
160 grams caster sugar
320 grams eggs
45 grams trimoline
320 grams cake flour
9.5 grams baking powder
320 grams praline paste (66% fruity
    hazelnut/almond)
160 grams milk
160 grams clarified butter, 55°C

Light Dulcey Horchata Mousse:
750 grams milk, scalded
170 grams brown rice, ground until
    texture of coarse polenta
1 stick cinnamon
30 grams gelatin, bloomed in 180
    grams warm water
3 grams vanilla seeds
1.5 kilograms Valrhona Dulcey,
    melted
1.5 kilograms heavy cream, whipped
    to soft peaks

Praline-Milk Chocolate Crémeux:
310 grams milk
310 grams heavy cream
80 grams yolks
60 grams sugar
280 grams Valrhona Bahibe milk
    chocolate
188 grams praline paste (60%)

Caramelized Hazelnuts:
50 grams ground cinnamon
10 grams vanilla powder
5 grams sea salt
625 grams sugar
500 grams hazelnuts
50 grams water
2.5 grams cocoa butter

Puffed Rice:
250 grams puffed rice
100 grams Valrhona Opalys white
    chocolate
10 grams salt

To Assemble and Serve:
150 grams Valrhona Opalys white
    chocolate
100 grams cocoa butter

METHOD

For the Praline Cake:
In a bowl, combine zest with sugar, followed by eggs and trimoline. Sift in flour and baking powder. In a separate container, combine praline and milk, using an immersion blender to emulsify. Add praline mixture to bowl, followed by hot butter, stirring to combine. Cover and rest in refrigerator 12 hours. Heat oven to 350°F. Prepare a raplette with a #4 bar. With the raplette, spread and flatten dough onto a silicone mat. When dough is smooth and level, bake 8 to 10 minutes; cool. Cut into 2-inch squares, cover, and reserve.

For the Light Dulcey Horchata Mousse:
In a storage container, combine milk, rice, and cinnamon. Cover and refrigerate overnight, at least 8 hours. Remove cinnamon stick, transfer to blender, and purée. Strain through a chinois lined with cheesecloth, squeezing to extract as much rice flavor as possible. Scale 750 grams of strained rice milk, and add to pot over medium-low heat. Add gelatin, vanilla, and Dulcey. Emulsify with an immersion blender. When mixture reaches 35°C, transfer to a bowl, and fold in whipped cream. Cover and chill.

For the Praline-Milk Chocolate Crémeux:
In a pot, combine milk, cream, yolks, and sugar. Heat to 85°C. In a double boiler, melt chocolate and praline. Add melted chocolate mixture to hot milk mixture, and emulsify with immersion blender. Cast into square insert molds and freeze.

For the Caramelized Hazelnuts:
Heat oven to 315°F. In a large bowl, combine cinnamon, vanilla, salt, and 500 grams sugar; reserve. Onto a parchment-lined sheet tray, spread hazelnuts. Warm in oven for about 10 minutes. In a small saucepot, combine water and remaining sugar, and bring to boil. Remove hazelnuts from oven and pour syrup over nuts, stirring to coat them evenly. When crystallized, transfer nuts to a separate pot and cook over medium heat until golden and caramelized. Add cocoa butter, stir to combine, and immediately cast into reserved bowl with sugar mixture. Toss to coat. Spread on silicone mat, let cool, cover, and reserve.

For the Puffed Rice:
In a bowl, combine all ingredients. Onto an acetate sheet, spread into a ¼-inch layer. Let set, and break into interesting shapes.

To Assemble and Serve:
Top a Praline Cake cube with a frozen square of Praline-Milk Chocolate Crémeux. Cast 60 grams of Light Dulcey Horchata Mousse into a square mold. Cake first, insert cake-crémeux into mousse. The mousse should rise to the top and the cake should set just below the lip of the mold. Spread clean with an offset spatula; freeze. In a double boiler, combine white chocolate and cocoa butter, and heat to 45°C. Load a power sprayer with warm chocolate mixture, and spray onto unmolded dessert. Let thaw in refrigerator 2 hours. Garnish with Puffed Rice and Caramelized Hazelnuts.

Featured Ingredient: Valrhona chocolate

Peru, feeds your soul

Three Peruvian restaurants among World´s 50 best:
Central, Astrid & Gastón and Maido.

Cebiche

peru.info

SAVORY

PHOTO: ANTOINETTE BRUNO

Matthew Accarrino

SPQR | San Francisco, CA

 **MATTACCARRINO**

MOST INFLUENTIAL COOK WITH WHOM YOU'VE WORKED: I've learned from every cook and chef I've ever worked with, sometimes what to do and others what not to do. Keep your eyes open.

A DISH YOU MAKE THAT'S INSPIRED BY ANOTHER CULTURE: In a sense, I use Italy as an inspiration for my cooking at SPQR. Really, I'm focused on ingredients of great quality. I'm interested in regional ingredients—that is, American, West Coast, and Californian products—that represent the Italian fundamentals of quality, seasonality, and locality.

IF YOU COULD EAT AT ANY RESTAURANT IN THE WORLD TONIGHT, IT WOULD BE: Le Restaurant du Pavillon de France circa 1939. You asked.

FAVORITE INDUSTRY INSTAGRAM ACCOUNT: What's Instagram?

FAVORITE COOKBOOK: The French Laundry Cookbook by Thomas Keller

Born in the Midwest and raised on the East Coast, Matt Accarrino spent his early years scouring the lower rungs of the Jersey restaurant scene, washing dishes, prepping ingredients, and learning the ropes. Humble work, sure, but Accarrino had his sights set high.

That may be why, in addition to attending the Culinary Institute of America, Accarrino earned a B.A. in hospitality management from Fairleigh Dickinson University. It's certainly why he traveled to Italy to work at Michelin-starred Antonello Colonna. Back in the United States, Accarrino worked his way through Metrazure, Oceana, and Per Se, where he was recruited to be opening sous chef. A meeting with Tom Colicchio in late 2005 found Accarrino in the heart of the Craft empire, and assigned to an influential post that eventually took him to the West Coast.

Taking the helm at SPQR, Accarrino brought years of technical acumen and respect for product, craft, and heritage that continues to define his cuisine. Amidst the (inevitable and adoring) national coverage, Accarrino took top honors at San Francisco's Cochon 555, was named a 2010 StarChefs San Francisco Rising Star, and earned a spot on *Food & Wine*'s "Best New Chef" list in 2014. His team has earned a Michelin star for SPQR two years in a row, and Accarrino (somehow) found time to write his first book, SPQR: Modern Italian Food and Wine in 2012.

SPAGHETTI WEST COAST

Roll deep. Roll often. Roll your pasta skills forward with two of the West Coast's primo pasta makers: Portland's Jenn Louis and San Francisco's Matt Accarrino. Attendees will work on rustic frascarelli, plump dumplings, and smoked doughs in this flour-filled, hands-on workshop.

Presented by MTucker and Vollrath

SMOKED PASTA, SEA URCHIN, SMOKED BACON, AND QUAIL EGG

Chef Matthew Accarrino of SPQR | San Francisco, CA
Adapted by StarChefs
Yield: 4 to 6 servings

INGREDIENTS

Smoked Durum Flour:
100 grams durum flour

Smoked Pasta:
200 grams 00 flour, plus additional for dusting
Pinch salt
3 eggs, beaten
1 tablespoon water, plus additional as needed

To Assemble and Serve:
150 grams smoked bacon, diced ¼-inch and rendered, bacon fat reserved
100 grams sea urchin
58 grams Parmesan cheese, finely grated, plus additional for garnish
58 grams butter
Black pepper
Smoked sea salt
Quail eggs, cooked in 64.5°C water bath

METHOD

For the Smoked Durum Flour:
Place a piece of cheesecloth in a stovetop smoker and lay the flour on top. Cover tightly with foil and smoke the flour 20 minutes. Remove flour from heat and remove the foil; cool. The flour will be darkened. Sift to remove any lumps.

For the Smoked Pasta:
In the bowl of a stand mixer fitted with a hook, combine 100 grams Smoked Durum Flour, 00 flour, and salt. Mix on low speed, slowly adding eggs until the dough comes together and adding enough water to moisten the dough. Turn the dough onto well floured work surface and knead by hand for several minutes. Flatten the dough into a flat rectangle, wrap in plastic wrap, and rest 30 minutes. Set up a pasta machine on a large work surface. Unwrap the dough and divide into 3 pieces. Roll each piece into a thin pasta sheet, dusting as needed, and cut into noodles. Shake the noodles loose and place them on a tray. Cover with a slightly damp towel and reserve.

To Assemble and Serve:
Bring a pot of salted water to a boil and cook Smoked Pasta until al dente, about 3 to 4 minutes; drain, reserving a small amount of the pasta water. In a sauté pan over medium flame, heat 2 tablespoons bacon fat and add bacon and pasta. Stir in sea urchin and toss to combine. Add a bit of pasta cooking water to create a sauce. Sprinkle in Parmesan and add butter. Toss to combine and season with salt and pepper. Place pasta into a serving bowl and garnish with Parmesan, black pepper, and a quail egg.

Featured Equipment: Vollrath Mirage Pro Induction Range, Hobart stand mixer

PHOTO: ANTOINETTE BRUNO

PHOTO: ED ANDERSON

 JENNLOUISPDX 🐦 JENNLOUIS

MOST INFLUENTIAL COOK WITH WHOM YOU'VE WORKED: Jamie Bissonnette. His attention to flavor building always inspires me, and he is a great collaborator.

COOLEST TECHNIQUE YOU'VE LEARNED FROM ANOTHER CHEF: I met a chef in Israel who was so open with her food and how she made it. She cooked all vegetarian, and her focus was very straightforward and flavorful. She brought me into the kitchen and showed me how she charred her eggplant, simmered her squash, and how simple her process was with such a restrained hand. Her honesty and transparency were as inspirational as her delicious food.

IF YOU COULD EAT AT ANY RESTAURANT IN THE WORLD TONIGHT, IT WOULD BE: Trattoria da Cesare in Rome

FAVORITE INDUSTRY INSTAGRAM ACCOUNT: @ChefJeremyFox

FAVORITE COOKBOOK: <u>Persiana: Recipes from the Middle East & Beyond</u> by Sabrina Ghayour

CHEF WITH WHOM YOU'D MOST LIKE TO COLLABORATE: Trevor Kunk. I adore his focus on produce and the flavors and textures he coaxes from ingredients.

Jenn Louis
Lincoln | Portland, OR

Many things might be learned at an Outward Bound base-camp, deep in the North Carolina woods. Usually, they don't involve wanting to become a chef. But then, Jenn Louis' story isn't that ordinary. A wayward teenage artist who'd done her fair share of traveling (Europe, North and South America, several months in Israel), Louis found herself cooking at Outward Bound and (coincidentally) had the kind of epiphany the program is intended for: she found her discipline.

After studying at the Western Culinary Institute of Portland, Louis began work as a line cook at the prominent local restaurant Wildwood. From there, an inspired Louis opened Culinary Artistry, a full-service catering company that provided everything from valet service and floral arrangements to an array of menu concepts. It's now one of the top event planning companies in Portland, with a reputation for sustainability.

Still ambitious eight years later, Louis and now husband David Welch opened Lincoln Restaurant, a refined-rustic, seasonal, and local reflection of the Pacific Northwest that's earned her semifinalist positions on the 2010 and 2011 James Beard "Best Chef, Northwest" lists and a StarChefs Rising Stars Award. In 2011, she and Welch opened soulful food and cocktail spot Sunshine Tavern in Portland's Southeast Division district. At Sunshine, Louis's sustainable, product-based passions shine through and earned her a spot on *Food & Wine*'s 2012 "Best New Chefs" list.

PHOTO: ED ANDERSON

SEMOLINA FRASCARELLI
Chef Jenn Louis of Lincoln | Portland, OR
Adapted by StarChefs
Yield: 6 servings

INGREDIENTS

Semolina Frascarelli:
910 grams semolina
1 quart ice water, plus additional as
  needed

To Assemble and Serve:
Salt
Warm tomato sauce

METHOD

For the Semolina Frascarelli:
Spread half the semolina on a sheet tray, leaving a 3-inch border around the edges. With a bench scraper in one hand, dip the other hand into the container with ice water. Let large droplets fall onto the semolina from the scraper. Do not shake or wiggle the scraper, as the water droplets will be too small. When several large droplets have scattered, use the bench scraper to turn semolina over onto itself to form small dough chunks. Transfer dough chunks to a mesh sieve or strainer and allow unabsorbed flour to fall back onto the sheet pan. The remaining dough chunks are the frascarelli. Place them on a separate parchment-lined sheet tray. Repeat process, until all the semolina has been used. Cover and store frascarelli in the refrigerator for up to 3 days.

To Assemble and Serve:
In large pot of boiling salted water, cook frascarelli until tender; drain. Serve with warm tomato sauce.

Featured Equipment: Vollrath Mirage Pro Induction Range

David Bazirgan

Dirty Habit | San Francisco, CA

David Bazirgan is known for his work on western shores, helming Fifth Floor, and now Dirty Habit, in San Francisco. But Bazirgan's story begins on the East Coast. With classically humble beginnings, washing dishes in his hometown of Newburyport, Massachusetts, Bazirgan went on to study French technique at the Cambridge School of Culinary Arts.

After graduating, Bazirgan worked through a number of renowned Boston-area restaurants, including Stan Frankenthaler's Salamander and Todd English's Olives. But his most important Boston connection was Chef Barbara Lynch, his would-be mentor. Taking note of Bazirgan's drive, Lynch connected him with his first job out of culinary school at Boston's prestigious Galleria Italiana. Before moving to San Francisco in 2003, Bazirgan was chef de cuisine at Lynch's No. 9 Park, where he helped craft the first of their acclaimed seven- and nine-course tasting menus.

After his tenure under Lynch, Bazirgan was ready for the City by the Bay. Before Fifth Floor, which earned three and a half stars from *The San Francisco Chronicle*, Bazirgan was executive chef at Chez Papa Resto at Mint Plaza, Baraka in Potrero Hill (where he earned a 2005 StarChefs San Francisco Rising Star Award), and Elisabeth Daniel in Jackson Square. Now, with the progressive, bar-anchored, small-plates Dirty Habit, Bazirgan finds himself unleashed from the constrictions of tasting menus and able to let his creativity run free, in a slightly more relaxed—but food-serious—context.

DON'T BIN IT, $PIN IT: BY-PRODUCT UTILIZATION

Waste reduction is trending right now. If you're not turning your scraps into a flying-off-the-pass Thursday night special, then you're behind the times (and probably running high food costs). In this hands-on workshop, Dirty Habit Chef David Bazirgan will give you the tips and techniques you need to transform trim, peelings, and odd bits into delicious, cost-effective dishes.

Presented by Hobart

BAZSF DIRTYHABITSF

MOST INFLUENTIAL MENTOR WITH WHOM YOU'VE WORKED: Barbara Lynch. Lynchie cooked with so much passion, it still resonates with me today.

COOLEST TECHNIQUE YOU'VE LEARNED FROM ANOTHER CHEF: Take a whole head of garlic, break it into cloves, sandwich two mixing bowls with garlic inside, and shake the shit out of it for 20 seconds. You get a whole head of peeled garlic.

A DISH YOU MAKE THAT'S INSPIRED BY ANOTHER CULTURE: Crispy soft shell crab stuffed with green curry sausage and atchara (fermented green papaya), and fresh banana ketchup. It's inspired by my sous chef Francis Ang's Filipino heritage.

IF YOU COULD EAT AT ANY RESTAURANT IN THE WORLD TONIGHT, IT WOULD BE: Hartwood in Tulum, Mexico

CHEF WITH WHOM YOU'D MOST LIKE TO COLLABORATE: Ken Oringer. I love his style and still think back to 1997 before we opened No. 9 Park, we went to Clio for dinner and I was thinking, "Holy shit. This is so fucking good." We have cooked together, but a real collaboration dinner would be sick.

EVERYTHING SAUSAGE, ROOT VEGETABLE PICKLE, AND APPLE MUSTARD

Chef David Bazirgan of Dirty Habit | San Francisco, CA
Adapted by StarChefs
Yield: 35 servings

INGREDIENTS

Infused Milk:
Vegetable oil
½ medium onion, coarsely chopped
1 medium carrot, coarsely chopped
1 clove garlic, coarsely chopped
1 bay leaf
4 sprigs thyme
2 liters milk

Everything Sausage:
Sausage casings
1 kilogram chicken meat scraps
1 kilogram duck meat scraps
1 kilogram foie gras scraps
500 grams quail meat scraps
500 grams pork fatback
3 eggs
12 egg whites
50 grams all-purpose flour
30 grams cornstarch
100 grams salt
1 gram ground clove
2 grams ground nutmeg
5 grams ground cinnamon

Root Vegetable Pickle:
400 grams celery root scraps, finely chopped
400 grams carrot scraps, finely chopped
400 grams parsnip scraps, finely chopped
1 liter rice wine vinegar
1 liter water
30 grams salt
50 grams sugar

Apple Mustard:
500 grams apple scraps
100 grams cider vinegar
200 grams sugar
20 grams salt
50 grams Dijon mustard
200 grams yellow mustard seeds, blanched
Salt

METHOD

For the Infused Milk:
In a saucepan, heat oil and sweat vegetables and aromatics. Add milk awnd steep for 1 hour. Strain and chill.

For the Everything Sausage:
Prepare sausage casings for stuffing. In a Hobart food processor, process remaining ingredients with

PHOTO: ANTOINETTE BRUNO

1¾ cups Infused Milk until smooth. Pass forcemeat through a tamis. Stuff sausage casings with forcemeat. Heat a large pot of water to 64°C. Prepare an ice bath. Cook sausages in hot water for 20 minutes. Transfer links to ice bath. Hang in refrigerator for 3 days or freeze up to 2 months.

For the Root Vegetable Pickle:
In a bowl, combine root vegetables. In a pot, bring remaining ingredients to boil. Pour hot pickling liquid over vegetables. Let sit overnight at room temperature.

For the Apple Mustard:
In a saucepan, add apple, vinegar, sugar, and salt and cover with water. Cook over medium heat until apple is soft. Remove from heat and stir in mustard. Transfer to a blender and purée; strain. In a bowl, fold mustard seeds into purée. Season with salt.

To Assemble and Serve:
Prepare and heat grill. Remove Everything Sausage from casing and sear on grill. Serve with Root Vegetable Pickle and Apple Mustard.

Featured Ingredients: Fossil Farms quail and duck
Featured Equipment: Hobart food processor and mixer with meat grinder attachment

Jose Garces
Garces Group | Philadelphia, PA

Jose Garces grew up in Chicago, raised by his Ecuadorian parents. He credits his interest in cooking to his mother, whom he vividly remembers helping in the kitchen after school when he was young. After graduating from local Kendall College for culinary school, Garces went on to apprentice at La Taberna del Alabardero in Marbella, Spain. He later moved to New York to work in the kitchens of some of the city's most well known restaurants: the Rainbow Room, the Four Seasons, 57/57, and Bolivar. Garces emerged as a true talent under the tutelage of Chef Douglas Rodriguez, often cited as "the godfather of Nuevo Latino cuisine." While working with Rodriguez at his two popular restaurants, Pipa and Chicama, Garces earned the respect of both his peers and the dining public.

In 2000, Garces was invited to Philadelphia to serve as executive chef, first at Restaurateur Stephen Starr's Cuban-influenced Alma de Cuba and, later, at El Vez. In January 2004, Garces was recognized as one of "Philly's New Star Chefs" by *Philadelphia Magazine*, and just one month later *Restaurant Hospitality Magazine* honored him with a similar award. That same year StarChefs recognized Garces with a Rising Star Chef Award. In 2009, he went on to compete in and win season two of "The Next Iron Chef."

Presently, Garces is at the helm of an ever-expanding Garces Group, a collection of 17 restaurants that span the country. This fall he'll make his New York debut as a restaurateur with the opening of tapas bar Amada in New York's Brookfield Place. He is also the founder of the Garces Foundation, a nonprofit that serves underprivileged immigrant communities in Philadelphia.

BREAK THE BANK PAELLA

Paella is tailor-made for the large format, family-style eating that's sweeping American dining rooms. Learn how to put on the ultimate show (crispy socarrat included) with an uber-luxe, break the bank paella. Attendees will fire up pans alongside Iron Chef Jose Garces, who'll bring the bling (and technique) to this Spanish classic.

Presented by Foods from Spain, the region of Valencia, and Paderno USA

CHEFJOSEGARCES

COOLEST TECHNIQUE YOU'VE LEARNED FROM ANOTHER CHEF: My paternal grandmother, Mamita Amada, is the undisputed empanada master. It was an absolute revelation when I learned the technique for the green plantain dough for her empanadas de verde. She showed me, step by step, the techniques for boiling the plantains, ricing them, and then overworking the riced plantains to activate their natural starches. The result is a soft, elastic dough that doesn't contain any flour, butter, or shortenings.

A DISH YOU MAKE THAT'S INSPIRED BY ANOTHER CHEF: Puffed morcilla with chimichurri, raisins, and orange that we serve at Volvér. In 2013, my culinary team and I took a trip to Spain and visited Restaurante Víctor Gutiérrez. Chef Gutiérrez hails from Peru, so the menu featured flavors from his native country but always utilized the best of Spain's stellar products. One of the courses was a morcilla chip, which I thought was a genius application. We adopted the idea but added an Argentine twist in terms of the accompanying flavors.

IF YOU COULD EAT AT ANY RESTAURANT IN THE WORLD TONIGHT, IT WOULD BE: Asador Etxebarri. Two standout dishes for me were the flawless grilled head-on prawns from the Catalan seaside town of Palamós, and a perfectly smooth, reduced milk ice cream surrounded by a red fruit infusion. The hint of smoke in the ice cream was unexpected and unforgettable.

FAVORITE COOKBOOK: Francis Mallmann's Seven Fires: Grilling the Argentine Way

SEAFOOD PAELLA

Chef Jose Garces of Garces Group | Philadelphia, PA
Adapted by StarChefs
Yield: 4 servings

INGREDIENTS

Clam-Squid Ink Broth:
1 quart clam juice
1 tablespoon squid ink
1 cup caramelized onions

Seafood Paella:
5 cockles, cleaned
5 mussels, cleaned
5 jumbo shrimp, peeled with head on
5 scallops, foot removed and sliced
  in half
2 ounces calamari, cut into ½-inch
  rings
¼ cup frozen peas
¼ cup julienned piquillo peppers
½ cup finely diced onion
1 cup Calasparra rice
2 tablespoons olive oil

Parsley Salad:
4 ounces cherry tomatoes, halved
1 bunch parsley, leaves picked
1 red onion, thinly sliced
2 tablespoons Sherry vinaigrette
½ cup fava beans, blanched and
  shelled

To Assemble and Serve:
4 toasted baguette slices
2 tablespoons paprika aïoli

METHOD

For the Clam-Squid Ink Broth:
In a saucepan, combine all ingredients. Over medium heat, bring to a simmer, and cook 1 hour. Remove from heat and cool slightly. Pour mixture into a blender and purée until smooth.

For the Seafood Paella:
Heat oven to 350°F. Place a 14-inch paella pan over medium heat. When pan is hot, add olive oil and then onions. Cook until tender, about 2 minutes. Add Calasparra rice and toast 2 minutes, until all grains are coated in oil. Place remaining ingredients in pan, along with 2¼ cups Clam-Squid Ink Broth. Move ingredients around so that the rice and broth are evenly distributed. When liquid comes to a simmer, cover with foil and place paella pan in the oven. Cook approximately 15 minutes, then remove foil cover. Cook 10 minutes more, until rice is cooked through and the bottom begins to brown and crisp.

For the Parsley Salad:
Toss all ingredients together right before paella is finished cooking in oven.

To Assemble and Serve:
Remove Seafood Paella from oven. Slather baguette slices with paprika aïoli. Garnish paella with Parsley Salad and baguette slices.

Featured Ingredients: Spanish olive oil and Sherry vinegar
Featured Cookware: Paderno black carbon steel paella pan

PHOTO: DARYL AND MINDI HIRSCH

PHOTO: MEGAN SWANN

Markus Glocker

Bâtard | New York, NY

A summer job does not always a profession make. But for Markus Glocker, summers spent working at his uncle's Austrian hotel were stepping stones to destiny. He knew right away he wanted to be in the family business—hospitality.

Except, where his uncle took care of room, Glocker was more interested in board. He attended culinary school in Linz, Austria, and having already shown a talent and discipline suited to the fine arts (Glocker studied classical music as a young student), he excelled under the singular pressures of the kitchen. After graduating, Glocker brought that joy-of-precision mentality to Restaurant Vier Jahreszeiten in Munich, Germany, where he worked as a commis chef.

Fully immersed in the industry, Glocker honed his skills everywhere he could, from three Michelin-starred Restaurant Eckart Witzigmann in Berlin to Charlie Trotter's in Chicago, and all the way back in Austria to work at the two Michelin-starred Restaurant Steirereck in Vienna. Hopping the pond to the United States, Glocker made a name for himself at Gordon Ramsay's New York flagship, where he earned a 2010 StarChefs Rising Stars Award. In 2014, Glocker joined forces with iconic New York restaurateur Drew Nieporent to open Bâtard, which earned the title of James Beard's "Best New Restaurant" in 2015. At Bâtard, Glocker's years of cooking crystallize with a cuisine defined as much by ebullient, rustic Austrian heritage as Glocker's refined precision and an ingrained, family-style love of hospitality.

SIMPLICITY REFINED: TECHNIQUES FROM BÂTARD

Markus Glocker's résumé exemplifies fine dining—at its finest. In his hands-on workshop, Glocker will take attendees on a journey from his Austrian roots to his modern TriBeCa restaurant, Bâtard, stripping away excess to reveal the core of elegant cuisine.

Presented by Fresh Origins

 📷 🐦 **MARKUSGLOCKER**

MOST INFLUENTIAL MENTOR WITH WHOM YOU'VE WORKED: I've been fortunate enough to work with numerous people who've taught me valuable lessons in several areas. For example, Charlie Trotter for culinary excellence and discipline, Eckart Witzigmann for bold flavors, and Drew Nieporent for business.

A DISH YOU MAKE THAT'S INSPIRED BY ANOTHER CULTURE: The quail ballotine dish with sauerkraut, crispy pumpkin seeds, and Sauternes raisins is a dish that represents tradition, trend, and finesse all at the same time.

IF YOU COULD EAT AT ANY RESTAURANT IN THE WORLD TONIGHT, IT WOULD BE: Restaurant Steirereck in Vienna. I believe it's one of the most amazing restaurants of our time.

CHEF WITH WHOM YOU'D MOST LIKE TO COLLABORATE: I'd love to collaborate with Chef Magnus Nilsson of Fäviken, since I think his approach to both food and restaurants is so absolutely unique.

QUAIL BALLOTINE, SAUERKRAUT, SMOKED CHICKEN VINAIGRETTE, AND PUMPKIN SEED BRITTLE

Chef Markus Glocker of Bâtard | New York, NY
Adapted by StarChefs
Yield: 8 servings

INGREDIENTS

Sauerkraut:
1 head green cabbage, thinly sliced
100 grams salt
50 grams sugar
25 grams caraway seeds
150 grams Champagne vinegar

Quail Ballotine:
8 butchered quail, breasts and legs
    separated
2 grams salt
2 grams sugar
2 grams pink salt
250 grams skinless chicken breast filet
100 grams heavy cream
25 grams foie gras nuggets, seared and
    cooled
4 grams tarragon leaves
4 grams oregano leaves
25 grams golden raisins, soaked in sweet
    wine

90 grams equal parts onion/celery/carrot
    brunoise, blanched 30 seconds
Salt
Black pepper

Smoked Chicken Vinaigrette:
Pumpkin seed oil
1 head garlic, thinly sliced
8 shallots, thinly sliced
200 grams maitake mushrooms, thinly
    sliced
375 milliliters dry white wine
2 quarts brown chicken jus
20 chicken wings, roasted, hot smoked
    20 minutes
Beer vinegar

Pumpkin Seed Brittle:
Oil for frying
225 grams pumpkin seeds
Salt
Black pepper
175 grams sugar
175 grams water

To Assemble and Serve:
40 grams rendered prosciutto fat, hot
Minced chives
Black pepper
Olive oil
Maldon sea salt
8 quail eggs, cooked sunny side up
Fresh Origins Petite Watercress Pink Ice
    micro greens

For the Sauerkraut:

In a storage container with a lid, combine all ingredients, cover, and cure 3 days. Rinse Sauerkraut thoroughly, drain, and season, as necessary.

For the Quail Ballotine:

Remove skin from quail breasts and cut out breast bone. Lightly pound quail breasts; cover and refrigerate. Coat legs with a mixture of salt, sugar, and pink salt; cure 1 hour. Confit legs until tender. Pick meat, discarding skin and bones. Heat the water bath of an immersion circulator to 70°C. In a food processor, grind chicken while slowly streaming heavy cream to make a mousse. In a bowl, combine 125 grams mousse with foie gras, herbs, drained raisins, blanched mirepoix, and 75 grams meat from quail leg confit. Season with salt and pepper; chill. To assemble 4 ballotines, lay out 4 lengths of plastic wrap and place tenderized quail breasts on top, slightly overlapping them in pairs. Pipe a quarter-sized bead of farce (37.5 grams) onto each quail breast, 2 beads per ballotine. Tightly roll up each ballotine in plastic wrap. Cook sous vide 30 minutes; chill.

For the Smoked Chicken Vinaigrette:

In a rondeau, heat oil and sweat garlic, shallots, and mushrooms. When shallots are translucent, add white wine. When alcohol has cooked out, add chicken jus and smoked wings. Bring to simmer, skimming off any impurities that rise to the surface. Reduce by half, strain, and cool the smoked chicken wing reduction. Scale the reduction and measure out equal parts pumpkin seed oil and beer vinegar. In a storage container, combine equal parts reduction, oil, and vinegar; emulsify.

For the Pumpkin Seed Brittle:

In a deep fryer, heat oil to 350°F. Fry seeds until puffy and golden; drain on paper towels. In a heavy skillet, combine sugar and water. Cook down until liquid is syrupy, add pumpkin seeds and cook until glazed. Pour brittle onto a parchment-lined sheet tray in an even layer. Season with salt and pepper; let cool to set.

To Assemble and Serve:

Into a bowl with 200 grams Sauerkraut, pour hot fat and mix gently. Season with chives and black pepper and arrange equal portions on serving plates. Slice Quail Ballontine into ¼-inch rounds, and lay 3 slices next to sauerkraut. Spoon 2 tablespoons Smoked Chicken Vinaigrette around ballotine on each plate. Glaze the ballotine slices with olive oil and sprinkle with sea salt. Place a fried quail egg on top of one of the slices on each plate. Finish with pepper and micro greens.

Featured Ingredients: Fresh Origins petite watercress pink ice, Fossil Farms quail and foie gras
Featured Plateware: Steelite Rene Ozorio

On Top of the World's Finest Cuisine!

Tuna Tonnato.
Micro Bitter Mix™
Cucumbers pickled and raw
Tomatoes
Toasted Parmesan Bread
Chef Shola Olunloyo

400+ Microgreens, Petite™ greens,
Edible Flowers, Tiny Veggies™ &
Herb Crystals®

FRESH ORIGINS
MicroGreens ®

Steelite welcomes the 2015 award winning Rising Star Chefs to the 10th Annual International Chefs Congress

Wabi Sabi by Rene Ozorio

Check out these chefs & their amazing creations at the Art of Presentation Pop Up

Sunday, October 25th	Monday, October 26th	Monday, October 26th	Tuesday, October 27th
11:00am - 2:00pm	*11:00am - 2:00pm*	*6:00pm - 8:00pm*	*11:00am - 2:00pm*

Daniela Soto-Innes
Cosme • New York, NY

Mattie McGhee
Range • Washington DC

John daSilva
Spoke • Boston, MA

Lee Wolen
Boka • Chicago, IL

For more information contact marketing@steeliteusa.com or visit www.steelite.com
800-367-3493 • New York • Chicago • Atlanta • New Castle, PA

steelite
INTERNATIONAL

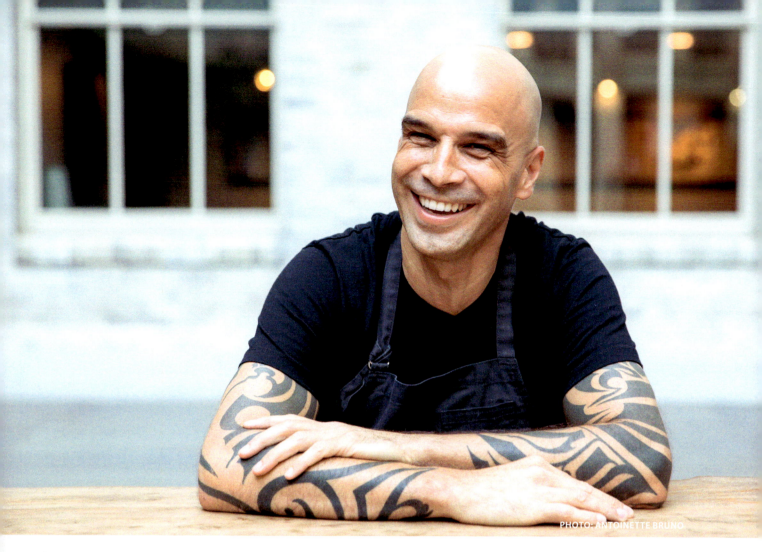

PHOTO: ANTOINETTE BRUNO

 **MOURAD_LAHLOU**

MOURADLAHLOU

COOLEST TECHNIQUE YOU'VE LEARNED FROM ANOTHER CHEF: The art of preserving from Joyce Goldstein

A DISH YOU MAKE THAT'S INSPIRED BY ANOTHER CHEF: An egg dish inspired by Alain Passard of L'Arpège.

IF YOU COULD EAT AT ANY RESTAURANT IN THE WORLD TONIGHT, IT WOULD BE: Asador Etxebarri

FAVORITE INDUSTRY INSTAGRAM ACCOUNT: Bonjwing Lee, @ulteriorepicure; and Aaron Arizpe, @pocketfork

CHEF WITH WHOM YOU'D MOST LIKE TO COLLABORATE: Michel Bras

PLATE YOUR OWN ODE TO THE MICHEL BRAS SALAD

It's a dish that has inspired careers and awoken creative urges. It's been studied, replicated, and exalted. It's Michel Bras' Gargouillou. In the spirit of Open Source Cooking, Chef Mourad Lahlou is bringing a chock-full-of-micros, Moroccan-inspired mise-en-place to his hands-on workshop, where attendees will prepare and plate their own ode to the most famous salad in the world.

Presented by Steelite International

Mourad Lahlou

Mourad | San Francisco, CA

Mourad Lahlou traveled to the United States from Marrakesh, Morocco, in 1985 to study macroeconomics at San Francisco State University. At that time, Lahlou was more into numbers than food. He only began cooking to ease the loneliness he felt while studying far from home. Working from memories of watching his mother prepare Moroccan dishes, Lahlou began to experiment for small groups of friends and professors.

After receiving his master's degree in economics, Lahlou decided to try his hand at cooking. He opened Kasbah in San Rafael, California, and in 1998 *The San Francisco Chronicle* named Lahlou a "Rising Star Chef." But Lahlou wanted to create a modern restaurant where he could revolutionize Moroccan cuisine. So he conducted an extensive search for a San Francisco location and closed Kasbah to open Aziza in November 2001. At Aziza, Lahlou strives to innovate his native cuisine, unravelling the stereotypes surrounding it and sharing its fine dining potential. In 2007, he was named a StarChefs Rising Star, and in 2009, Aziza was awarded three and a half stars from *The San Francisco Chronicle*.

With successful stints on Food Network's "Iron Chef America" and a PBS series on Moroccan cuisine, Lahlou published his first cookbook in 2011, <u>Mourad: New Moroccan</u>. Earlier this year the chef opened a second restaurant called Mourad, earning high praise from critics and the public. Serving family-style meals, he showcases his innovative meld between modern techniques and tradition.

BAY AREA GARGOUILLOU À LA MAROCAINE
Chef Mourad Lahlou of Mourad | San Francisco, CA
Adapted by StarChefs
Yield: 4 servings

INGREDIENTS

Merguez Broth:
4 gallons poultry stock, reduced by ¼
5 pounds merguez, seared
Xanthan gum
Salt

Burnt Lemon Purée:
3 lemons, halved lengthwise
1 liter simple syrup
10 grams agar agar

Tomato Gelée:
2 cups clear tomato water
½ cup bonito flakes
1 tablespoon chermoula powder
1½ sheets gelatin, bloomed
Kosher salt

Harissa:
8 pasilla chiles
4 dried New Mexico chiles
4 dried chipotle chiles
1 cup extra virgin olive oil
⅛ teaspoon black pepper
2 teaspoons kosher salt
1 tablespoon plus ½ teaspoon ground cumin
⅛ teaspoon cayenne
2 cloves garlic, grated
¼ cup Champagne vinegar
2 tablespoons chopped parsley
2 tablespoons chopped cilantro
2 tablespoons lemon juice

Vadouvan Quinoa:
Kosher salt
2 cups quinoa
3 quarts rice bran oil
½ cup white sesame seeds, toasted
½ cup black sesame seeds, toasted
2 teaspoons Madras curry powder

To Assemble and Serve:
Grapeseed oil
1 lemon cucumber, cut into bite-sized
    pieces, skin charred
4 cauliflower florets, blanched
4 Romanesco florets, blanched
1 kohlrabi, peeled and thinly sliced
1 yellow squash, thinly sliced
    lengthwise (8 slices)
4 baby turnips, blanched
Fleur de sel
Chickpea purée
Chilled watercress purée thickened with
    xanthan gum
1 avocado, scooped with a melon baller,
    balls charred with torch
16 red grapes, charred with a torch
8 pickled baby chanterelles
8 pickled ramp bulbs
8 husk cherries, halved
4 cubes and 8 thin slices pickled
    watermelon rind
12 zucchini ribbons in kombu brine
12 cubes compressed watermelon
Urfa-cumin roasted carrots
Champagne vinegar-braised radishes
Kale oil
Berbere-spiced walnut crumble
2 tablespoons basil seeds, bloomed
Medjool date purée thickened with
    xanthan gum
Whipped salted crème fraîche
16 thin slices peel from house-preserved lemons
1 red jalapeño, seeds removed, thinly sliced
Fresh Origins micro greens

METHOD

For the Merguez Broth:
Over medium heat, combine stock and sausage, and reduce by one-third. Pass mixture through a chinois into a separate pot set over ice bath. Remove fat from surface. Over low heat, bring to a simmer. Scale broth and record weight. Measure 1 percent of that weight in xanthan gum. Transfer broth to a blender and slowly increase speed until vortex forms. Add xanthan; blend 3 minutes. Strain mixture through a chinois and season with salt. Vacuum seal broth several times until air bubbles are eliminated and broth is clear.

For the Burnt Lemon Purée:
In a cast iron pan over high heat, char lemons, pulp side down, until blackened. Transfer to a container with simple syrup and steep 1 hour. Transfer to blender, purée, and pass through a chinois into a pot over medium heat. Add agar agar and bring to a boil. After 30 seconds, transfer mixture to a bowl set over an ice bath. When chilled and firmly set, cut into cubes, and purée. Pass though a chinois and into a squeeze bottle.

For the Tomato Gelée:
Over low heat, bring tomato water to a simmer, skimming solids that surface. Add bonito flakes and chermoula, remove from heat, and cover. After 1 hour, strain into a separate pot and bring to a simmer. Stir in gelatin. Strain through a cheesecloth-lined chinois into a container. Cool until solidified. Break with a fork before serving.

For the Harissa:
Combine chiles and cover with boiling water. Place a small plate on top to keep chiles submerged, and cover with plastic wrap. Soak chiles 1 hour, until softened. Drain chiles, reserving liquid. Let sediment settle, then measure ½ cup liquid. Pull stems off chiles and remove seeds and ribs. In a food processor, purée chiles, adding liquid as needed. Add olive oil and blend until smooth. Add black pepper, salt, cumin, cayenne, and garlic. Blend to a smooth paste. Add vinegar and blend for 30 seconds. Add additional chile liquid if too thick. Pass through a chinois into a bowl and stir in parsley, cilantro, and lemon juice. Season with salt.

For the Vadouvan Quinoa:
In a large pot of boiling water, cook quinoa until tender; drain. Onto a paper towel-lined sheet tray, spread quinoa and cool. Heat oil to 350°F. Fry quinoa until crisp, drain on paper towels, and cool. Transfer to a bowl with sesame seeds and curry. Mix well and season with salt.

To Assemble and Serve:
To a pan over low heat, add a few drops grapeseed oil, followed by cucumber, cauliflower, Romanesco, kohlrabi, squash, and turnips. Sauté until barely warm. Add 2 tablespoons Merguez Broth, stirring constantly until pan is almost dry. Drain on a paper towel-lined sizzle platter. Season with fleur de sel; keep warm. Using a demitasse spoon, place a dollop of chickpea purée onto a large white serving plate with a dimple and make swoosh. Repeat with the watercress purée. Around the dimple of the plate, arrange 3 pieces of cucumber from reserved sautéed vegetables, 2 avocado balls, 4 grapes, 2 chanterelles, 2 ramp bulbs, 1 cauliflower floret, 1 Romanesco floret, 4 cherry halves, 1 kohlrabi slice, 1 cube pickled watermelon rind, 2 squash slices, 3 ribbons brined zucchini, 2 slices pickled watermelon rind, 3 cubes compressed watermelon, 1 baby turnip, 2 roasted carrots, and 4 braised radishes. Place 2 tablespoons Tomato Gelée in the dimple of the plate and drizzle with kale oil. Arrange 2 teaspoons walnut crumble and 2 teaspoons Vadouvan Quinoa around vegetables. Add 2 teaspoons basil seeds, and a few dots each of date purée, crème fraîche, Burnt Lemon Purée, and Harissa. Place 4 slices preserved lemon peel on the arranged vegetables. Garnish with the jalapeño and assorted micro greens.

Featured Ingredients: Fresh Origins micro greens and Kalettes
Featured Plateware: Steelite International

For the full recipe, visit www.starchefs.com.

PHOTO: NICK BERARD

Tory Miller

Estrellón | Madison, WI

[Instagram] MILLS608 [Twitter] GRAZELETOILE

COOLEST TECHNIQUE YOU'VE LEARNED FROM ANOTHER CHEF: It was actually at the first ICC I ever went to. Joël Robuchon was there, and he used a vacuum sealer to seal duck and foie gras in a cabbage leaf. Watching that happen in person was just incredible.

A DISH YOU MAKE THAT'S INSPIRED BY ANOTHER CULTURE: I had this pastry in Spain that was basically like a fried croissant filled with pastry cream, and I'd never had anything like it before. It was delicious. I thought to myself, I have to bring this back, so it's on the menu at Estrellón.

IF YOU COULD EAT AT ANY RESTAURANT IN THE WORLD TONIGHT, IT WOULD BE: I still haven't been to The French Laundry. It's the pinnacle of cuisine for chefs in my era.

FAVORITE INDUSTRY INSTAGRAM ACCOUNT: Jamie Bissonnette, @JamieBiss. He's one of my buddies, so it's always fun to see what he's doing in the kitchen and out.

FAVORITE COOKBOOK: Jerusalem by Yotam Ottolenghi and Sami Tamimi. It's gorgeous, and it's such an inspiring cookbook to read during the summer.

CHEF WITH WHOM YOU'D MOST LIKE TO COLLABORATE: Danny Bowien, definitely. We're both adopted and love adapting different cuisines, so our styles would work very well together. Also, he's just a really cool person, so it would be a blast to cook with him.

Madison, Wisconsin, isn't known as a culinary mecca, but Tory Miller has created a small gustatory oasis with his four restaurants: L'Etoile, Graze, Sujeo, and Estrellón. Miller specializes in dishes made from locally grown, sustainable, organic ingredients, executed in part through a rigorous "put-by" system, in which he preserves summer produce for use year round.

Before Miller was a devotee to sustainability, he was a graduate of New York City's French Culinary Institute (now the International Culinary Center). Looking for training and experience in professional kitchens, he worked in several of New York's best restaurants, including Eleven Madison Park and Judson Grill, before arriving at L'Etoile to work as Odessa Piper's chef de cuisine. In 2005, Miller purchased the restaurant with his sister and business partner, Traci Miller. Seven years later he earned L'Etoile's second James Beard Award for "Best Chef, Midwest."

Miller is an active member of Slow Food USA and Chefs Collaborative. He is a regular Terra Madre attendee, and has participated in Citymeals-on-Wheels and Autism Speaks benefits in New York. Miller works closely with Wisconsin Homegrown Lunch, advocating fresh, local foods in the school system, and he has spent time working with middle school students, teaching them to identify and cook with local ingredients and how to plant and tend a garden.

RABBIT, THE OTHER OTHER WHITE MEAT

Do you really know rabbit? In his hands-on workshop, Chef Tory Miller will take the rabbit on a cross-cultural culinary journey through Korea, France, and Spain (with extra help from Sherry vinegar). Attendees will learn how to break down and transform their formerly furry friends into delicious, culturally rooted dishes.

Presented by Sherry Vinegar from Spain and Fossil Farms

ROASTED RABBIT, CHARRED CARROTS, MARCONA ALMONDS, AND SHERRY VINEGAR SALMUERA

Chef Tory Miller of Estrellón | Madison, WI
Adapted by StarChefs
Yield: 4 Servings

INGREDIENTS

Sherry Vinegar Salmuera:
1 cup Sherry vinegar
2 tablespoons finely chopped shallot
1 teaspoon finely chopped garlic
1 cup water
1 tablespoon kosher salt
½ tablespoon extra virgin olive oil
1 teaspoon cracked black pepper

Rabbit:
2 rabbits, butchered and separated
  into loins and legs
Hot smoked pimentón
Olive oil

Carrots:
1 pound carrots
1 tablespoon coriander seeds, toasted
  and crushed
Kosher salt

To Assemble and Serve:
1 teaspoon finely chopped chives
1 teaspoon finely chopped parsley
¼ cup Marcona almonds, toasted and
  coarsely chopped

METHOD

For the Sherry Vinegar Salmuera:
In a bowl, whisk together all ingredients.

For the Rabbit:
Prepare and heat grill. Season rabbit loins with pimentón and drizzle with olive oil. Grill loins over high heat, about 2 minutes per side; let rest, keeping warm. Season rabbit legs with pimentón. Grill over low heat 50 minutes to 1 hour, until tender, basting every 15 minutes with Sherry Vinegar Salmuera; let rest, keeping warm.

For the Carrots:
Heat oven to 375°F. Place carrots in a hotel pan and sprinkle with coriander seeds. Completely cover carrots with salt. Bake carrots 1 hour, or until tender with a little crispness in the center. When cooled, dust off salt. Heat plancha until very hot. Place carrots on plancha and char on all sides. Keep warm.

To Assemble and Serve:
Arrange Rabbit loins and legs and Carrots on serving plate. Drizzle with ½ cup Sherry Vinegar Salmuera for each serving. Garnish with chives, parsley, and Marcona almonds.

Featured Ingredients: Spanish Sherry vinegar, Fossil Farms rabbit

PHOTO: SAMANTHA EGELHOFF

Shola Olunloyo

StudioKitchen | Philadelphia, PA

 STUDIOKITCHEN1 STUDIOKITCHEN

MOST INFLUENTIAL MENTOR WITH WHOM YOU'VE WORKED: Georges Perrier. He emphasized the elements of taste over presentation.

COOLEST TECHNIQUE YOU'VE LEARNED FROM ANOTHER CHEF: Reinforcing flavors on multiple levels through stratification. Alain Ducasse and Sean Baker.

A DISH YOU MAKE THAT'S INSPIRED BY ANOTHER CHEF: "Jaune Flamme." It's tomatoes cooked in fermented peach juice with burrata and green coriander seeds. It was inspired by Sean Baker, formerly of Verbena in San Francisco.

IF YOU COULD EAT AT ANY RESTAURANT IN THE WORLD TONIGHT, IT WOULD BE: Asador Etxebarri in Spain

FAVORITE COOKBOOK: Le Livre de Michel Bras

CHEF WITH WHOM YOU'D MOST LIKE TO COLLABORATE: Jeremy Fox of Rustic Canyon in Santa Monica. His food is elemental and refined without intellectual complications.

Shola Olunloyo is a talented, passionate, and resourceful chef, and a distinguished member of the Philadelphia restaurant community. He's carved out a creative niche and reputation for himself in an industry where it's hard to get a foothold, let alone make an impact. Now known to the Philly food world as just Shola, Olunloyo was born in England and raised in both Europe and West Africa. Never one to follow a traditional path, Olunloyo embarked on a self-designed apprenticeship that included employment in several countries, from Italy and France to countries throughout Southeast Asia. Picking up techniques, flavor profiles, and traditions along the way, Olunloyo was also developing what would become a kind of culinary credo.

Back in Philadelphia, Olunloyo found an outlet in writing about food and working as a private chef and caterer. But his passion and curiosity weren't quite satisfied, so the chef moved to New York City, where working as a private chef allowed him to save more for a future investment. Additionally, selling all of his bicycles (Olunloyo had been an avid cyclist) earned him roughly $15,000 in seed money, which the chef invested in his small, experimental project, StudioKitchen. From StudioKitchen, or "SK," Olunloyo develops and plays with culinary concepts, global foods, and cutting-edge technology in an approachable laboratory setting. There he sees ideas to fruition, from concepts for restaurants to innovations for food service equipment manufacturers.

SUBMERGED: NEXT LEVEL SOUS VIDE COOKING

If all you've done is wade in the shallow end of sous vide cooking, get ready for a deep dive into advanced techniques. In his hands-on workshop, StudioKitchen's Shola Olunloyo will give attendees the tools they need to elevate, optimize, and expand their sous vide skills.

Presented by PolyScience Culinary

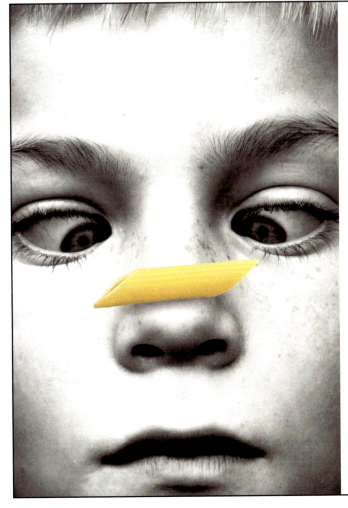

FERMENTED PINEAPPLE TEPACHE

Bartender Eamon Rockey of Betony | New York, NY
Adapted by StarChefs
Yield: 4 liters

INGREDIENTS

2 pineapples, peeled,
   cut into chunks, and
   skins reserved
200 grams piloncillo
   sugar
4 liters water

TEPACHE

09.05.15

METHOD

Combine pineapples,
skin, sugar, and water
in a large container
(more piloncillo sugar
may be added to
achieve a higher level
of sweetness, or left to
ferment for a higher
level of alcohol). Cover
with cheesecloth and
store in a cool place.
Let ferment and allow
to rest for 2 days. Strain
and chill. Serve over ice.

PHOTO: ALIZA ELIAZAROV

 **EAMONROCKEY**

MOST INFLUENTIAL MENTOR WITH WHOM YOU'VE WORKED: My dad. My father and mother were both chefs. They're the reason that I got into this industry to begin with. I remember very early on, my dad would work with very sharp knives at home on a great big butcher's block. He'd show me how to work neatly, to clean as I cooked, to focus, stand up straight, and organize my "station" in an efficient fashion to get the most out of every motion. These are values that I use and teach every day.

COOLEST TECHNIQUE YOU'VE LEARNED FROM ANOTHER CHEF: Leo Robitschek priming a glass with an effervescent liquid to ensure that when you pour something with fat or protein into it, it will instantly produce a stable, firm foam.

A DRINK YOU MAKE THAT'S INSPIRED BY ANOTHER CULTURE: Ju Lip: Korean Soju, Ginger, Beer, and Shiso. It's inspired by classic flavors of Southeast Asia, not to mention, some of the most delicious food I've experienced here in the city in K-Town.

FAVORITE COCKTAIL REFERENCE: The Fine Art of Mixing Drinks by David A. Embury

Eamon Rockey

Betony | New York, NY

When you grow up in a small town—in this case, Hattiesburg, Mississippi—there's a chance you'll find yourself at closer quarters with your parents. If your parents are both working chefs, there's a chance you'll end up like Eamon Rockey, which is to say, fully immersed in the business. Think of it this way—by 14, Rockey was working at Sakura, Hattiesburg's only sushi restaurant.

Decamping from Mississippi, Rockey studied at the Culinary Institute of America in Hyde Park, New York, where he anticipated graduating as a cook. Instead, he was lured away by the romance of wine and beverage. Moving to New York City to get professional, Rockey was hired at Gilt in 2006 and began working under his first mentor, Chris Day. The next year found him at Eleven Madison Park, where he not only upped his service game but was promoted to captain and bartender.

With experience in some of New York's top kitchens, including Atera, Rockey helped open Compose in Tribeca in a managerial role. After managing and developing the beverage program at Scandinavian-inspired Aska, Rockey was poised to open Betony with Bryce Shuman in 2013. The restaurant quickly earned rave reviews and nods, including "Restaurant of the Year" from *Esquire*, a Michelin star, and a spot on *Wine Enthusiast*'s "100 Best Wine Restaurants" list.

FERMENTATION GOES FINE DINING

Fermentation penetrates every elegant inch of the menu at Betony—from the savory side, courtesy of Chef Bryce Shuman, to the cocktail program from General Manager Eamon Rockey. In their hands-on workshop, attendees will harness Alto-Shaam technology to refine the funk in vinegars, charcuterie, pickles, and more.

Presented by Alto-Shaam

ALASKA SOCKEYE SALMON, BUTTERMILK BEURRE BLANC, AROMATIC FLOWERS, SHOOTS, AND SEEDS

Chef Shola Olunloyo of StudioKitchen | Philadelphia, PA
Adapted by StarChefs
Yield: 4 Servings

INGREDIENTS

Beurre Blanc:
2 cups fish fumet
1 cup cooking liquid from mussels
½ cup vermouth
½ cup white wine
1 cup buttermilk
4 ounces cultured butter, cold, diced
Salt

Salmon:
80 grams fine sea salt
40 grams sugar
800 grams water
200 grams yuzu juice
Four 6-ounce fillets Alaska sockeye salmon
Olive oil

To Assemble and Serve:
Green coriander seeds
Nasturtium leaves
Sorrel
Cilantro flowers
Fennel pollen
Purple basil
Radish seed pods
Chervil
Sun gold tomato
Flaked sea salt

METHOD

For the Beurre Blanc:
In a saucepan over medium-low heat, combine fish fumet, mussel jus, vermouth, white wine, and buttermilk. Simmer until mixture is syrupy. Add butter, 1 cube at a time, whisking constantly to emulsify. Season with salt and keep warm.

For the Salmon:
In a pot over low heat, combine salt, sugar, and half the water. Stir until salt and sugar dissolve. Remove from heat and add remaining water. When temperature of brine falls below 42°F, stir in yuzu juice. Heat the water bath of an immersion circulator to 52°C. In a shallow container, brine salmon 45 minutes. Drain, rinse, and pat salmon dry with paper towels. Transfer each piece of salmon to a vacuum bag with 1 tablespoon olive oil. Cook salmon sous vide 12 minutes or until salmon just flakes. Rest 5 minutes.

To Assemble and Serve:
Transfer Salmon to plate and garnish with coriander seeds, nasturtium, sorrel, flowers, pollen, basil, radish pods, chervil, and tomato. Sprinkle flaked salt on top. Tableside, pour a small pool of Beurre Blanc on the side.

Featured ingredient: Alaska sockeye salmon
Featured Equipment: PolyScience Culinary Chef Series Immersion Circulator, Chamber Vacuum Sealer

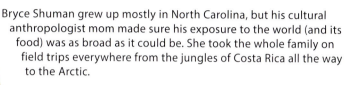

Bryce Shuman

Betony | New York, NY

PHOTO: SIGNE BIRCK

Bryce Shuman grew up mostly in North Carolina, but his cultural anthropologist mom made sure his exposure to the world (and its food) was as broad as it could be. She took the whole family on field trips everywhere from the jungles of Costa Rica all the way to the Arctic.

A passion for food thoroughly ingrained, Shuman began cooking at a local restaurant (where he would meet his future wife, Jenn). Shuman's next step took him across the country to San Francisco, where he studied at the California Culinary Academy during the day and worked at Wolfgang Puck's Postrio at night.

After graduating, Shuman joined the staff at Rubicon, where he was mentored by 2005 and 2007 San Francisco Rising Stars Chef Stuart Brioza and Pastry Chef Nicole Krasinski (now of State Bird Provisions). Returning to the East Coast, Shuman joined the team at Eleven Madison Park, where he worked for six years, was promoted to executive sous chef, and oversaw a staff of 40. Now at the helm of Betony, Shuman's pure, clean, and imaginative cooking is the culmination of a well traveled culinary journey to self-discovery. In 2015, he earned a StarChefs Rising Star Chef Award for his work at Betony.

 **BRYCESHUMAN**

MOST INFLUENTIAL MENTOR WITH WHOM YOU'VE WORKED: Daniel Humm. He taught me that if you want something and push very, very hard, nothing is out of reach.

COOLEST TECHNIQUE YOU'VE LEARNED FROM ANOTHER CHEF: Kevin Farley from Cultured Pickle Shop in Berkeley, California, taught me about the glory of pickling garlic in miso. Kevin let me taste the garlic he had been pickling in his own miso and fermenting for two years! Now, we have some garlic in miso fermenting here at Betony. It is a mere seven months old.

A DISH YOU MAKE THAT'S INSPIRED BY ANOTHER CULTURE: A skate curry hors d'oeuvre that's inspired by Thai culture and flavors. The concept started with my interest in cooking with bones of creatures—either using them as vessels to eat food, or to eat the bones themselves. We found the cartilage of skate could be treated in a way that it becomes a crispy, delicious seafood chip. To make the aforementioned dish, we clean and poach the cartilage from skate, and then puff it in very hot oil until it's crispy. We then make a thick emulsion with green curry paste, green curry oil, and lots of fresh herbs like Thai basil and cilantro. Once the skate and emulsion are completed, we finish the dish with fresh lime, three types of basil, and a pickled chile.

IF YOU COULD EAT AT ANY RESTAURANT IN THE WORLD TONIGHT, IT WOULD BE: Sobadokoro Rakuichi in Hokkaido, Japan. I often crave cold soba noodles, and I hear Tatsuru Rai's are the best.

CHEF WITH WHOM YOU'D MOST LIKE TO COLLABORATE: I'm particularly interested in chefs that excel at fermentation (the folks at the Cultured Pickle Shop), baking (Chad Robertson of Tartine Bakery), and maintaining a larder (Kyle and Katina Connaughton, who are about to open a farm, inn, and tasting menu restaurant, Single Thread). I'm also a great admirer of chefs operating at the highest level of technical precision in fine dining: Rasmus Kofoed, Grant Achatz, René Redzepi, and Ferran Adrià. On a personal level, I love Stuart Brioza and Nicole Krasinski, from whom I learned so much, and Christopher Kostow, because we always have a good time together.

'NDUJA, FERMENTED CARROT, AND CIABATTA

Chef Bryce Shuman of Betony | New York, NY
Adapted by StarChefs

INGREDIENTS

'Nduja: (Yield: One 900-gram sausage)
500 grams pork shoulder, cut into small pieces and
   refrigerated
500 grams pork fatback, cut into small pieces
   and refrigerated
200 grams Calabrian chile
30 grams Aleppo pepper
5 grams black pepper
20 grams smoked paprika
5 grams fennel seed
32 grams kosher salt
3 grams pink salt
15 grams yogurt
Pig's bladder

Celery Vinegar: (Yield: 2 kilograms)
353 grams corn sugar
1.392 kilograms celery juice
482 grams Champagne yeast

Fermented Carrots: (Yield: 20 carrots)
55 grams salt, dissolved in 200 grams
   room temperature water
900 grams carrot juice
40 grams fresh ginger
10 grams coriander seeds
65 grams scallion greens
15 grams savory
10 grams Fresno chiles
20 carrots

Pickled Red Onions: (Yield: 100 grams)
4 grams grapeseed oil
100 grams red pearl onions, sliced
20 grams Champagne vinegar
1 gram salt

Ciabatta Poolish:
980 grams water, 18.3°C
980 grams all-purpose flour
15 grams yeast

Ciabatta: (Yield: 6 loaves)
1.4 kilograms water, 31.1°C
32 grams malt syrup
8 grams honey
1.18 kilograms bread flour
1.08 kilograms all-purpose flour, plus additional for dusting
64 grams yeast
80 grams salt
Salt water

Torn Ciabatta Croutons: (Yield: 200 grams)
75 grams extra virgin olive oil
2 cloves garlic
3 sprigs thyme
Salt

To Assemble and Serve: (Yield: 1 serving)
Fennel fronds
Baby arugula leaves
Curly mustard leaves
Watercress leaves
Oxalis leaves
Olive oil

METHOD

For the 'Nduja:

Prepare and heat an Alto-Shaam smoker to 21.1°C. Through a meat grinder fitted with the largest die, grind pork shoulder and fatback. In a blender, combine peppers, paprika, fennel, salts, and yogurt. Blend on high until completely smooth and pass through a chinois. Transfer to a large mixing bowl. Using gloves, combine with ground pork mixture by hand until smooth. Place a 1-inch layer of the mixture into hotel pans and smoke for 2 days; let cool. Mix again until the texture is uniform. Using a sausage press, stuff mixture into a pig's bladder, creating sausages that are 26 centimeters long and 5 centimeters wide. Truss with butcher's twine and hang in a curing chamber at 12.78°C for 1 month.

For the Celery Vinegar:

Whisk sugar into celery juice and bring its gravity to 1.068. Temper to 20°C. Introduce the yeast and incubate at 20°C for 2 to 3 weeks. At this point, it's a cider. Label and date the jar, and place in a dark, fairly humid, and moderately warm environment, about 26.6 to 29.4°C. Age for 4 to 5 weeks. When the vinegar has matured to a desirable product, use a spigot to dispense it without agitating the sediment that has settled. Reserve some to use as a starter for the next batch. Refrigerate vinegar and let settle. Filter vinegar through a cheesecloth and place in a sterile container.

For the Fermented Carrots:

In a bowl, combine brine and carrot juice. Add ginger, coriander, scallion greens, savory, and chiles. Gently place carrots in fermentation vessel and cover with pickling mixture. Ferment at 17.78°C for 2 weeks.

For the Pickled Red Onions:

In a small sauté pan over high heat, heat oil until shimmering. Add onions and sauté briefly until just hot. Add vinegar and salt. Toss and immediately transfer to a container; cover with lid. After 5 minutes, drain onions and store in a pint container.

For the Ciabatta Poolish:

In the bowl of a stand mixer fitted with a dough hook, mix all ingredients until combined. Transfer poolish to a grease-sprayed metal bowl and cover with plastic wrap. Chill for at least 2 hours. Bulk-ferment 10 to 12 hours. The poolish should be bubbly.

For the Ciabatta:

Heat oven to 232.2°C. In the bowl of a 40-quart mixer fitted with a hook, mix water, malt syrup, honey, and 1.58 kilograms Ciabatta Poolish. Add all dry ingredients and mix on low 5 minutes. Flip dough. Mix 1 minute on medium. Wrap dough in plastic and bulk-ferment in a grease-sprayed metal bowl until doubled in size, about 90 minutes. Gently punch down dough, tri-fold, and allow to rise for 60 minutes. Carefully transfer dough to a heavily floured table. Shape into a rectangle, then portion into loaves. Shape each loaf and transfer to generously floured linen. Rest 35 to 40 minutes. Gently flip each loaf off of its linen onto a large, floured, parchment-lined sheet tray. Spray the loaves with salt water, and let sit 5 minutes uncovered. Fill a hotel pan with water and place on bottom rack of oven. Bake loaves on middle rack 5 minutes. Remove water and bake 7 minutes more. Remove from oven and cool.

For the Torn Ciabatta Croutons:

Tear 200 grams Ciabatta into small pieces. To a large sauté pan over medium heat, add oil, garlic, and the torn Ciabatta. Allow bread to color slightly. Add thyme and toss to color bread evenly. Drain on a rack lined with C-fold napkins. Season with salt. The croutons should be pale golden on the outside but still have a soft bread texture on the inside.

To Assemble and Serve:

Prepare and heat grill. Spread 35 grams 'Nduja on the bottom of a serving plate. Using a peeler, shave Fermented Carrots into thin ribbons. Carefully arrange 20 grams Fermented Carrots ribbons, 10 grams Pickled Red Onions, fennel fronds, arugula, mustard, watercress leaves, and Torn Ciabatta Croutons in a forest mosaic. Slice Ciabatta, brush with olive oil, and toast on grill. Serve with toast on side.

Featured Equipment: Alto-Shaam 767-SK/III Deluxe Control Smoker Oven and CTP6-10 Combi Oven

Kari Underly

Muscolo Meat Academy | Chicago, IL

Kari Underly is a third generation master butcher, who was introduced to the craft by her father at Underly's Market in Indiana. If it's not enough that Underly carved her way through the ranks to master butcher in a primarily male-dominated field, she's also a teacher, author, and businesswoman. Underly is the James Beard-nominated author of <u>The Art of Beef Cutting</u>, principal of Range, Inc. (a fresh-meat industry consultancy founded in 2002), and the founder of Muscolo Meat Academy, her most ambitious project to date. Underly's students are trained in whole animal butchery and charcuterie, and learn the business principles required to successfully run a butcher shop. Additionally, she is the resident meat expert at the Independent Grocers Alliance Coca-Cola Institute, where she trains and educates meat staff, butchers, and chefs.

Underly's work may be seen in the many "cuts of meat" posters on the walls of butcher shops and restaurants across the country. As part of the Beef Checkoff Program, she has been instrumental in creating and popularizing cuts such as the flat iron, Sierra cut, Denver cut, petite tender, and chuck eye country-style ribs. Although Underly performs many different roles, her favorite is that of an educator. Along with her book and school, Underly travels the nation giving lectures, teaching seminars, and training the next generation of chefs and charcutiers in the art of butchery.

 **KARIUNDERLY**

MOST INFLUENTIAL MENTOR WITH WHOM YOU'VE WORKED: My Polish grandmother, Cylia Underly, who taught me at an early age about how to use all the odd bits.

COOLEST TECHNIQUE YOU'VE LEARNED FROM ANOTHER CHEF: Removing the lamb femur bone from the leg by cranking the shank. I watched my lamb butcher on Taylor Street in Chicago do this one afternoon.

IF YOU COULD EAT AT ANY RESTAURANT IN THE WORLD TONIGHT, IT WOULD BE: Victor Churchill, Fine Family Butcher, established in 1876 in Sydney, Australia

FAVORITE INDUSTRY INSTAGRAM ACCOUNT: Craig Deihl, @cdeihl

MAKING A BUCK FROM CHUCK

Take the mystery out of the square cut chuck in Kari Underly's hands-on butchery workshop. She'll go from primal to subprimal with Master Purveyors beef, talk cooking methods, and explore different "grill-able" cuts to add to the menu. Build upon your chuck sensory palate, and leave with a few hidden gems you'll be proud to share with your customers.

Presented by WÜSTHOF

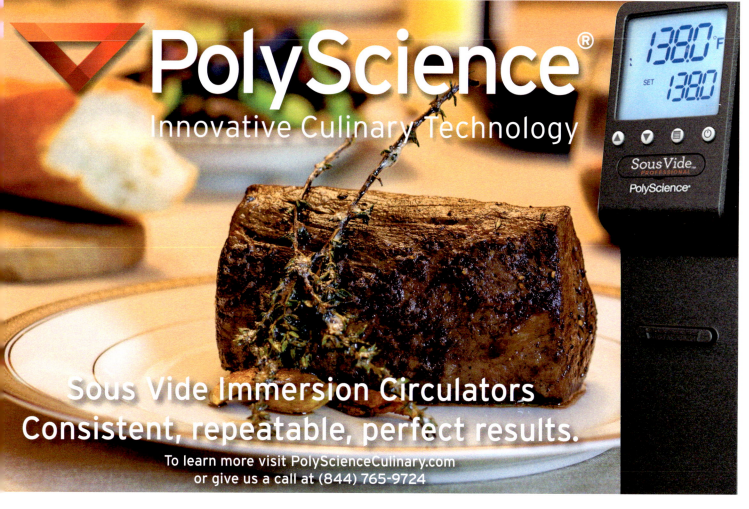

PASTRY

Monica Glass

Starr Catering Group | Philadelphia, PA

Growing up in West Chester, Pennsylvania, Monica Glass enjoyed experimenting in the kitchen alongside her parents, and her interest in cooking earned her the affectionate moniker "Chef Moni" among her friends at Pennsylvania State University.

Upon graduation, Glass moved to New York to embark on a career in public relations. But after a few years she decided to switch gears to what made her happiest: pastry. Heading straight to the top, she lobbied Pastry Chef Deborah Racicot of Gotham Bar and Grill for an opportunity to learn, and subsequently joined the team full time.

Glass' ambition to learn from the best led her next to Eric Ripert's Le Bernardin, where she continued to develop and refine her skills under esteemed Pastry Chef Michael Laiskonis. Growing into a leadership position of her own, Glass made the move to Philadelphia, where she helmed the pastry department at 10 Arts Bistro & Lounge at the Ritz Carlton. It was around this time she was diagnosed with celiac disease, causing her (heartbreakingly) to reevaluate the viability of a career in pastry. Instead of giving up, she decided to meet the challenge head on, forging a new identity as an innovative gluten-free pastry chef.

After four years with the Ritz Carlton, Glass brought her skills to a new setting at Chef Mike Stollenwerk's Fish, and then to Ken Oringer's Clio in Boston. In 2015, Glass moved back to Philadelphia to tackle the role of executive pastry chef with the juggernaut that is Starr Catering Group.

FLOUR POWER: POSSIBILITIES IN THE GLUTEN-FREE KITCHEN

Learn the finer points and particles of gluten-free baking with the Ideas in Food duo Aki Kamozawa and Alex Talbot, along with Monica Glass, who just so happens to be equal parts celiac and badass pastry chef. Kamozawa and Talbot will discuss the building blocks and flour blends essential to gluten-free pastry, and Glass will elevate the basics into a fine-dining-worthy composed dessert.

Presented by California Walnuts

PHOTO: GABE

 CHEFMONI

MOST INFLUENTIAL MENTOR WITH WHOM YOU'VE WORKED: Michael Laiskonis. Not only is the breadth of his knowledge so expansive, but he's incredibly humble and generous in sharing his wealth. He really helped me refine my skills and also expanded my scope of what is possible with pastry.

A DISH YOU MAKE THAT'S INSPIRED BY ANOTHER CULTURE: I love perusing Chinatown and Asian markets, so I guess my inspiration is often drawn from things I discover there. I once made an umeboshi sorbet the star of a dish, and paired it with togarashi macadamia nuts, aloe granita, hibiscus-poached pineapple, and a black sesame tuile.

IF YOU COULD EAT AT ANY RESTAURANT IN THE WORLD TONIGHT, IT WOULD BE: Parachute in Chicago, Uncle Boons in NYC, or Toro in Boston

FAVORITE INDUSTRY INSTAGRAM ACCOUNT: Chris Ford, @butterloveandhardwork

FAVORITE COOKBOOK: The Flavor Bible, Grand Livre De Cuisine: Alain Ducasses's Desserts and Pastries by Frédéric Robert, Chez Panisse Fruit by Alice Waters, and On Food and Cooking by Harold McGee

LA RHUBARBE: RHUBARB, LABNEH MOUSSE, CUCUMBER SHERBET, WALNUT-QUINOA GRANOLA, MEYER LEMON-SAKE KASU CURD, AND QUINOA TUILE

Pastry Chef Monica Glass of Starr Catering Group | Philadelphia, PA
Adapted by StarChefs

INGREDIENTS

Cucumber Sherbet: (Yield: 1 quart)
400 grams milk
150 grams sugar
50 grams glucose syrup
4 grams ice cream stabilizer
600 grams cucumber juice
Lime juice
Salt

Labneh Mousse: (Yield: 1 quart)
75 grams sugar
350 grams heavy cream
7½ grams vanilla extract
7½ grams silver gelatin, bloomed
375 grams labneh

Meyer Lemon Meringues:
(Yield: 1½ quarts)
20 grams egg white powder
100 grams water
50 grams Meyer lemon juice
150 grams sugar
50 grams isomalt
Zest of 1 lime

Crispy Quinoa: (Yield: 1 pint)
220½ grams quinoa
Salt
Oil for frying

Walnut-Quinoa Granola:
(Yield: 1 quart)
180 grams honey
113 grams butter, melted
50 grams light brown sugar
½ vanilla bean, scraped
162½ grams rolled oats
375 grams walnuts, chopped
3 grams cinnamon
¼ teaspoon salt

Meyer Lemon-Sake Kasu Curd:
(Yield: 1 quart)
4 eggs, blended and strained
200 grams sugar
200 grams Meyer lemon juice
Zest of 4 Meyer lemons
3 grams salt
150 grams sake kasu
113 grams butter
1 sheet silver gelatin, bloomed

Poached Rhubarb: (Yield: 1½ quarts)
800 grams rhubarb, peeled and
    chopped on a bias
600 grams sugar
1 vanilla bean
120 grams orange juice
40 grams grenadine

20 grams purple beet juice
2 grams salt

Rhubarb Compote: (Yield: 1 pint)
300 grams sugar
500 grams rhubarb, peeled and diced
Juice of 1 to 2 limes
Beet juice

Rhubarb Soup: (Yield: 1 quart)
2 pounds rhubarb, roughly chopped
100 grams sugar
100 grams water
Juice of 2 lemons
Simple syrup
Salt

Quinoa Tuile: (Yield: 1 pint)
200 grams glucose
200 grams fondant
200 grams isomalt

To Assemble and Serve:
Maldon sea salt
Violas or other edible flowers

METHOD

For the Cucumber Sherbet:
In a medium saucepot, combine milk, sugar, and glucose and bring to a simmer. Whisk in stabilizer and heat to a boil, then cook 30 seconds. Pass base through a chinois and chill fully in an ice bath. Combine base and cucumber juice and season with lime juice and salt. Process in an ice cream machine according to manufacturer's instructions.

For the Labneh Mousse:
In a saucepot, combine sugar, 50 grams heavy cream, and vanilla; heat to dissolve sugar. Add bloomed gelatin and stir to fully incorporate. Pour labneh into a large bowl and whisk in cream-gelatin mixture. Whip remaining 300 grams cream to soft peaks and fold into labneh mixture. Transfer to a piping bag and pipe into desired molds. Chill mousse in refrigerator until set, then freeze solid. Temper in refrigerator before use.

For the Meyer Lemon Meringues:
In a deep container, combine egg white powder, water, and Meyer lemon juice and blend with an immersion blender. Transfer to the bowl of a stand mixer fitted with a whisk and begin whipping on medium-low speed. Meanwhile, in a small saucepot, combine sugar, isomalt, and lime zest; add just enough water to cover and cook to 240°F. When egg whites have reached medium peaks, continue to whip while streaming hot syrup into mixture. Continue whipping until stiff peaks form. Transfer meringue to a piping bag and pipe buttons onto a silicone baking mat. Dehydrate overnight in a low oven or dehydrator.

For the Crispy Quinoa:
Rinse quinoa. Set in a medium pot with an equal volume of water and a pinch of salt and bring to a boil. Reduce heat to low and cover pot; cook until water has been absorbed and quinoa is translucent. Spread quinoa onto a tray and dehydrate in a low oven or dehydrator until quinoa is dry on the outside but retains some moisture inside. In a saucepot, heat oil to 350°F. Fry quinoa in batches until crispy and puffed. Drain on paper towels and reserve in an airtight container.

For the Walnut-Quinoa Granola:
Heat oven to 300°F. In a small saucepot, combine honey, butter, brown sugar, and vanilla bean scrapings; bring to a boil over medium heat. Meanwhile, in a large bowl, combine oats, 162½ grams Crispy Quinoa, walnuts cinnamon, and salt. Pour hot honey mixture into dry ingredients and toss to coat. Spread granola on a parchment-lined sheet tray and bake until golden and crispy, 8 to 10 minutes.

For the Meyer Lemon-Sake Kasu Curd:
Heat the water bath of an immersion circulator to 167°F. In a vacuum bag, combine eggs, sugar, Meyer lemon juice and zest, salt, and sake kasu and compress fully. Cook sous vide 30 minutes. Transfer to a deep container and, with an immersion blender, emulsify in butter. Add gelatin to dissolve. Chill curd in an ice bath.

For the Poached Rhubarb:
Heat the water bath of an immersion circulator to 141.8°F. Combine all ingredients in a vacuum bag and cook sous vide 20 minutes, or until tender. Immediately transfer bag to an ice bath.

For the Rhubarb Compote:
In a small saucepot, cook sugar to soft ball, or 240°F. Add rhubarb and cook until softened and thickened like jam. Transfer compote to a food processor and process until smooth. Season with lime juice and color with beet juice.

For the Rhubarb Soup:
In a large bowl, combine rhubarb, sugar, and water and cover tightly with plastic. Set over a pot of simmering water and cook until rhubarb is soft and has released its juices. Pass liquid through a chinois. Season with simple syrup, salt, and lemon juice. Strain through a coffee filter to remove any particles. Chill.

For the Quinoa Tuile:
Line a sheet tray with a silicone baking mat. In a medium saucepot, combine glucose, fondant, and isomalt and cook to 320°F. Immediately pour onto prepared sheet tray; cool fully at room temperature. Heat oven to 350°F. Line a sheet tray with a silicone baking mat and lightly spray with nonstick spray. Break hardened sugar into pieces. In a spice grinder, combine sugar shards with 60 grams Crispy Quinoa and grind to a fine powder. Using a small sieve, sift tuile powder in an even layer over the prepared tray. Top with another silicone baking mat sprayed with nonstick spray and bake 2 minutes. Cool slightly before removing top silicone baking mat and pulling/breaking tuile as desired.

To Assemble and Serve:
Set a dome of Labneh Mousse in the center of a bowl. Pipe dots of Rhubarb Compote and Meyer Lemon-Sake Kasu Curd around the mousse. Place Poached Rhubarb and Walnut-Quinoa Granola on either side of mousse. Set a few Meyer Lemon Meringues and violas on top of other components, and sprinkle with Maldon sea salt. Scoop a ball of Cucumber Sherbet and place next to Labneh Mousse. Top with a Quinoa Tuile.

Featured Ingredients: California Walnuts, Peruvian quinoa
Featured Equipment: Hobart food processor

Aki Kamozawa & Alex Talbot

Ideas in Food | Bow, NH

Aki Kamozawa and Alex Talbot, the duo behind Ideas in Food, met in the kitchen of Clio in Boston in 1997, and have been cooking and brainstorming together ever since. Kamozawa and Talbot care about the explanations behind cuisine. They specialize in sharing creative techniques with the culinary community—clarifying both why and how to express oneself through food. And though they tend to focus on modern ingredients, equipment, and innovative approaches, they remain grounded in the fundamentals of technique and a deep appreciation for ingredients.

Before it reached its current status, Ideas in Food began in December 2004 as an under-the-radar blog. Originally a digital notebook to record the couple's work, it evolved into a clearing house for ideas gleaned from restaurants, blogs, books, people, and the interactions and accidents of everyday life. The blog now has a cult-like professional following.

In 2010, Kamozawa and Talbot crystallized their ideas in book form. Ideas in Food: Great Recipes and Why They Work blends stories, science, and recipes, all aiming to teach chefs and cooks how to unleash their imagination. The couple also has contributed essays to both Food and Philosophy and The Kitchen as Laboratory, and wrote a regular online column for *Popular Science* from 2008 to 2009. In fall 2013, Kamozawa and Talbot released Maximum Flavor, a cookbook dedicated to revolutionizing home cooking. Their latest work, Gluten-Free Flour Power—released in early 2015—tackles the ever-expanding challenge of making delicious gluten-free food. Rivaling their written contributions to the culinary conversation are their lecturing appearances, from episodes of "Foodography" on the Cooking Channel and the Flemish Primitives to the StarChefs International Chefs Congress, and beyond.

PHOTO: ANTOINETTE BRUNO

 **IDEASINFOOD**

COOLEST TECHNIQUE YOU'VE LEARNED FROM ANOTHER CHEF:
Aki: At Clio, with Ken Oringer, we used a lot of finely cut herbs, and I was amazed to realize how much flavor such a small addition could add to a dish. They had to be sliced perfectly, with a very sharp knife, and they made all the difference in the finished dish.
Alex: Brining scallops before cooking them from Wylie Dufresne.

A DISH YOU MAKE THAT'S INSPIRED BY ANOTHER CHEF:
Alex: Japanese yams and cheese dish inspired by the traditional aligote potatoes made famous by Michel Bras

IF YOU COULD EAT AT ANY RESTAURANT IN THE WORLD TONIGHT, IT WOULD BE:
Aki: Charcoal BYOB in Yardley, PA
Alex: Del Posto

FAVORITE INDUSTRY INSTAGRAM ACCOUNTS:
Aki: Elise Kornack, @takerootbklyn; and Iliana Regan, @elizabethrestaurant

CHEF WITH WHOM YOU'D MOST LIKE TO COLLABORATE:
Aki: David Lebovitz or Dan Lepard. They are both so knowledgeable and create such beautiful food. Frankly, I'd love to put the two of them together in a kitchen to collaborate and just be able be there and soak things in.
Alex: Francisco Migoya. He's a thinker and a fabulous technician.

CARROT CAKE

Chefs Aki Kamozawa and Alex Talbot of Ideas in Food | Bow, NH
Adapted by StarChefs
Yield: One 9-inch, three-layer cake

INGREDIENTS

Glazed Walnuts:
1 cup California walnuts
¾ cup sugar
½ cup plus 2½ tablespoons water
⅜ teaspoon fine sea salt
2 teaspoons unsalted butter, sliced

Gluten-free Flour Blend:
700 grams cornstarch
500 grams tapioca starch
300 grams white rice flour
200 grams brown rice flour
200 grams nonfat milk powder
100 grams potato flour
20 grams xanthan gum

Cake:
1 tablespoon baking powder
1¼ teaspoons baking soda
¾ teaspoon fine sea salt
1¼ cups light brown sugar, packed
1 cup sugar
4 large eggs
1½ cups vegetable oil
¼ cup heavy cream
1 tablespoon vanilla paste or pure
  vanilla extract
1 tablespoon finely chopped candied
  ginger
Zest of 2 large oranges
1½ teaspoons ground cinnamon
¾ teaspoon grated nutmeg
½ teaspoon ground cardamom
3 cups firmly packed shredded carrots

Cream Cheese Frosting:
2 pounds plus 3 ounces cream cheese,
  room temperature
1½ cups heavy cream
2½ cups powdered sugar, sifted
½ teaspoon fine sea salt
½ teaspoon grated nutmeg

METHOD

For the Glazed Walnuts:
In a small saucepan, combine walnuts, sugar, water, and ¼ teaspoon salt. Bring to a boil over medium-high heat, then reduce to a simmer for 5 minutes. Remove from heat, cover, and let walnuts steep for 20 minutes. Heat oven to 350°F. Drain walnuts and discard syrup. Transfer to a medium bowl and toss with butter and remaining ⅛ teaspoon salt. Spread walnuts on a parchment-lined baking sheet and bake 15 to 20 minutes, rotating the pan once, until walnuts are a deep golden brown. Remove from oven and cool completely, until crisp. Keep walnuts in an airtight container at room temperature for up to 2 weeks.

For the Gluten-free Flour Blend:
In a bowl, whisk to combine all ingredients. Sift to remove any lumps.

For the Cake:
Heat oven to 350°F. Lightly butter three 9-inch round cake pans, then line with parchment paper. In a medium bowl, whisk together 2⅓ cups Gluten-free Flour Blend, baking powder, baking soda, and salt. In the bowl of a stand mixer fitted with a paddle, mix brown sugar, sugar, and eggs on medium-low until thoroughly combined. Add oil, cream, vanilla, candied ginger, orange zest, cinnamon, nutmeg, and cardamom. Beat on low until just combined. Add carrots and the Glazed Walnuts and mix until just incorporated. Divide batter evenly among cake pans and smooth surface with a small offset spatula. Tap cake pans on the countertop a few times to help settle contents. Bake cake layers 20 minutes, rotate, and bake 10 minutes more. The internal temperature of the cake should be 205°F. Cool cake in pans on a rack for 15 minutes. Then invert onto a rack, remove parchment, and cool completely.

For the Cream Cheese Frosting:
In the bowl of a stand mixer fitted with a whisk, combine cream cheese, cream, powdered sugar, salt, and nutmeg. Whip on medium speed until light and fluffy.

To Assemble and Serve:
Place one Cake round onto a cardboard cake circle. With an offset spatula, evenly spread about ¾ cup Cream Cheese Frosting over the top, leaving a ¼-inch border around the circumference. Repeat with the second layer. For the third layer, use ¾ cup frosting again but spread so it falls over the edge. Spread a thin layer of frosting around the sides to make a crumb coat. Rinse spatula under warm water and wipe dry before applying the final coat. Swirl remaining frosting onto cake in pretty patterns or pipe small rosettes along the border. Refrigerate at least 30 minutes to set frosting. Bring cake to room temperature before serving.

Featured Ingredient: California Walnuts

PHOTO: ANTOINETTE BRUNO

Kriss Harvey

The Bazaar by José Andrés | Los Angeles, CA

⊙ **KRISSHARV3Y** 🐦 **KRISSHARVEY**

MOST INFLUENTIAL MENTOR WITH WHOM YOU'VE WORKED: That's easy. Sylvain Guyez, my pastry chef at the Ritz Carlton, Pentagon City. Not a day goes by that I don't do something that he taught me.

COOLEST TECHNIQUE YOU'VE LEARNED FROM ANOTHER CHEF: Polishing my chocolate molds with a cotton ball that's been soaked in 91 percent alcohol. It gives my chocolates their signature shine.

A DISH YOU MAKE THAT'S INSPIRED BY ANOTHER RESTAURANT: The Vanilla Pillow is inspired by the small cake I recently had at Cyril Lignac in Paris. The recipes are all mine, but the lightness and flavor the pastry chef achieved was remarkable.

IF YOU COULD EAT AT ANY RESTAURANT IN THE WORLD TONIGHT, IT WOULD BE: As far as eating at any restaurant in the world, I don't care anything about that. I'm not even interested in food, and I basically eat the same foods over and over. I'm very basic in that regard.

FAVORITE INDUSTRY INSTAGRAM ACCOUNT: Gary Rulli, @Emporio_Rulli

FAVORITE COOKBOOK: Au Cœur des Saveurs by Frederic Bau. It's a complete book of chocolate, small cakes, and desserts, and even though it's 20 years old, it still looks great today.

Executive Pastry Chef Kriss Harvey brings innovative flavor combinations, avant-garde techniques, and more than 20 years of experience to the pastry menus at The Bazaar by José Andrés at the SLS Hotel in Los Angeles.

A New York native, Harvey trained under some of the world's most highly regarded chefs. He began his career in the Cacao Barry Chocolate Academy near Philadelphia, spending time under the tutelage of Master Chocolatier Pascal Janvier. With a desire to fine-tune his knowledge in French pastry, Harvey moved to Paris, where he studied with legendary Pastry Chefs Christophe Felder at the Hôtel de Crillon and M.O.F. Emmanuel Ryon of École Gastronomique Bellouet Conseil. He continued his international experience with a stint in Spain, working with Pastry Chef Oriol Balaguer of El Bulli and Oriol Balaguer Pastry. Harvey also studied with M.O.F. chocolatier and candy maker, Pierre Mirgalet.

Throughout his career, Harvey assumed pastry positions at some of the country's finest establishments, including The Ritz Carlton in Washington, D.C., NoMI in the Park Hyatt Chicago, and at Bartolotta Ristorante Di Mare at the Wynn Resort in Las Vegas. He consults on various pastry menus around the country, such as for the James Beard Award-nominated NOCA in Phoenix. Harvey joined The Bazaar by José Andrés in spring 2013, where he works closely with Andrés and Think Food's team to create forward-thinking, innovative desserts that remain true to the group's modernist style.

THE CHOCOLATE CAKE OF YOUR DREAMS

Update your dessert menu's best seller: chocolate cake. In his hands-on workshop, Pastry Chef Kriss Harvey will help expand your repertoire to include the chocolate cake of your dreams—one that's beautiful (thanks to precise mold work and finishing), decadent (courtesy of a trio of Valrhona chocolates), and irresistible (guests just can't say no).

Presented by Valrhona

THE CHOCOLATE CAKE OF YOUR DREAMS
Pastry Chef Kriss Harvey of The Bazaar by José Andrés | Los Angeles, CA
Adapted by StarChefs
Yield: 2 small cakes or 25 individual cakes

INGREDIENTS

Ganache:
340 grams Valrhona Pur Caraibe chocolate féves
110 grams Valrhona Jivara féves chocolate féves
4 grams fleur de sel
240 milliliters milk, scalded

Moelleux:
160 grams invert sugar
80 grams glucose syrup
260 grams room temperature eggs, beaten
100 grams room temperature egg yolks
250 grams heavy cream, scalded
300 grams Valrhona Pur Caraibe chocolate féves
90 grams bread flour, sifted

Feather Light Mousse:
550 grams milk, scalded
9 grams powdered gelatin, bloomed in 36 grams water
650 grams Valrhona Illanka chocolate féves
1.1 kilograms whipped cream

To Assemble and Serve:
Red cocoa butter
Broken plaque of chocolate from a structure sheet

METHOD

For the Ganache:
In a heatproof bowl, combine chocolates and salt. Slowly pour in hot milk, stirring constantly with a rubber spatula until combined and glossy. Pour ganache into silicone pomponette molds with a heart-shaped ring mold framing them. Freeze.

For the Moelleux:
Heat oven to 177°C. In a heatproof bowl, combine invert sugar and glucose syrup. Warm over a double boiler. Add eggs and yolks, lightly stirring, until mixture reaches 55°C. Transfer to the bowl of stand mixer fitted with whisk. Whip until combined; reserve. Pour hot cream into bowl with chocolate. Stir to combine. Fold in one-third of the egg mixture, followed by the remaining two-thirds. Fold in flour. Using a raplette, spread mixture onto a silicone mat until 5 millimeters thick. Bake 8 minutes. Let cool completely; freeze.

For the Feather Light Mousse:
In a bowl, combine hot milk and gelatin. Pour into small bowl with chocolate. Stir to combine. When temperature of mixture falls to 40°C, fold in cream. Transfer to piping bag.

To Assemble and Serve:
Pipe Feather Light Mousse into heart-shaped silicone molds until two-thirds full. Insert Ganache and pipe more mousse to cover. Finish with Moelleux cut to fit mold. Blast freeze at -35°F for 4 hours. Remove from molds. Spray with red cocoa butter and let defrost in refrigerator. Decorate with broken plaque of chocolate.

Featured Ingredient: Valrhona chocolate
Featured Equipment: Hobart stand mixer

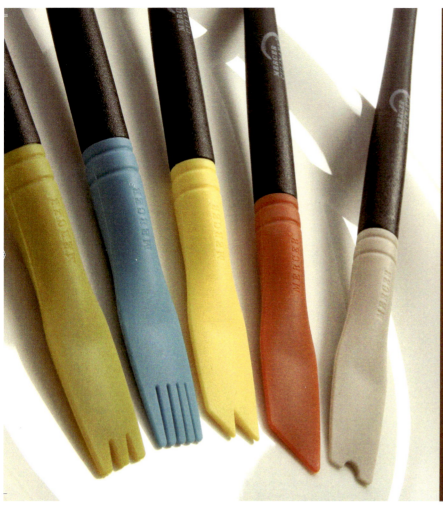
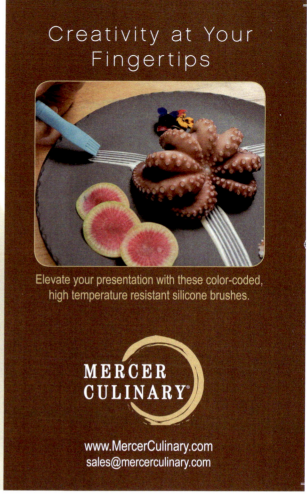

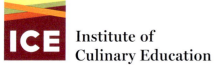

Michael Laiskonis

Institute of Culinary Education | New York, NY

PHOTO: STEPHEN KENNY

Michael Laiskonis is one of the preeminent chefs working in pastry today. He first rose to prominence during his eight year tenure as executive pastry chef of Le Bernardin, during which time the restaurant earned four stars from *The New York Times* and three Michelin stars. Known for exquisite, modern desserts that balance art and science with a nod to the classics, Laiskonis' renown is an apt reflection of his introduction to the craft. He was a visual arts major who discovered that the techniques and traditions he studied translated well to the discipline and creativity of pastry.

Laiskonis found the perfect venue for his creative vision at Le Bernardin, where he was named one of America's "Top 10 Pastry Chefs" by *Pastry Art & Design* in 2002 and 2003 and was *Bon Appétit*'s "Pastry Chef of the Year" in 2004. Laiskonis was a 2006 StarChefs Rising Star and a recipient of James Beard's "Outstanding Pastry Chef" award in 2007. He's a consultant for Ritz Carlton and Starbucks, and has been the creative director of The Institute of Culinary Education since 2012. In 2014, Laiskonis received IACP's "Culinary Professional of the Year" Award. His writing has been published in *Gourmet*, *Saveur*, *The Atlantic*, The Huffington Post, and the 2011 anthology <u>The Kitchen as Laboratory</u>, as well as on his own blogs.

As a luminary and leader, Laiskonis strives to inspire the next generation of pastry chefs to tell more personal stories and guide them toward finding their own voices.

GENETICS, ORIGIN, AND PROCESS: UNDERSTANDING CHOCOLATE

A deeper, more nuanced understanding of chocolate awaits. Join Pastry Chef Michael Laiskonis to explore the impact of varietal, origin, and processing on a finished chocolate—how it tastes and, ultimately, how it's best used. Attendees will assemble bonbons alongside Laiskonis, pairing distinct chocolate flavor profiles with fillings that complement or contrast with the chocolate base.

Presented by Institute of Culinary Education

📷 🐦 MLAISKONIS

MOST INFLUENTIAL MENTOR WITH WHOM YOU'VE WORKED: Eric Ripert. From earlier chefs, I learned about passion and discipline (and even how not to do things), but with Eric came the realization that being a great chef is more than just being a good cook. It's how you carry yourself in life. I still hear his voice in my head when I have to make important decisions.

COOLEST TECHNIQUE YOU'VE LEARNED FROM ANOTHER CHEF: I've really been loving Sam Mason's techniques of using nitro-frozen inclusions in his ice creams. His version of Neapolitan is genius.

A DISH YOU MAKE THAT'S INSPIRED BY ANOTHER PASTRY CHEF: I'm working a lot with bean-to-bar chocolate these days, so my head has been deep in commercial formulations, but I'm also talking with a lot of artisan chocolate makers, comparing notes, and soaking up some of their knowledge and experience. At the end of the day, every chocolate is different: a blend of the inherent qualities of the bean and the instincts of the chocolate maker.

CHEF WITH WHOM YOU'D MOST LIKE TO COLLABORATE: I think a collaborative synergy between a chef and pastry chef can create a result greater than the sum of its parts. I think it would be fun to work with Paul Liebrandt. I've been a fan of his for years.

PHOTO: LAUREN DEFILIPPO

HOMAGE TO MAILLARD: ROASTED WHITE CHOCOLATE, PISTACHIO FINANCIER, AND APRICOT CARAMEL

Pastry Chef Michael Laiskonis of Institute of Culinary Education | New York, NY
Adapted by StarChefs
Yield: 10 servings

INGREDIENTS

White Chocolate Crémeux:
130 grams whole milk
10 grams glucose syrup
1 stick cinnamon
1 gram soluble coffee granules
2 grams grated orange zest
2 sheets gelatin, bloomed
170 grams Valrhona Dulcey white
    chocolate, melted
50 grams banana
180 grams heavy cream (35% fat)

Pistachio Financier:
140 grams sweetened pistachio paste
30 grams brown butter
30 grams sucrose
4 eggs
20 grams all-purpose flour
1 gram salt

Apricot Caramel:
200 grams heavy cream (35% fat)
130 grams sucrose
50 grams glucose syrup
100 grams apricot purée
5 grams cocoa butter
1 gram citric acid
15 grams butter

Lime Meringue:
32 grams sucrose
75 grams water
35 grams lime juice
2 sheets gelatin, bloomed

Browned Milk Solids:
1 kilogram heavy cream (35% fat)
60 grams nonfat milk powder

METHOD

For the White Chocolate Crémeux:
In a saucepot, bring milk to a boil. Add glucose, cinnamon, coffee, and orange zest. Remove from heat and infuse 15 minutes. Strain, return to a boil, and stir in gelatin. Remove from heat and slowly incorporate white chocolate. Add banana and cream, and emulsify with an immersion blender for 2 minutes. Transfer to silicone molds and freeze.

For the Pistachio Financier:
In a bowl, combine all ingredients. Pass through a chinois and transfer to a siphon and charge twice. Dispense into paper cups, making sure not to leave air pockets. Place in microwave and cook on high for 30 to 40 seconds.

For the Apricot Caramel:
In a saucepot, combine cream, sucrose, and glucose, and cook to 110°C. Add apricot purée and cook to 106°C. Stir in cocoa butter, citric acid, and butter. Remove from heat and cool.

For the Lime Meringue:
In a saucepot, combine sucrose and water, and bring to a boil. Add remaining ingredients, stirring to dissolve gelatin. Transfer mixture to the bowl of a stand mixer fitted with a whisk, and whip to soft peaks. Place a silicone mat within a 12-centimeter frame. Spread meringue evenly to fill frame. Freeze to fully set. Portion into 5-millimeter cubes and freeze.

For the Browned Milk Solids:
In a saucepot over low heat, combine cream and milk powder. Slowly reduce until the solids have browned and separated from the clarified butter fat. Carefully drain Browned Milk Solids through cheesecloth, squeezing to extract excess fat. Reserve.

To Assemble and Serve:
Unmold Roasted White Chocolate Crémeux and place 1 portion on serving plate. Tear off small pieces of Pistachio Financier and arrange on and around crémeux. Arrange Lime Meringue cubes and bits of Browned Milk Solids similarly. Dot plate sparsely with Apricot Caramel.

Featured Ingredient: Valrhona chocolate

PHOTO: ANTOINETTE BRUNO

Rachel Sundet

State Park | Cambridge, MA

For Rachel Sundet, the journey to food began with a (sweet) parental shove. A Columbia University graduate with a degree in anthropology and some professional ambivalence, the Boston native decamped to London in 2003 to live with her grandmother and embark on some soul searching. Encouraged by parents who saw her potential, Sundet found herself looking to culinary school. To test the waters, she took a position as an unpaid intern at Upstairs on the Square in Cambridge, Massachusetts, where she fell in love with the kitchen.

After a year abroad at Leith's School of Food and Wine, Sundet returned to Upstairs for two years. She then moved to Seattle and got a job working the line at Brasa with Chef Tamara Murphy, and (simultaneously) the morning pastry gig at Macrina Bakery. Broadly skilled, and with then boyfriend, Tyler, Sundet spent eight months learning to make cheese on a goat farm in Maine, and followed that experience into working as cheesemonger at Formaggio Kitchen in Cambridge. Sundet couldn't manage to stay away from the kitchen, though. When Tyler started cooking at Hungry Mother and a part time pastry position opened up, she jumped at the opportunity. After almost a year, Sundet took the helm of the Southern-inflected pastry menu. In late 2013, the pair, now married, helped open State Park, a stylized dive and cocktail den with elevated American cuisine. In 2015 Sundet was named a StarChefs Rising Star Pastry Chef.

CVAP FOR SWEETS

Pastry Chef Rachel Sundet has commandeered her Cambridge restaurant's CVap for her own sweet purposes: silky custards, steamed puddings, and light-as-air cheesecakes. In this hands-on workshop, Sundet will show attendees how to fully flex the power of steam in the pastry kitchen.

Presented by Winston Industries

SUNDET13 STATEPARKBAR

MOST INFLUENTIAL MENTORS WITH WHOM YOU'VE WORKED: Amanda Lydon and Susan Regis. They had such different styles but both made incredible food. It was great to be exposed to multiple ways of being successful in the kitchen.

COOLEST TECHNIQUE YOU'VE LEARNED FROM ANOTHER CHEF: To get every bit of product out of the food processor: scrape as much as possible out, and then turn on the motor one more time. It shoots the last bits out to the side so it's easy to get it all out.

IF YOU COULD EAT AT ANY RESTAURANT IN THE WORLD TONIGHT, IT WOULD BE: Test Kitchen, South Africa

FAVORITE INDUSTRY INSTAGRAM ACCOUNT: @massimobottura

PHOTO: ANTOINETTE BRUNO

SALTED BUTTERSCOTCH CUSTARD, CRANBERRY-SPARKLING WINE GRANITA, PICKLED AND DEHYDRATED CRANBERRIES, AND CHANTILLY

Pastry Chef Rachel Sundet of State Park | Cambridge, MA
Adapted by StarChefs
Yield: 8 servings

INGREDIENTS

Salted Butterscotch Custard:
1¼ cups heavy cream
1 cup whole milk
½ cup dark brown sugar, loosely packed
1⅛ teaspoons fine sea salt
3 tablespoons Demerara sugar
3 tablespoons water
96 grams egg yolks
1 teaspoon JR Watkins pure vanilla extract

Cranberry-Sparkling Wine Granita:
½ cup fresh cranberries
¼ cup vanilla sugar
2 tablespoons honey, plus additional as needed
1 pinch salt
1 cup sparkling white wine
1 tablespoon lemon juice, plus additional as needed

Dehydrated Cranberries:
1 cup fresh cranberries
Zest of 1 orange
Zest of 1 lime
¼ cup sugar

Pickled Cranberries:
¼ cup dark brown sugar, packed
1 pinch salt
1 cup red wine vinegar
¼ cup fresh cranberries, ends trimmed and cut
    in half on their equator

Chantilly:
1 cup heavy cream
1 tablespoon powdered sugar
1 teaspoon pure vanilla extract

For the Salted Butterscotch Custard:

In a heavy saucepan over medium heat, combine cream, milk, brown sugar, and salt. Stir until sugar dissolves and milk scalds; remove from heat. In a separate saucepan, combine Demerara sugar with water. Over low heat, slowly melt the sugar. Continue cooking over medium heat to caramelize. When the caramel is deep golden brown and the bubbles are big and syrupy, slowly add cream mixture, whisking to combine. In a medium bowl, combine egg yolks with vanilla and whisk to combine. Stream caramel-cream mixture into yolk mixture, whisking constantly. Strain through a chinois into a nonreactive, heatproof container. Adjust seasoning—the salt should be assertive, but not overpowering. Set CVap to steam at 200°C with zero browning. Evenly divide custard into 8 bowls and steam for 30 minutes, or until set. Cool at room temperature 10 to 15 minutes; cover and chill.

For the Cranberry-Sparkling Wine Granita:

In a medium saucepan, combine cranberries, vanilla sugar, honey, 1 cup water, and salt. Cook over medium-high heat until cranberries burst and are very tender. Transfer mixture to blender and purée. Strain through a chinois—it should have body, but be pourable; adjust consistency with water as needed. Whisk in the wine and lemon juice. Taste and adjust for sweetness with honey or lemon. Pour into a shallow pan and place in freezer. Every 15 to 20 minutes, use a fork to break up the forming ice crystals. The finished product should be evenly sized magenta crystals. Fluff with a fork before serving.

For the Dehydrated Cranberries:

Line a mesh dehydrator rack with parchment paper. In a food processor, pulse cranberries a few times, until evenly and finely chopped. Scrape into a bowl and add zests and sugar. Toss to coat. Evenly spread coated cranberries on the lined rack. Dehydrate on medium-high heat 6 to 8 hours, stirring periodically, until completely dry and crisp.

For the Pickled Cranberries:

In a saucepan over medium heat, dissolve sugar and salt in vinegar. Increase heat and bring to a boil. Into a shallow quarter hotel pan with cranberries, pour the hot pickling liquid. Cover the surface with parchment paper. Rest at room temp at least 30 minutes, then refrigerate. The cranberries are ready to serve, but will continue to intensify and deepen in flavor the longer they sit in the pickling liquid.

For the Chantilly:

In a bowl, combine all ingredients and whip to soft peaks.

To Assemble and Serve:

Place a quenelle of Chantilly in the center of custard. Top with Cranberry-Sparking Wine Granita, a few Pickled Cranberries, and a dusting of Dehydrated Cranberries.

Featured Ingredient: J.R. Watkins pure vanilla extract
Featured Equipment: Winston CVap

Indulgent Coffee Moments to Enhance Your Guest's Experience

Nespresso provides the Ultimate Coffee Experience with a variety of portioned premium Grand Cru coffees that work in perfect harmony with our state-of-the-art business machines and milk frothing solutions. Treat your guests to the perfect Espressos, Cappuccinos. Lattes and other coffee drinks with the simple touch of a button.

DRINK

PHOTO: DANIEL KRIEGER

Talia Baiocchi

Punch | New York, NY

Graduating from New York University armed with degrees in journalism and political science, Talia Baiocchi promptly abandoned the idea of attending law school. Culinary common sense swept in, it seems, and pointed Baiocchi squarely in the direction of Italy, where she worked the Piedmontese wine harvest in 2006 and traveled to every wine region she possibly could before resources ran out.

Returning home with less cash but more direction, Baiocchi soon got a job working at Italian Wine Merchants, fusing all she had learned abroad into a new career path. She also began writing Synesthesium, a blog covering topics from music and art to wine. Baiocchi's blog gained traction and attention, earning her the title of first-ever wine editor for Eater. Working for Eater, Baiocchi wrote about everything from restaurant wine programs to rappers' beverages of choice.

Over the course of her career, Baiocchi has also written a regular column for *Wine Spectator*, in addition to contributing to *The San Francisco Chronicle*, *Decanter*, *Bon Appétit*, and *Wine & Spirits*. She is currently the editor-in-chief of the online drink and culture magazine PUNCH and the author of Sherry: A Modern Guide to the Wine World's Best Kept Secret, which is why it's no surprise *Time Out* called Baiocchi one of New York's "New Wine Prophets," or that she made *Forbes*' "30 Under 30" list in 2013.

THERE'S SOMETHING ABOUT SHERRY

It's been a good five years for Sherry, an industry favorite that's finally made its way into the hearts and palates of your guests. No small thanks to Talia Baiocchi, who literally wrote the book on Sherry. Along with Sommelier Ashley Santoro, Baiocchi will lead a tasting workshop on the varietals and nuances of this golden, 3,000-year-old Spanish tradition.

Presented by Wines from Spain

📷 🐦 **TALIABAIOCCHI PUNCH_DRINK**

WINE LISTS YOU REFERENCE FOR INSPIRATION: Juliette Pope's list at Gramercy Tavern, which Jon Bonné wrote about for Punch recently (I happen to agree with him wholeheartedly); Pascaline's list at Rouge Tomate (reopening very soon); Jeff Kellogg's incredible list of Italian wines at Maialino; and the many other sommeliers in the country running small, but super passionate lists, like Dana Frank at Ava Gene's, Taylor Parsons at Republique, Justin Vann at Public Service, and many more.

IF YOU COULD SIT AT ANY BAR IN THE WORLD TONIGHT, IT WOULD BE: Bar Manteca in Cádiz, Spain. It's a Sherry bar serving exceptional cured meats just steps from the beach. It's no frills. Just a place where you go drink glasses of Sherry for barely more than a Euro and eat chicharrones and jamón and olives with a mix of locals that span generations. It's one of my favorite bars in the world.

WINE AND SPIRIT YOU'RE MOST EXCITED ABOUT: Mezcal on the spirits side. And on the wine side, I drink so broadly it's always hard to choose one place. But I continue to be surprised and delighted by the wines coming out of Sicily—particularly the eastern part of the country (Vittoria, Etna).

Ashley Santoro

The Standard East Village | New York, NY

Curating the wine list for some of New York City's finest and most iconic eateries is no small chore. It takes a special, intuitive understanding to really stand out. Enter Sommelier Ashley Santoro, who had a humble introduction to the industry, bussing tables at the age of 15. Now, Santoro, the former wine director of Casa Mono and Bar Jamón, is the wine director at The Standard East Village, The Standard Café, and Narcissa.

Initially dreaming of law school, Santoro switched paths after working a banquet position at a hotel and went on to earn a bachelor's degree in food and beverage management from Johnson & Wales University. It was after college when Santoro fell in love with wine. A case of post-graduate confusion led her to Italy and, ultimately, Umbria, where she lived and worked (but mostly ate and drank). Deep in the in the heart of Italy and Italian wine tradition, Santoro couldn't resist the call of the grape. After her Italian juice awakening, Santoro settled back in the United States to pursue a career in wine. In addition to her work at The Standard, she also devotes time to traveling and teaching wine courses. Santoro has been featured in numerous publications including *The New York Times* and *Wine & Spirits Magazine*.

PHOTO: GABI PORTER

 **ASHLEY_SANTORO**

MOST INFLUENTIAL SOMMELIERS WITH WHOM YOU'VE WORKED: While I've only worked events with Jordan Salcito and Pascaline Lepeltier, I would say that both those ladies make me want to step up my game. They're humble, confident, and outstanding leaders in their positions.

IF YOU COULD SIT AT ANY BAR IN THE WORLD TONIGHT, IT WOULD BE: Ma Cuisine in Beaune, France. They have a crazy awesome collection of wines with prices that allow you drink some of the finest Burgundy without going completely broke.

FAVORITE INDUSTRY INSTAGRAM ACCOUNT: For sure Michael Madrigale from Bar Boulud and Boulud Sud, @mikemadrigale

FAVORITE WINE REFERENCE: The Oxford Companion to Wine by Jancis Robinson and The Wines of Burgundy by Clive Coates

WINE YOU'RE MOST EXCITED ABOUT: I've been gravitating toward the Savoie. I think it's a very unappreciated region that produces some really affordable, delicious wine.

PHOTO: GREG POWERS

Juan Coronado

The Pour Group | New York, NY

An 18-plus year veteran of the food and wine industry, Juan Coronado got his start surrounded by Champagne as a sommelier for Bubble Lounge in New York and San Francisco. He shared his knowledge beyond the lounge by teaching "Champagne 101" for *The New York Times*.

Soon, the industry had Coronado looking beyond bubbles to the world of spirits. He expanded his expertise to sake and tequila and eventually served as *The New York Post*'s go-to tequila expert. Coronado's next move took him to Hell's Kitchen, where he opened Sortie, a forerunner in mixology innovation and creativity. Other creative collaborations included Braai and the Hennessey House of Mixing Academy.

Recognized as a gifted bartender, Coronado won several rum-specific cocktail awards in 2005, 2006, and 2012, as well as the Classic Martini Contest at the Astor Center in 2008. Mentored by Rum Master Señor William Ramos, Coronado eventually joined the Bacardi team as a brand ambassador. He was also the cocktail innovator in charge of creating "all things liquid" for José Andrés' Think Food Group, where he most recently launched the pisco-centric bar program at China Chilcano. Coronado has been featured in publications ranging from *GQ*, *Saveur*, and *The Washington Post*. In 2014, he co-founded The Pour Group, a food, beverage, and events consulting company.

FLIGHT OF THE PISCOS

You'll go so far beyond the pisco sour in this tasting workshop with bartender and spirits champion Juan Coronado. Learn about the great eight grapes (Quebranta, Italia, Negra Criolla, Torontel, Mollar, Moscatel, Uvina, Albilla) that give Peruvian piscos their character, and how best to mix and match with each nuanced spirit.

Presented by PROMPerú

 **JUAN_E_CORONADO**

MOST INFLUENTIAL SOMMELIER WITH WHOM YOU'VE WORKED: Lucas Paya for his ability to connect wines from the Old World with the New World, and his ability to pin-point specific characteristics in people's palates to select the perfect wine for them.

COCKTAIL LISTS YOU REFERENCE FOR INSPIRATION: I like to let loose to my creative process. The best part of my job is to create my own inspiration.

IF YOU COULD SIT AT ANY BAR IN THE WORLD TONIGHT, IT WOULD BE: Oscar Bar in Fukuoka, Japan

FAVORITE INDUSTRY INSTAGRAM ACCOUNT: Camper English, @alcademics

FAVORITE WINE/COCKTAIL REFERENCE: The Savoy Cocktail Book by Harry Craddock

SPIRIT YOU'RE MOST EXCITED ABOUT: Definitely pisco

WAIKIKI BEACH
Bartender Juan Coronado of The
Pour Group | New York, NY
Adapted by StarChefs
Yield: 1 cocktail

INGREDIENTS

1½ ounces Macchu Pisco
¾ ounce coconut water
½ ounce lime juice
½ ounce pandan syrup
Activated charcoal

METHOD

In a shaker with ice, combine all ingredients and shake. Double strain into a chilled coupe.

Featured Ingredient: Peruvian pisco

PHOTO: STACY GOLDBERG

Julie Dalton
Wit & Wisdom | Baltimore, MD

Like many students, Julie Dalton waited tables in college, and the savvy scholar soon realized she could earn more money if she knew a thing or two about wine. But even with that early insight to the perks of oenology, Dalton spent 12 years working in the biotech industry before she struck out on a new career path paved with grapes. She began working for an importer in 2010, but eventually realized hospitality was her true calling.

For Dalton, the intrigue of wine is its ability to be a unifier, encompassing and connecting subjects as far ranging as weather, religion, taxonomy, and botany. After completing her Advanced Sommelier Certification from the Court of Master Sommeliers, she helped Michael Mina and Rajat Parr open Wit & Wisdom, a tavern in the Four Seasons Hotel in Baltimore, Maryland. Dalton is also a Certified Wine Educator through the Society of Wine Educators and is in the process of completing her Diploma in Wine and Spirits through the Wine and Spirits Education Trust.

Dalton represented the Mid-Atlantic region at the National Young Sommelier Competition through the Chaîne des Rôtisseurs in 2010, and the Washington, D.C. area for the Guild of Sommeliers in Champagne after winning the Ruinart Challenge for the Mid-Atlantic in 2012. Dalton also competed and earned the runner-up spot in both the 2012 and 2013 StarChefs Somm Slam at the International Chefs Conference, and she was named a 2014 StarChefs D.C.-area Rising Star Sommelier.

ESOTERICA: WINES ON THE FRINGE

Somms Julie Dalton and Brent Kroll are teaming up at ICC this year to introduce you to your new favorite wine—one with a little cool-kid-cache. They're bringing in lesser-known producers from under-explored regions (Uruguay, Spain, South Africa, and beyond) that will add intrigue and value to your wine list.

 JULIEMDALTON

MOST INFLUENTIAL SOMMELIER WITH WHOM YOU'VE WORKED: Although not a sommelier, and although he eschews formal wine education and certifications, Mitchell Pressman has contributed most to my philosophy about wine. When I moved to Baltimore in 2000, he hired me on the spot at his Chesapeake Wine Company. I was only an enthusiast working there part-time while I was in the biotech industry. He helped me nurture my passion for wine and become the wine professional that I am today.

WINE LISTS YOU REFERENCE FOR INSPIRATION: Other Mina properties like RN74, Michael Mina, and Bourbon Steak. I also look to NYC's Eleven Madison Park and Seattle's Canlis.

IF YOU COULD SIT AT ANY BAR IN THE WORLD TONIGHT, IT WOULD BE: Pabu in San Francisco

FAVORITE SOMMELIER INSTAGRAM ACCOUNTS: @pascalinelepeltier and @corkhoarder

FAVORITE WINE REFERENCE: The World Atlas of Wine by Hugh Johnson and Jancis Robinson

WINE YOU'RE MOST EXCITED ABOUT: Not to be redundant, but Champagne is my reason for living. Period. It's delicious, and it makes me smile from the inside out.

Brent Kroll

Neighborhood Restaurant Group | Washington, D.C.

PHOTO: ANTOINETTE BRUNO

Brent Kroll's restaurant experience has spanned the nation. He has spent time working for the Michael Mina Restaurant Group, which put him behind the corkscrew at Saltwater at the MGM Grand in Detroit and Bourbon Steak at the Fairmont Turnberry Country Club in Miami. He also worked at the classic Italian Casa Tua in South Beach. In 2008, this state-hopping somm and Michigan native settled in Washington, D.C., and landed a position with renowned restaurateur Ashok Bajaj. Kroll oversaw the wine program at Ardeo + Bardeo and later at the Oval Room, where he met mentor Madeline Triffon, who instilled in him a deep-rooted sense of hospitality. In 2010, Kroll accepted the position of wine director at Ardour at The St. Regis Hotel.

Today, Kroll is the wine director for the Neighborhood Restaurant Group, which includes 16 distinctive chef-driven restaurants, a bakery, a butcher shop, and a retail wine shop. Kroll oversees the wine programs at each of the group's concepts, creating compelling and distinctive beverage programs for restaurants, such as Red Apron and Iron Gate. He also leads staff training and creates singular beverage programming and events. He has been featured in *The Washingtonian* and *DC Modern Luxury*. Kroll competed like a champ in both the 2010 and 2011 StarChefs Somm Slams at the International Chefs Congress. In 2014, he was named a StarChefs Rising Star Sommelier for the greater Washington, D.C. area.

BTKROLL

MOST INFLUENTIAL SOMMELIER WITH WHOM YOU'VE WORKED: Madeline Triffon. I was a young server when I worked with her, and she gave me a lot of perspective. Watching her in a dining room shaped how I view a prolific sommelier.

WINE LISTS YOU REFERENCE FOR INSPIRATION: There are sommeliers that I admire for their palate and ability to assess wine, but I try not to look at anyone else's list when building one.

IF YOU COULD SIT AT ANY BAR IN THE WORLD TONIGHT, IT WOULD BE: A bar in Spain that does a perfect gin and tonic

FAVORITE HOSPITALITY QUOTE: "Most guests won't remember what wine they drank in a year. They will remember how you made them feel."

WINE YOU'RE MOST EXCITED ABOUT: Assyrtiko

PHOTO: ALIZA ELIAZAROV

Fred Dexheimer

Rx Wine Lab | Durham, NC

Transient jobs after high school, in places like Nantucket and Jackson Hole, and a natural knack for all things wine gave Fred Dexheimer the skills he needed to land a job at the famed cellar of Daniel in New York City. From that prestigious point of entry, Dexheimer worked the front lines at New York's Gramercy Tavern and the BLT Restaurant Group, where Dexheimer won a 2005 StarChefs New York Rising Stars Award. He also has contributed to publications such as *The New York Times, Wine Spectator, Food & Wine,* and *Wine Enthusiast.* An avid cocktail enthusiast and accomplished bartender, Dexheimer has also shared his creations with national publications from *Bon Appétit* to *People.*

Founding wine and beverage consulting company Juiceman Consulting in 2009, Dexheimer's industry impact continued to expand. Clients have included Wines of Chile, Wines of Southwest France, Max Brenner Chocolate, Grand Hyatt New York City, and StarChefs, for whom Dexheimer has overseen four previous Somm Slams at the International Chefs Congress. Along with his numerous consulting gigs, Dexheimer heads Rx Wine Lab in Durham, North Carolina—a wine bar with a carefully curated vino program with intimate sommelier-patron interaction, including with the famous ingenue himself. Dexheimer is one of only 230 Master Sommeliers in the world, and the only one based in the Carolinas.

THE ART OF COFFEE HARMONIZATION

Coffee blends—with their aromas, terroir, acidity, and bitterness—have all the nuances of fine wines, and those blends are integral to fine-dining experiences everywhere. Join Master Sommelier Fred Dexheimer in a come-one-come-all coffee break, where you'll learn how to pair Nespresso coffees with spirits, chocolate, and wines.

Presented by Nespresso

 **FREDDEXMS**

MOST INFLUENTIAL SOMMELIERS WITH WHOM YOU'VE WORKED: Craig Hanna of Wauwinet in Nantucket gave me a shot as a 22-year-old, wet-behind-the-ears kid who was thirsty to learn about wine. Jean-Luc le Dû gave me a shot to move to NYC and work in the epic wine cellar at Restaurant Daniel. Paul Grieco believed in a young, brash kid who wanted to take the NYC wine scene by storm and hired me as a cellar rat and bartender at Gramercy Tavern. Best restaurant experience ever!!! Chris Cannon is a very unique personality because he is an amazing restaurateur who knows more about wine than most sommeliers. He gave me a shot, then fired me. We still talk! I would say Chuck Simeone is the most influential person I ever worked under. Chuck taught me how to play the buying game, how to taste wine in many facets, how to be an operator, how to work clean and have a meticulous wine list and cellar. He taught me the world of being a multi-unit buyer. He is a badass!

COCKTAIL LISTS YOU REFERENCE FOR INSPIRATION: I am getting to be old school. I still look to Flatiron Lounge and Pegu for inspiration.

IF YOU COULD SIT AT ANY BAR IN THE WORLD TONIGHT, IT WOULD BE: Gramercy Tavern's window seat. Hands down!

SPIRIT YOU'RE MOST EXCITED ABOUT: Green Chartreuse for over a decade now

STACK YOUR
BAR
WITH NEW YORK STATE

Build the depth, breadth, and quality of your bar program with spirits from New York State—home to some of the country's most distinct gins, rums, whiskeys, vodkas, and liqueurs. Learn more about New York State spirits, including purchasing information and availability, by contacting the New York State Distillers Guild via **newyorkstatedistillersguild@gmail.com**.

Eben Freeman
AvroKO Hospitality Group | New York, NY

Native New Yorker Eben Freeman has worked in the city's food and beverage industry for nearly two decades. Beginning as a stock boy at Crossroads Wine & Spirits while attending New York University, Freeman has bartended in the West Village, on the Lower East Side, in Midtown at Palladin (when Wylie Dufresne was in the kitchen), in Brooklyn, and at the fast-paced Spring Lounge in Soho. His performance at Spring Lounge so impressed the proprietors that they asked him to become a partner in their new venture in Hell's Kitchen, The Collins Bar. There, Freeman developed his first cocktail program and spirit selection. He later joined the team at wd~50 when it opened in 2004.

Possessing a thorough understanding of wine, spirits, and classic cocktails, Freeman's innovative, cutting-edge drinks employ the latest scientific methods with a focus on fresh ingredients, underutilized spirits, and a playful, culinary character. He met Pastry Chef Sam Mason while managing the bar at wd~50, and together they opened Tailor, which was known as much for its food as for its imaginative cocktails.

In 2010, Freeman signed on as director of bar operations and innovation at Altamarea Group, where he joined forces with Michael White to open The Butterfly, a bar that featured all of Freeman's greatest cocktail hits. Freeman left his position with Altamarea in 2014, and is presently with the chic design and concept firm, AvroKO, as beverage director.

NEGRONIS WITH THE O.G. HOMIES

Drop the mic. Just not into one of the eight negronis you're drinking. For this tasting workshop, AvroKO's Eben Freeman has assembled some of bartending's O.G. homies (Jim Meehan, Toby Maloney, Katie Stipe) to mix their favorite riffs on the classic combo of Campari, gin, and vermouth. For good measure, their protégées (Nacho Jimenez, Jeff Bell, James Beck, and Natasha David) will throw down their own versions. Out.

Presented by Campari

 **EBENFREEMAN**

MOST INFLUENTIAL BARTENDER WITH WHOM YOU'VE WORKED: Stanislav Vadrna introduced me to Japanese technique, Wylie Dufresne opened my mind to possibilities, and Sam Mason taught me how to have fun at a high level.

COCKTAIL LISTS YOU REFERENCE FOR INSPIRATION: Tony Conigliaro & Matthew Bax

IF YOU COULD SIT AT ANY BAR IN THE WORLD TONIGHT, IT WOULD BE: The Artesian, London

FAVORITE INDUSTRY INSTAGRAM ACCOUNT: @jeffreymbell

FAVORITE COCKTAIL REFERENCE: Cocktail Guide and Ladies Companion, 1941 by Crosby Gaige

SPIRIT YOU'RE MOST EXCITED ABOUT: Hpnotiq

Nacho Jimenez

The Daily | New York, NY

Bartender Ignacio "Nacho" Jimenez has been part of the hospitality business for the past 13 years, a journey that started from the bottom and has ended up at the top. Jimenez has held nearly every front-of-house position—from backwaiter, host, runner, and sommelier assistant to waiter, barback, and finally bartender. This breadth of work experience is also reflected in the range of venues through which Jimenez has journeyed, including small neighborhood restaurants, dive bars, and Michelin-starred restaurants. Such reach and range have given Jimenez the uncanny ability to view the industry from many perspectives.

Jimenez began bartending at New York's Madam Geneva, where he was first introduced to craft cocktails in a fast-paced environment. After a year and half, he was extended the opportunity to tend bar at Saxon + Parole, where Naren Young and Linden Pride took him under their wing and showed him the myriad roles, skills, and joys that come with the job. Young taught Jimenez knowledge and appreciation for spirits, fresh produce, and technique. Linden taught him the meaning of the word hospitality, redefining for Jimenez his job behind the bar. These lessons eventually took Jimenez to the The Daily, where he has been mixing and overseeing bar operations for the past three years.

PHOTO: MEGAN SWANN

 THEDAILYNYC

MOST INFLUENTIAL BARTENDERS WITH WHOM YOU'VE WORKED: Naren Young and Linden Pride. Even though I've been in the industry for quite some time, it wasn't until I met the pair that I learned a whole different level of hospitality and attention to detail. Their experience, passion, and understanding of the industry is what, to this day, keeps me motivated to continue to improve each day.

COCKTAIL LISTS YOU REFERENCE FOR INSPIRATION: While places like PDT, Attaboy, The Dead Rabbit, and Mace are definitely inspiring, I think there's a lot to learn from every cocktail bar. Whether this is something positive or negative, they all contribute to my experience and growth in this industry.

IF YOU COULD SIT AT ANY BAR IN THE WORLD TONIGHT, IT WOULD BE: The Broken Shaker in Miami

FAVORITE COCKTAIL REFERENCES: Beverage Media, Difford's Guide, PUNCH, *Imbibe*, and Liquor.com

SPIRIT YOU'RE MOST EXCITED ABOUT: I am always SUPER excited about Mezcal. I think the tradition, integrity, and sustainability in which the spirit is produced is something to admire and be passionate about.

CAMPARINETTE

Bartender Eben Freeman of AvroKO Hospitality Group | New York, NY
Adapted by StarChefs
Yield: 1 cocktail

INGREDIENTS

1 ounce Campari
1 ounce Carpano Antica Formula vermouth
1½ ounces Tanqueray gin
Flaming orange coin

METHOD

In a Gallone mixing glass, combine Campari, vermouth, and gin. Add ice and swirl for 20 seconds. Strain into chilled coupe. Garnish with flaming orange coin.

SOLERA NEGRONI

Bartender Nacho Jimenez of The Daily | New York, NY
Adapted by StarChefs
Yield: 1 cocktail

INGREDIENTS

½ ounce Dolin dry vermouth
¾ ounce Dolin rouge vermouth
½ ounce Campari
1 ounce Lustau Amontillado Sherry
Lemon twist

METHOD

In a Yarai mixing glass, combine vermouths, Campari, and Sherry. Add ice and stir. Strain into a rocks glass filled with ice. Garnish with lemon twist.

Toby Maloney
The Violet Hour | Chicago, IL

Toby Maloney began his career with more basic training than razzle dazzle. The future bartender, beverage guru, and trend setter spent some time in culinary school in San Francisco, where he began collecting the skills and techniques he would later bring to bear during New York City's cocktail revival. But it's not just schooling that makes Maloney such an invaluable player in the cocktail game.

Over the course of his career, Maloney has traveled the world, seeking out the most visceral of epicurean experiences. His wanderings have led him from the beaches of Thailand, where he concocted Sang Thip cocktails, to the boisterous traditions of Oktoberfest, where Maloney pulled beers for a rosy-cheeked and happy crowd. He was a founder of Chicago's original cocktail den, The Violet Hour, and helped launch The Park Hyatt Tokyo's New York Bar before opening The Patterson House in Nashville and Pouring Ribbons in New York City.

He was one of the founders of taste-making Alchemy Consulting in 2004, and has since moved on from the firm. While Alchemy's purview was strictly cocktailian, Maloney was the company's "philosophical guide." In all of his projects, he brings to the table every lesson learned from a life in the industry—from doorman and dishwasher to busboy, waiter, cook, and bar back. In 2014, he was nominated for James Beard's "Outstanding Bar Program" at The Violet Hour, finally taking the medal home in 2015.

TOBYCOCKTAIL   TOBYPMALONEY

MOST INFLUENTIAL BARTENDER WITH WHOM YOU'VE WORKED: I'm not sure how to answer this question, so I'm going to hijack it. The bartenders that I get to work with at The Violet Hour and The Patterson House are the most influential to me. I am amazed, learn new things, and look at cocktails differently every time I get submissions from them.

COCKTAIL LIST YOU REFERENCE FOR INSPIRATION: Joaquín Simó's lists. His cocktails are stunningly creative. He has these wistful, Proustian anecdotes about how the drink came together. When I drink one or look at his specs, I imagine a rambling story about crushed rose bushes and the diesel motor running the cotton candy machine at a county fair.

IF YOU COULD SIT AT ANY BAR IN THE WORLD TONIGHT, IT WOULD BE: There is a bar on the south end of the Zona Romantica in Puerto Vallarta called La Palapa that has ice-cold beer, Havana Club 7, or a blended Daiquiri, and a view of the sunset that cannot be beat.

FAVORITE INDUSTRY INSTAGRAM ACCOUNT: Alex Day, @APDay, has a great account that isn't just about cocktails. It's a very human view of what we do. You can see the love he has for the people in this industry, not just the booze.

James Beck

The Patterson House | Nashville, TN

PHOTO: BRIAN REDAHAN

A son of Enterprise, Alabama, James Beck enrolled as a mechanical engineering student at the University of Mobile before spending five years on the road as a touring guitarist for various musicians and bands. He finally landed in Nashville in 2010 and chose to call it home.

The Patterson House had recently opened and it was there that Beck—who until this point hardly consumed alcohol at all—had two drinks that changed the course of his career and life. He was enraptured by the cocktails and fascinated by their mixing, history, and quality. Soon afterward, he joined the bar's ranks. Beck was trained from the ground up at The Patterson House under the aegis of renowned barman Toby Maloney and his opening staff. Two cocktails and four and a half years later, Beck holds the distinction of being the longest-tenured bartender at The Patterson House.

While still playing music, Beck's value to the bar's institutional memory is without rival, and in a town that is constantly changing, he's a source of comfort and familiarity for guests he's served over the last several years. Beck remains active in helping push the beverage program to new heights, keeping The Patterson House in the national spotlight and in the best possible expression of itself.

JAMESBECK JAMES_BECK

MOST INFLUENTIAL BARTENDER WITH WHOM YOU'VE WORKED: Toby Maloney. He was the creative mind behind the bar that taught me how to drink properly. Working with him for the last few years has been incredibly inspirational and fun, the parts I remember at least. And I'm sure the parts I don't were great too.

IF YOU COULD SIT AT ANY BAR IN THE WORLD TONIGHT, IT WOULD BE: Would it be fair to say any beer/tequila/taco shack on a beach in Mexico? Failing that, I'd love to go spend a few more hours at Attaboy.

FAVORITE COCKTAIL REFERENCE? The Flavor Bible. In terms of creating cocktails, it's somewhat like having an incredibly intelligent friend standing next to you saying "try this" whenever you're in a rut.

SPIRIT YOU'RE MOST EXCITED ABOUT: Over the past year or two, my preferences have shifted from whiskey to rum and tequila. More than half my drinks start with rum. I could also sip on Zacapa 23 or Don Julio Blanco all day.

DON'T PUSH ME

Bartender Toby Maloney of The Violet Hour | Chicago, IL
Adapted by StarChefs
Yield: 1 cocktail

INGREDIENTS

¾ ounce coconut- and cocoa nib-infused Ford's Gin
¾ ounce Plantation pineapple rum
¾ ounce Cynar
¾ ounce Dolin Blanc vermouth
St. Elizabeth Allspice Dram
Orange pigtail

METHOD

In a mixing glass, combine all ingredients; add ice. Stir and strain into a Nick and Nora glass rinsed with St. Elizabeth Allspice Dram. Garnish with an orange pigtail.

Featured Glassware: Steelite Nick & Nora

DEE-DELY-DEE

Bartender James Beck of The Patterson House | Nashville, TN
Adapted by StarChefs
Yield: 1 cocktail

INGREDIENTS

1½ ounces coconut- and cocoa nib-infused Ford's Gin
1 ounce Baglio Baiata Alagna vermouth bianco
1 ounce Luxardo Bitter
13 drops Peychaud's bitters
1 whole egg
Cinnamon stick

METHOD

In a shaker, combine gin, vermouth, Luxardo, Peychaud's, and egg. Dry shake. Add ice, vigorously shake, and double strain into a coupe. Garnish with sparked cinnamon.

THE EXTRAORDINARY
ITALIAN TASTE

Products of Italy, often imitated, never duplicated

ITALIAN TRADE AGENCY
ICE - Italian Trade Commission

Italian Trade Commission - 33 E 67th Street, New York, NY 10065 T.212.980.1500 newyork@ice.it www.italtrade.com

PHOTO: SHANNON STURGIS

Jim Meehan

Mixography, Inc. | Portland, OR

With a justifiable reputation as a thinker, perfectionist, savvy businessman, and writer to boot, Jim Meehan's made his mark on cocktail culure. But he didn't start out with a proverbial silver stirring spoon in his cocktail glass. Long Island Iced Teas and Alabama Slammers were the name of the game when Meehan began his bartending career in 1995 as a student at the University of Wisconsin.

In 2001, he moved to the finer cocktail climes of New York, where he honed his skills in fine dining and developed his palate at Five Points and Pace. Three years later, he showcased his budding talents behind the bar at both Gramercy Tavern and Audrey Saunder's Pegu Club, and in 2007, he was named a StarChefs Rising Star Mixologist.

PDT has received numerous awards with Meehan at the helm, including a 2009 Spirited Award for "World's Best Cocktail Bar" at Tales of the Cocktail and a 2012 "Outstanding Bar Program Award" from the James Beard Foundation. In 2011, the bar published its James Beard Award-nominated The PDT Cocktail Book, solidifying Meehan's stature and influence.

Mixing things up, Meehan left New York and brought his cocktails with him out west to Portland, Oregon, where he operates a consulting firm, Mixography Inc. He has joined former PDT cohort Sean Hoard at the Stray Dog pop-up at Big Trouble Bar, released a PDT cocktail app, and landed a book deal with Ten Speed Press. His book, _Meehan's Manual_, is set for release in 2016.

  MIXOGRAPHY

MOST INFLUENTIAL BARTENDER WITH WHOM YOU'VE WORKED: Audrey Saunders mentored me as a bartender from 2005 on. She took what she learned from Dale DeGroff and transformed our industry at the Pegu Club and beyond.

COCKTAIL LISTS YOU REFERENCE FOR INSPIRATION: Sean Muldoon and Jack McGarry's at the Dead Rabbit, Eryn Reece's at Death & Co, Ryan Chetiyawardana's at Dandelyan in London, Tash Conte's menu at Black Pearl in Melbourne, and many more.

IF YOU COULD SIT AT ANY BAR IN THE WORLD TONIGHT, IT WOULD BE: My own at PDT. I live in Portland now and miss it terribly.

FAVORITE INDUSTRY INSTAGRAM ACCOUNT: My man Jeffrey Bell, @jeffreymbell, takes some serious photos. I have to give it to him.

FAVORITE COCKTAIL REFERENCE: David Wondrich just rewrote Imbibe! It was already the best cocktail book ever written, and now it's even better.

SPIRIT YOU'RE MOST EXCITED ABOUT: I'm watching what Steven Soderbergh is doing with Singani 63 very closely. Really cool to have someone with his talents in our field.

Jeff Bell

PDT | New York, NY

Born and raised in the Pacific Northwest, Jeff Bell began his career in the hospitality industry washing dishes and bussing tables—as you do—at the age of 18. Sensibly, he was not enamored of a life elbow-deep in suds. Bell first stepped behind the bar in Seattle at the age of 21, while studying philosophy at the University of Washington, dividing his time between metaphysics and mixing.

After graduating in 2007, Bell knew bartending was his calling and moved to New York City to hone his craft among the best and brightest. He met PDT's Jim Meehan in 2010 while bartending at Maialino in the Gramercy Park Hotel. Meehan recognized Bell's potential and offered him one shift a week as a barback. Bell jumped at the opportunity, pulling a strenuous five nights at Maialino and one at PDT.

When a bartending position opened at PDT in fall 2010, Bell received his due promotion. Since then, he's fully committed himself to PDT, essentially taking over for Meehan and helping to earn a 2012 James Beard "Outstanding Bar Program" Award. On the rise, Bell was named a 2013 StarChefs Rising Star Bartender and won first place—after an unprecedented tie-breaker—in the 2013 United States Bartenders' Guild and Diageo World Class U.S. Bartender Competition. Certified national phenom, the "2013 U.S. Bartender of the Year" has been traveling with Diageo, representing PDT, and sharing his skills and knowledge on a global level.

PHOTO: SHANNON STURGIS

JEFFREYMBELL

MOST INFLUENTIAL BARTENDER WITH WHOM YOU'VE WORKED: I've obviously learned an incredible amount in my time at PDT, but I would not have found the job or been able to stand out if I hadn't worked for Jay Flemming in Seattle. He taught me all of the basics of tending bar and how to be a consummate host. The glamorization of our industry has attracted a lot of people who lack that background and understanding of how to properly serve guests.

WINE LIST YOU REFERENCE FOR INSPIRATION: Thomas Pastuszak of the NoMad. In the words of Pete Wells: "The wine list is tempting both in mainstream regions and off the beaten path." He curates a list of wines that allows the geeks to geek out and has plenty within the average diners comfort zone. With this approach, he doesn't alienate any of his guests and gives them the option to be adventurous or to play it safe.

IF YOU COULD SIT AT ANY BAR IN THE WORLD TONIGHT, IT WOULD BE: Bar High Five in Tokyo. Hidetsugu Ueno is a gracious host and is the best technical bartender I've ever seen work. He executes cocktails with a kind of precision that doesn't exist in the United States, or the rest of the world.

PHOTO: NICK BROWN

PHOTO: NICK BROWN

EAST INDIA NEGRONI

Bartender Jim Meehan of Mixography, Inc. | Portland, OR
Adapted by StarChefs
Yield: 1 cocktail

INGREDIENTS

2 ounces Banks 5 Island rum
¾ ounce Campari
¾ ounce Lustau East India Sherry
Orange twist

METHOD

In a mixing glass, combine all ingredients; add ice. Stir and strain into a rocks glass filled with one large ice cube. Garnish with orange twist.

ABCDEF

Bartender Jeff Bell of PDT | New York, NY
Adapted by StarChefs
Yield: 1 cocktail

INGREDIENTS

½ ounce Aperol
1½ ounces Beefeater gin
¼ ounce Campari
¾ ounce Dolin dry vermouth
½ ounce Encanto pisco
1 barspoon Fernet Branca

METHOD

In a mixing glass, combine all ingredients; add ice. Stir and strain into a chilled coupe.

Pisco is Peru

Pisco sour, a tasty timeless
national cocktail.

peru.info

Perú

PHOTO: MEGAN SWANN

Katie Stipe

Grand Army | Brooklyn, NY

As a young woman with a penchant for performance, Katie Stipe traded the neon lights of her Las Vegas hometown for the bright lights of the Big Apple. For Stipe (as for many would-be performers), pursuing a career in performing arts meant auditioning during the day and working the bar at night.

As Stipe worked her way through the bar scene, she soon realized she had a natural talent for crafting cocktails. In 2003, she was hired by Julie Reiner to work at her Art Deco cocktail den, Flatiron Lounge. Stipe worked with Reiner for three and a half years, honing her craft and fine-tuning her palate, eventually becoming head bartender and manager.

With enough confidence to take center stage, Stipe left Flatiron in 2007 to open The Bourgeois Pig in the East Village, where she served as beverage director. In 2008, Stipe reunited with Reiner to help her open Clover Club in Brooklyn.

Stipe eagerly took the opportunity to invest herself in yet another spirit-culinary concept at the Northern European restaurant Vandaag, where she created a market-driven cocktail list with a focus on genevers and aquavits. She's also worked at Brooklyn favorites The Shanty, Prime Meats, and Long Island Bar. For several years, Stipe has worked as a consultant for Diageo, and has crafted the beverage programs at Eventi Hotel for L'Amico and The Vine. Most recently, Stipe joined the team at newly opened Grand Army bar, also in Brooklyn.

MOST INFLUENTIAL BARTENDER WITH WHOM YOU'VE WORKED: I am currently working on a consulting project with Yana Volfson and have to say it has been an absolute pleasure. We have different influences and techniques when it comes to developing cocktails, and we found that when our two worlds collided creatively we developed some innovative and lovely recipes. She is a spirit like I have never met.

IF YOU COULD SIT AT ANY BAR IN THE WORLD TONIGHT, IT WOULD BE: Las Teresas in Seville drinking Manzanilla and eating jamón. No question. Then head to see a Flamenco performance.

FAVORITE COCKTAIL REFERENCE: The greatest addition to our industry, as of late, has been sevenfifty.com.

SPIRIT YOU'RE MOST EXCITED ABOUT: Avua Amburana Cachaça. I look forward to mixing with it going into the fall and winter months. All its cinnamon, warm earthy tones play well with Amontillado and Oloroso Sherries and, of course, brown spirits. It can also be used as a modifier to add layers of spice.

PHOTO: ALIZA ELIAZAROV

MOST INFLUENTIAL BARTENDER WITH WHOM YOU'VE WORKED: Katie Stipe takes the cake. She has this incredibly calm demeanor behind the bar, which is so lovely to watch, and her palate is outrageous.

COCKTAIL LISTS YOU REFERENCE FOR INSPIRATION: I love the menu at Maison Premiere. Their wine list is gorgeous. Honeycut in L.A. has this delightfully whimsical menu that I love to reference. Any bar that has a cocktail named "Crop Top" gets an A+ in my book.

IF YOU COULD SIT AT ANY BAR IN THE WORLD TONIGHT, IT WOULD BE: The corner table by the window at Le Mary Celeste in Paris, drinking one of their fantastic all-natural wines and nibbling on grilled octopus.

FAVORITE INDUSTRY INSTAGRAM ACCOUNT: @Punch_Drink. Those ladies have a good time!

SPIRIT YOU'RE MOST EXCITED ABOUT: Brandy. Pear brandy specifically. It is such a perfect expression of its fruit. I like to sip Clear Creak Pear Brandy chilled. It's heaven.

Natasha David

Nitecap | New York, NY

If Natasha David seems to bring something a little more cosmopolitan to the bar, it's for good reason. David was born in Germany and grew up in an eclectic household, with musician parents who had her globetrotting from one opera house to another.

By the time she was 18, David was more than equipped to handle fast-paced culture hub New York City. Enrolling at New York University to pursue a theater degree, David supported herself with a job at an Irish pub. What might seem like a fairly unglamorous situation was a mini-revelation for David, who began working behind the bar less as a means to an end than an end in itself.

David didn't stay pub-side for long. Talented and ambitious, she was assistant general manger and bar manager at The Corner Shop Café in Noho by her senior year, and the gigs haven't stopped. From the opening staff at Woodson & Ford (where she worked with Lynette Marrero and Jim Kearns), David went on to mix Italian at Maialino and Pulino's, Scandinavian at Vandaag, absinthe-happy at Maison Premiere, and just happy at Prime Meats. She also has worked with Brian Miller at Diageo's New York headquarters, and taught bartending classes at Haven's Kitchen. Following a successful stint at Demi Monde, David is now head bartender and co-owner of rowdy, unassuming Nitecap on the Lower East Side, part of the Proprietors LLC powerhouse, for which she is also a consultant.

CAFFÉ CAMPARI

Bartender Katie Stipe of Grand Army | Brooklyn, NY
Adapted by StarChefs
Yield: 1 cocktail

INGREDIENTS

1 ounce Lustau Solera Reserva brandy
½ ounce Carpano Antica
½ ounce Cocchi Americano
1 ounce espresso bean-infused Campari
Lemon peel

METHOD

In a mixing glass, combine brandy, Carpano Antica, Cocchi Americano, and infused Campari. Add ice and stir. Strain into a coupe. Garnish with expressed lemon peel.

HOT FLASH

Bartender Natasha David of Nitecap | New York, NY
Adapted by StarChefs
Yield: 1 cocktail

INGREDIENTS

1 ounce Rittenhouse rye whiskey
1 ounce Bonal Gentiane Quina
½ ounce Campari
¼ ounce raspberry syrup
Lemon twist

METHOD

In a mixing glass, combine whiskey, Bonal, Campari, and raspberry syrup. Add ice and stir. Strain into a rocks glass with a large ice cube. Garnish with lemon twist.

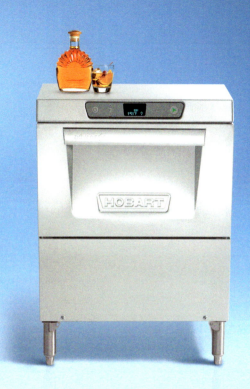

Geoff Kruth

Guild of Sommeliers | Petaluma, CA

Graduating from Sonoma State University with a degree in computer science, Geoff Kruth moved to Silicon Valley to pursue a career in the ever-burgeoning tech industry. By proximity alone, wine became a hobby, then a passion, and finally a career change, with Kruth enrolling at the International Culinary Center (then the French Culinary Institute) in New York. Before returning to California, Kruth became assistant wine director at Balthazar in Manhattan, overseeing the entirety of their extensive, high-profile wine program. With mentors like Fred Dame and Chris Goodhart behind him, Kruth rose quickly, and in 2008 became one of fewer than 150 people who (at the time) had earned the title Master Sommelier.

A 2009 StarChefs Napa-Sonoma Rising Star and now a wine director at the Michelin-starred Farmhouse Inn and Restaurant in Forestville, California, Kruth has also been the wine consultant for the Kapalua Wine and Food Festival in Hawaii for several years. As chief operating officer for the nonprofit Guild of Sommeliers, Kruth helped found the annual "Top Somm" competition, furthering the Guild's mission of advancing wine culture with a fun, professional edge.

WHAT IS IT? MYSTERY WINE TASTING

Explore two wine regions with Geoff Kruth, a Master Sommelier and the fearless leader of a little organization known as the Guild of Sommeliers. Put your palates to the test as Kruth pours wines from … well, we can't say. What we can tell you is that by the end of the workshop, you'll have a much deeper understanding of two exciting regions.

Presented by Steelite International

 GEOFFKRUTH 🐦 GKRUTH

MOST INFLUENTIAL SOMMELIER WITH WHOM YOU'VE WORKED: The late Chris Goodhart had a significant impact on my wine aesthetics, and Fred Dame has been a career mentor.

WINE LIST YOU REFERENCE FOR INSPIRATION: A16 in San Francisco. I don't like every wine on the list, but it's Shelley Lindgren's personal journey, and she buys wines that she likes regardless of what's on trend.

IF YOU COULD SIT AT ANY BAR IN THE WORLD TONIGHT, IT WOULD BE: I love drinking Champagne at half price after 10pm at Corkbuzz in New York.

FAVORITE INDUSTRY INSTAGRAM ACCOUNT: I mostly follow photographers and @TheFatJewish.

FAVORITE WINE REFERENCE: GuildSomm.com

WINE YOU'RE MOST EXCITED ABOUT: Regional Italian white wines. They offer tremendous value, and I never get tired of drinking them. Also Champagne because it's Champagne.

EXPLAINING WINES from SPAIN
FOUR GRAPES TO KNOW

IF YOU LIKE SUBTLE UNOAKED PINOT GRIGIO...

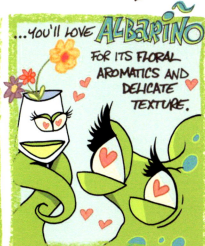

...YOU'LL LOVE ALBARIÑO FOR ITS FLORAL AROMATICS AND DELICATE TEXTURE.

IF YOU'RE A FAN OF TART, HERBAL SAUVIGNON BLANC...

...YOU'll ADORE VERDEJO'S LUXURIOUS MOUTHFEEL AND TANGY TROPICAL FLAVORS.

DO YOU ENJOY SOFT RIPE REDS LIKE MERLOT OR SHIRAZ?

THEN YOU'LL FALL FOR GARNACHA'S MEATY FLAVORS OF STRAWBERRY JAM AND WHITE PEPPER.

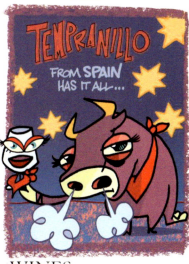

TEMPRANILLO FROM SPAIN HAS IT ALL...

IT COMBINES MALBEC'S FRUITY CHARM, WITH THE EARTHY COMPLEXITY OF PINOT NOIR, AND AGES AS GRACEFULLY AS CABERNET.

DON QX

AND THAT'S NOT ALL— SPAIN HAS DOZENS MORE WINE GRAPES TO EXPLORE.

pedro Ximénez
Godello
Monastrell
Mencía
Bobal

PHOTO: MEGAN SWANN

TJ Lynch

Mother's Ruin | New York, NY

TJ Lynch found his calling as a bartender at the tender age of 9, when he started making gin and tonics for his parents and their friends. Albeit not his finest work, the act of mixing drinks struck a chord with Lynch. However, his first endeavors into the industry were as a chef, not a bartender. Lynch cooked for seven years and eventually co-owned his own restaurant, Red Maple, in Baltimore, Maryland. After realizing his passion for beverage, he took off his toque, made a permanent leap behind the bar, and moved to New York City.

Lynch worked in some of the city's more established spaces, such as Highlands in the West Village. Bartending gigs turned into management positions, which later allowed him to become a consultant.

In 2011, Lynch opened influential hot spot Mother's Ruin in Nolita. A comfortable setting with a serious cocktail program, Mother's Ruin showcases Lynch's creativity and the culinary skills he amassed in the past two decades. Lynch's creations have been featured in publications such as *Cosmopolitan*, *Black Book*, *Imbibe*, *Ask Men*, and *Tasting Table*. In summer 2015, he opened a second bar, Lorenzo's, in Brooklyn.

SOUPED UP SLUSHIES

There's nothing easier, breezier, or more fun than slurping on a spiked slushy. Making a good frozen drink, with its integrity and ABV intact, is another story. Learn how you can bring banging slushies to your bar with the king of freeze, TJ Lynch, whose team at Mother's Ruin has mastered more than 300 slushy recipes.

Presented by Skyy Vodka

  MOTHERSRUINNYC

MOST INFLUENTIAL BARTENDER WITH WHOM YOU'VE WORKED: Toby Maloney

COCKTAIL LIST YOU REFERENCE FOR INSPIRATION: Jeffrey Morgenthaler's Clyde Common

IF YOU COULD SIT AT ANY BAR IN THE WORLD TONIGHT, IT WOULD BE: Bar Do Evori in Florianópolis, Brazil

FAVORITE OCKTAIL REFERENCE: The Bar Book: Elements of Cocktail Technique by Jeffrey Morgenthaler

SPIRIT YOU'RE MOST EXCITED ABOUT: The one that's in my hand

OMG, SHOES!

Bartender TJ Lynch of Mother's Ruin | New York, NY
Adapted by StarChefs
Yield: 1 cocktail

INGREDIENTS

1½ ounces Skyy vodka
¼ ounce pomegranate juice
¼ ounce aloe juice
½ ounce lemon juice
¼ ounce maraschino liqueur
Peychaud's bitters
Angostura bitters

METHOD

To a slushy machine, add vodka, pomegranate juice, aloe, lemon, maraschino, and a few dashes Peychaud's and Angostura bitters. Process and dispense the frozen cocktail into a rocks glass.

MAKE YOUR

HACCP

HAPPEN

HACCP plans are serious, time-consuming, and tedious. But once you complete one (and follow its protocols), you can cure, ferment, and sous vide to your heart's content. In this panel, you'll learn from two chefs who use HACCP as a necessary means to unleash their creativity. Josh Smith (New England Charcuterie) and Greg Biggers (Sofitel Chicago) will be joined by the USDA's own Thomas Collaro and Susan Isberg to help you overcome the pitfalls of achieving HACCP status.

 GREG_BIGGERS

MOST INFLUENTIAL COOK WITH WHOM YOU'VE WORKED: Erik Rollings, who I worked with at TRU. We were cooking on the same station, and he taught me a lot of technique and discipline early on in my career.

COOLEST TECHNIQUE YOU'VE LEARNED FROM ANOTHER CHEF: How to blanch a tomato properly: blanch in boiling water for eight seconds and let sit at room temperature. The skin peels off perfectly and the tomato doesn't get water logged.

IF YOU COULD EAT AT ANY RESTAURANT IN THE WORLD TONIGHT, IT WOULD BE: Takazawa in Tokyo

FAVORITE INDUSTRY INSTAGRAM ACCOUNT: @theartofplating

CHEF WITH WHOM YOU'D MOST LIKE TO COLLABORATE: Ryan Poli. That guy is just getting back to the States after a year of traveling the world and working in the BEST kitchens on the planet.

Greg Biggers

Sofitel Chicago Water Tower | Chicago, IL

Alabamian Greg Biggers grew up watching his mother prepare chicken and dumplings, a ritual linking food, love, and tradition in a way that's stuck with him. Before leaving Alabama, he worked under Chef Matthew Wood, who jump-started his passion for the professional kitchen.

Biggers studied at Johnson & Wales in South Carolina, but found hands-on work at Blossom Café and McCrady's more rewarding. A stage at TRU in Chicago would turn into a position as chef de partie under Rick Tramonto, which Biggers followed up with an executive sous chef gig at Morimoto in Philadelphia.

PHOTO: MEGAN SWANN

An expanding culinary repertoire under his belt, Biggers returned to Chicago to help open Tramonto's Steak & Seafood and RT Lounge. High-volume success would follow Biggers at Fulton's on the River, before he was picked to oversee Sofitel Chicago Water Tower's dining operations. His work at the hotel's Café des Architectes and the artisanal concept Chestnut Provisions earned him a 2015 StarChefs Chicago Rising Stars Award.

Thomas Collaro

United States Department of Agriculture | Waltham, MA

PHOTO: JEREMY ABRAHAMER PERLMAN

Thomas Collaro is no stranger to the food industry. He used to work among the ranks of line cooks before he exited the kitchen and jumped (cautiously) into food safety.

Collaro is now a Senior Investigator for the Food Safety and Inspection Service, which is the public health agency within the United States Department of Agriculture. The agency is responsible for ensuring that the nation's commercial supply of meat, poultry, and egg products is safe, wholesome, and correctly labeled and packaged. His everyday duties include investigating violations of the meat and poultry inspection laws, controlling violative products through detentions, civil seizures, and voluntary recalls, and helping ensure that appropriate criminal, administrative, and civil sanctions are carried out.

USDAGOV USDA

IF YOU COULD EAT AT ANY RESTAURANT IN THE WORLD TONIGHT, IT WOULD BE: El Tapeo de Cervantes, Malaga, Spain

RESTAURANT TREND YOU'RE EXCITED ABOUT: Upscale comfort food

FAVORITE INDUSTRY INSTAGRAM ACCOUNT: Who knew this was a thing?

WHO YOU LOOK TO FOR ADVICE OR INSPIRATION: Food Safety Discovery Zone!

MOST IMPORTANT PLACE TO INVEST MONEY IN YOUR BUSINESS: Food safety, of course.

Susan Isberg

United States Department of Agriculture | Waltham, MA

PHOTO: JEREMY ABRAHAMER PERLMAN

If sustainability and conscientious production are (relatively) new concepts in the food world at large, inspection isn't. Susan Isberg has been with inspection for almost a decade now. Since 2006, Isberg has worked as an Enforcement, Investigations, and Analysis Officer (EIAO) with the Food Safety and Inspection Service, the public health agency in the United States Department of Agriculture responsible for the safety of the nation's commercial supply of meat, poultry, and egg products.

Isberg's work has national—and vital—impact. In her duties as an EIAO, she conducts on-site consumer protection assessments to verify the design and proper functioning of a plant's food safety and process control systems. She also performs investigative work related to food processing and slaughter systems—meaning large scale food safety and handling issues are Isberg's day-to-day concern.

USDAGOV USDA

IF YOU COULD EAT AT ANY RESTAURANT IN THE WORLD TONIGHT, IT WOULD BE: El Tapeo de Cervantes in Malaga, Spain

RESTAURANT TREND YOU'RE EXCITED ABOUT: More chefs are getting into food safety! Although great food is an integral part of a restaurant's success, the increasing use of sanitation and employee training to help prevent foodborne illness—combined with awesome food—is making food safety cool!

FAVORITE INDUSTRY INSTAGRAM ACCOUNT: @moodyswaltham

MOST IMPORTANT PLACE TO INVEST MONEY IN YOUR BUSINESS: Food safety. Although not glamorous, if you do not have a safe product, your business will not prosper.

MOST INFLUENTIAL MENTOR WITH WHOM YOU'VE WORKED: Chef Charles Semail. He started me on the path to making my own charcuterie when I was 19.

COOLEST TECHNIQUE YOU'VE LEARNED FROM ANOTHER CHEF: Sous vide. Chef Ryan Hardy turned me onto this for putting out perfect meat for large numbers of guests.

IF YOU COULD EAT AT ANY RESTAURANT IN THE WORLD TONIGHT, IT WOULD BE: The French Laundry. Bucket list experience I've yet to have.

FAVORITE INDUSTRY INSTAGRAM ACCOUNT: @Victor_Churchill

FAVORITE COOKBOOK: Bar Tartine: Techniques & Recipes by Nicolaus Balla and Cortney Burns

Joshua Smith

New England Charcuterie | Waltham, MA

Chef Joshua Smith was just a local kid working at a Dean and Deluca in Charlotte, North Carolina, when one day, the butcher didn't show. Smith was thrown into the task and so began his long journey to becoming a charcutier. Smith worked his way up the West Coast before settling into the Four Seasons Olympic Hotel in Seattle. After cooking his way around northern California, an opportunity arose back in Charlotte at Nobles Restaurant Group, giving him the chance to dive deeper into charcuterie.

PHOTO: ALIZA ELIAZAROV

Smith then set up the food and beverage program for a resort in Lake Tahoe before landing in Boston in 2005 as the sous chef at the Four Seasons. After four years, Smith took the executive chef position at Michael Schlow's Tico, earning a spot on *Esquire*'s "Top 20 Best New Restaurant in America." Confident, Smith took a chance on his passions and founded New England Charcuterie in 2012, along with its storefront Moody's Deli & Provisions, where he earned a StarChefs Boston Rising Stars Artisan Award. In April 2015, he opened Backroom, an addition to Moody's with 50 seats, wine, cocktails, a rotisserie, and wood-fired oven.

HOW TO PAY
YOUR COOKS
$15
AN HOUR

There's no avoiding it. The $15 minimum wage is coming to your city. This business panel brings together chefs and hospitality head-honchos from across the country to discuss why and how they've spent more on employee wages—all while earning a profit. Tune in to find out how you can increase wages, morale, and the success of your business.

Will Blunt

StarChefs | Brooklyn, NY

 WILLBLUNT

Growing up in a political family in Washington, D.C., Will Blunt graduated from Georgetown University and spent time working for a Congressman on Capitol Hill before moving to New York City. He joined StarChefs when the company was in its infancy, and has been instrumental in making it the leading media company for culinary professionals.

As managing editor, Blunt wears many hats. He has been integral to the vision, development, and success of the International Chefs Congress. Blunt has helped build the StarChefs advertising client base from virtually nothing and has worked to maintain the integrity and authenticity of its promotions.

In his role as editor, Blunt is particularly involved with the growth of bartending content. His foresight was crucial in recognizing the importance and influence of mixology within the restaurant industry. Blunt works on the ground to contribute to tastings, interviewing many of the professionals featured on StarChefs. He also serves on the board of Careers through Culinary Arts Program and has worked with organizations such as Chefs for the Marcellus, Share Our Strength, and Partnership with Children.

PHOTO: AUTUMN STEIN

A DISH INSPIRED BY ANOTHER CULTURE: I have been playing around with injera and different berbere spice blends: We have a delicious organic barley injera at Amy's Mercado here in central Seattle.

IF YOU COULD EAT AT ANY RESTAURANT IN THE WORLD TONIGHT, IT WOULD BE: I think often of the delicious tajarin with sage butter at Anticatorre in Barbaresco, Piedmont. And if that was not possible, how about Le Cep in Fleurie, Beaujolais.

CHEF WITH WHOM YOU'D MOST LIKE TO COLLABORATE: I do it every day with my chef team at TD Restaurants, led by Eric Tanaka. We are a collaborative group and our passion for food and service is deeply rooted. They also have an awareness of their teams in terms of livable wages, healthcare, paid time off, advancement, education—all part of being a chef but often overlooked.

Tom Douglas

Tom Douglas Restaurants | Seattle, WA

If there's anything Tom Douglas has besides exceptional kitchen skills, it's persistence and enthusiasm for growing a business. In 1989, Douglas, along with his wife and partner Jackie Cross, opened their first and flagship restaurant, Dahlia Lounge in downtown Seattle. It was the beginning of the restaurant group that would 20-some years later include successful and diverse businesses all over Seattle and employ almost a thousand people at restaurants such as Etta's Seafood, Lola, Palace Kitchen, Serious Pie, and Cantina Lena.

PHOTO: ROBIN LAYTON

Douglas' hunger to make himself and his business better, more profitable, and more successful is unmatched. He's always keeping an eye out for bigger and more exciting projects, leading with his strong creative vision. Douglas received the "Outstanding Restaurateur" Award from the James Beard Foundation in 2012, one of the three James Beard medals he's won—the other two being "Best Chef Northwest" in 1994 and "Best Americana Cookbook" for Tom Douglas' Seattle Kitchen in 2001. In 2012, Douglas was named "Executive of the Year" by *Puget Sound Business Journal*.

IF YOU COULD EAT AT ANY RESTAURANT IN THE WORLD TONIGHT, IT WOULD BE: Sea Satin in Hora, Mykonos

RESTAURANT TREND YOU'RE EXCITED ABOUT: The media seems less starstruck (chef-struck?) and more interested with the integrity in which restaurants interact with the public. I would like to see more of that.

WHO YOU LOOK TO FOR ADVICE OR INSPIRATION: First, my dad. Second, my partners Steve Tzolis and Nicola Kotsoni.

WHAT YOU'VE LEARNED FROM A MISTAKE YOU'VE MADE: Do not open restaurants in neighborhoods you do not know or understand.

MOST IMPORTANT PLACE TO INVEST MONEY IN YOUR BUSINESS: Your colleagues

James Mallios

Amali | New York, NY

In the summer 2010, James Mallios, a longtime attorney, left his law career to pursue a path in the restaurant industry. Teaming up with Nicola Kotsoni and Steve Tzolis—law firm colleagues with similar goals and interests—the trio opened Amali on New York's Upper East Side in November 2011.

Presently, James Mallios is the managing partner of Amali and Amali Mou. He also serves as in-house council for the hotels and restaurants of Kotsoni and Tzolis, including Il Cantinori, Periyali, Bar Six, and The Bar Room. Team Amali boasts a remarkable track record of sustainability practices and community building, having worked with New York City schools to teach the health benefits of the Mediterranean diet and culinary traditions. Amali has been recognized by institutions such as *The New York Times*, *Time Magazine*, and the White House Press Office.

PHOTO: MALCOLM BROWN PHOTOGRAPHY

Christine Cikowski

Honey Butter Fried Chicken | Chicago, IL

PHOTO: CAROLINE HATCHETT

If most good cooking starts with some form of home cooking, Christine Cikowski took that to the next level. Cikowski is the chef and co-founder, along with Josh Kulp, of Chicago's Sunday Dinner Club.

However, before the two began their project, Cikowski gained formative experience at Blackbird and Milk & Honey Café. But even as she built her skillset, Cikowski envisioned something a little more intimate. With Kulp, the Sunday Dinner Club came to fruition, with multi-course dinners served in a home setting.

The dinner club not only vaulted the duo into the public eye, it was the birthplace of the item that would become their next professional focal point: honey butter fried chicken. In 2013, they opened a restaurant of the same name . When she's not cooking, fielding press inquiries, or receiving awards (including a 2015 StarChefs Rising Stars Award), Cikowski writes about food, travel, and the business philosophies that drive her home-cooked career.

 HONEYBUTTERCHI

IF YOU COULD EAT AT ANY RESTAURANT IN THE WORLD TONIGHT, IT WOULD BE: Verjus in Paris

CHEF WITH WHOM YOU'D MOST LIKE TO COLLABORATE: Vivian Howard. I like her style and her story.

RESTAURANT TRENDS YOU'RE EXCITED ABOUT: Restrained menus. The return of more casual food. Treating restaurant workers better.

WHAT YOU'VE LEARNED FROM A MISTAKE YOU'VE MADE: Undercharging for food and service. It only ends up hurting the business, and staff and chefs should be paid appropriately for their craft and labor. I've learned to price food and service what it is worth—fairly. Not less and not more.

Joshua Kulp

Honey Butter Fried Chicken | Chicago, IL

PHOTO: CAROLINE HATCHETT

Chicago is known for big flavors and progressive culinary strides. It's also home to a thriving grassroots food community—thanks to chefs like Josh Kulp. He and partner Christine Cikowski are founders of the city's beloved Sunday Dinner Club, a venture that brings chef-driven flavors to legions of fans in a comfortably accessible home-style setting.

Not that Kulp has always worked from home, so to speak. Before opening the Sunday Dinner Club, Kulp worked at Tweet and Restaurant Magnus in Wisconsin. Before that, he was a fifth grade teacher in the Bronx.

In 2013, SDC's success led to a new venture with Cikowski. They opened Honey Butter Fried Chicken, serving their popular rendition of a classic. Word of mouth, a 2014 *Chicago Tribune* Dining Award, a 2015 StarChefs Rising Stars Community Award have kept the chefs on the national radar, with Kulp's own writing (for publications like *Chicago Magazine*, *Chicagoist*, and his blog, *Parcook*) helping to keep the grassroots conversation going.

HONEYBUTTERCHI

IF YOU COULD EAT AT ANY RESTAURANT IN THE WORLD TONIGHT, IT WOULD BE: Besides my neighborhood taqueria, El Asadero, in Chicago, I'd love to spend another evening at Da Enzo Al 29 in Rome.

CHEF WITH WHOM YOU'D MOST LIKE TO COLLABORATE: I had a life changing meal at the Gramercy Tavern back when Tom Colicchio was at the helm and Claudia Fleming was slinging incredible pastries. The memory of sinking my teeth into his glazed pork belly and her raspberry dessert flight remains with me as the meal that changed the course of my life. I'd love to cook with them.

RESTAURANT TRENDS YOU'RE EXCITED ABOUT: Focus. I like restaurants that do one thing or a couple of things incredibly well.

MOST IMPORTANT PLACE TO INVEST MONEY IN YOUR BUSINESS: People and great ingredients.

MOST INFLUENTIAL MENTOR WITH WHOM YOU'VE WORKED: Chef Thomas Keller, like so many others would say. For me, it's his work ethic. It is a most humbling experience to watch someone like him still do everything himself.

A DISH YOU MAKE THAT'S INSPIRED BY ANOTHER CULTURE: We have Kombu-cured salmon with green papaya salad at Revel right now. It's the best kind of green papaya salad you will ever get.

FAVORITE INDUSTRY INSTAGRAM ACCOUNT: Chef Chris Consentino, @cockscombsf

FAVORITE COOKBOOK: I really enjoyed Bar Tartine by Nicolaus Balla and Cortney Burns. Great chefs and awesome food.

CHEF WITH WHOM YOU'D MOST LIKE TO COLLABORATE: The chefs from Parachute in Chicago, Johnny Clark and Beverly Kim. They have awesome Korean-fusion, and we could probably create something amazing together.

Rachel Yang
Joule | Seattle, WA

After graduating from Brown University in Providence, Rhode Island, with a degree in urban studies and visual arts, Rachel Yang enrolled at the Institute of Culinary Education in New York City to pursue her true passion: cooking. She mastered the classical techniques while working at some of the city's most formidable restaurants, including DB Bistro Moderne, Essex House, and Per Se. But it was during her time at the now closed D'Or Ahn that she found her distinct culinary voice— an intricate weave of her personal history as a Korean native and her experiences in fine dining.

PHOTO: JACKIE DONNELLY

Now based in Seattle, she and her chef-husband-business partner, Seif Chirchi, own three restaurants: Joule, Revel, and Trove. Highly praised and loved by local residents, Joule was named *Bon Appetit*'s "Best New Restaurant" in 2013. Trove, which features a noodle bar, Korean BBQ, and a parfait window, is one of *GQ*'s "Best New Restaurants of 2015," and Yang and Chirchi were nominees for James Beard's "Best Chef, Northwest."

CAREERS BEYOND THE

TRADITIONAL
—KITCHEN—

We're all addicted to this crazy, rewarding, merit-based industry, but a life on the line isn't for everyone. Meet four chefs who have chosen career paths in consulting, corporate cheffing, butchering, and managing F&B for pro-sports stadiums. In this business panel, you'll learn about the challenges and benefits of stepping out of a restaurant kitchen while staying wholly immersed in the industry we love.

Presented by Minor's

Antoinette Bruno

StarChefs | Brooklyn, NY

ANTOINETTEBRUNO ANTOINETTE_B

After Antoinette Bruno found success on Wall Street, she realized something was missing: an intimacy with food— the kind of closeness she felt living in Europe, working her way through school in restaurants. Bruno left the world of finance for the Chefs' Program at Ritz Escoffier in Paris. She earned her culinary chops working in southern France and then returned to the States.

In 1999, Bruno became CEO of StarChefs, refocusing its mission of supporting, connecting, and elevating chefs and their profiles in a fractious and competitive industry. In 2001, Bruno became Editor-in-Chief, leading StarChefs to become an industry authority on chefs, food trends, and the culinary world. The Rising Stars Awards were launched in 2002 as a platform for young chefs to be recognized broadly. And in 2006, Bruno and partner Will Blunt launched the StarChefs International Chefs Congress.

Bruno's photography has been featured in books, magazines, and dailies across the country. She holds a post-graduate degree from the London School of Economics and an MBA from Harvard Business School. Bruno was nominated for James Beard's "Best Multi-Media Feature" and "Best Food Website." She was elected to the board of Women Chefs and Restaurateurs in 2012.

PHOTO: ALIZA ELIAZAROV

Jill Conklin

Salt Block 8 | New York, NY

PHOTO: CRISTY QUINN

Earning a degree in food-applied science and nutrition, Jill Conklin has spent 20 years in the restaurant business working as an executive chef, a nutrition and food safety educator, a business development market manager, a product manager, and a philanthropic advisor.

As founder of Salt Block 8, she's found a way to bring her dizzying array of skills together, providing operations and business development services to the industry. Her long-simmering passion for gastronomy has translated into nonprofit work in areas such as global health, food systems, and economic development. Over the course of her career, she's worked with Chefs Move to School, The American Culinary Federation, School Nutrition Association and Foundation, the USDA, and as ambassador to the Global Child Nutrition Forum, the United Nations World Food Programme, and The Center for Excellence. Currently, Conklin serves as a board trustee of The Culinary Trust, an advisor-chair of IACP Youth Culinary Initiatives, and program director for SuperChefs Cookery.

 JILLPCONKLIN

IF YOU COULD EAT AT ANY RESTAURANT IN THE WORLD TONIGHT, IT WOULD BE: Honey & Co in London. Itamar Srulovich and Sarit Packer's cuisine is filled with flavors closest to my heart and reminiscent of the Sephardic foods I've spent years studying.

RESTAURANT TRENDS YOU'RE MOST EXCITED ABOUT: Dismantling the phenomena that good food can only be found in expensive restaurants. I am excited to watch how fresh-casual concepts are evolving, with the possibility that fresh, local, and sustainable can become affordable options.

WHAT YOU'VE LEARNED FROM A MISTAKE YOU'VE MADE: Providing a product that didn't have a demographic to support it. Business is a balance between that passion and the reality of market conditions.

MOST IMPORTANT PLACE TO INVEST MONEY IN YOUR BUSINESS: Your most valuable asset—staff—and his or her education.

Jennifer Cox

Levy Restaurants | Chicago, IL

PHOTO: LEVY RESTAURANTS

Jennifer Cox worked in the corporate world for seven years before starting a career in the food industry. Eventually, she found her true passion in cooking and pursued an associate degree in culinary arts from Kendall College in Chicago. She began her culinary journey by accumulating kitchen experience in Chicago restaurants, and then moved to San Francisco, where she deepened her love for Chinese cuisine at China Moon Cafe and honed her cooking and baking skills with Elizabeth Falkner.

In 2004, Cox was tapped by Compass Group to develop recipes for its healthy dining program and head their internal culinary training program. Three years later, she was asked by Joie de Vivre Hotels, Restaurants, and Spas to oversee 38 California hotel properties. Cox's latest position at Levy Restaurants as vice president of culinary involves oversight of daily operations of more than 120 locations nationwide.

 LEVY.RESTAURANTS
LEVYRESTAURANTS

MOST INFLUENTIAL MENTOR WITH WHOM YOU'VE WORKED: Barbara Tropp. She taught me it's OK to except and demand the details.

COOLEST TECHNIQUE YOU'VE LEARNED FROM ANOTHER CHEF: I learned how to make perfect rice from a prep cook named Rosa. No measuring. It works every time.

IF YOU COULD EAT AT ANY RESTAURANT IN THE WORLD TONIGHT, IT WOULD BE: Since I'm on the road right now, in my hotel room, eating Triscuits and Cracker Barrel cheese, the options are endless! Right now, Zuni Café's roasted chicken sounds yummy!

FAVORITE COOKBOOK: Fancy Pantry by Helen Witty. It's a pickling and preserving book.

CHEF WITH WHOM YOU'D MOST LIKE TO COLLABORATE: Carla Hall. We have a similar point of view about food, people, and kitchens.

Bridget McManus-McCall

Nestlé | New York, NY

Chef Bridget McManus-McCall's concerns stretch far beyond the confines of the kitchen. After earning degrees from St. John's University and the Culinary Institute of America in Hyde Park, New York, and Le Cordon Bleu in Paris, McManus-McCall became the director of sales and marketing for Lackmann Culinary Services in 2004.

She left Lackmann in 2008 to serve as corporate executive chef for the Nestlé Corporation. She is a Chef2Chef business development manager at Nestlé Professional, which manufactures and distributes a variety of bases, sauces, gravies, entrées and sides, sandwiches, snacks, and desserts. Nestlé Professional's foodservice brands include Minor's, Stouffer's, Stouffer's Lean Cuisine, Chef-Mate, Maggi, Trio, Nestlé Carnation, and Nestlé Toll House. Having a background in catering, marketing, event planning, and cooking, McManus-McCall is well suited to understanding the needs of clientele from large scale commercial and noncommercial culinary operations.

PHOTO: THOMAS COOK II

ART
OF THE

DEAL

What does a good restaurant deal look like? More importantly, how can you spot a bad (really bad) restaurant deal? If you want to open your own restaurant, you can't afford to miss this panel with Mark Stone, the man who made Morimoto restaurants a global reality; Hilda Staples, who runs some of Mid-Atlantic's most successful restaurants; Marcus Samuelsson (no intro needed); and San Francisco's Richie Nakano, who's bouncing back from signing a shitty contract.

Mark Stone

Petrus International | New York, NY

PHOTO: ALIZA ELIAZAROV

After earning a degree in history from Harvard in 1980, Mark Stone embarked on a career that would bring him into contact with a wide range of industries, including finance, commodities, health care, tech, and even plant desalination. With a wealth of experience behind him, Stone founded Petrus International, Inc. in 1992, a consulting company that eventually opened a door into the world of hospitality and to work across the globe in Asia.

It wasn't until 2008, when Stone became the president of MM Management LLC, that he came into direct contact with the food industry. For the next eight years he successfully oversaw and directed Chef Masaharu Morimoto in his many business endeavors, giving Stone invaluable exposure to the ins and outs of the restaurant world and its transactions. Today, his sole focus is on Petrus International, Inc., which brings in clients from both national and international backgrounds.

DREAM PROJECT: Red Rooster Harlem. It's everything I've ever wanted to create in a restaurant. It combines music, culture, art, delicious food, and captures the essence of the Harlem community.

FIRST FOOD JOB: Besides being an apprentice to my grandmother Helga, I worked at Tidbloms in Göteborg, Sweden.

WHERE YOU WANT TO GO FOR CULINARY TRAVEL: I want to travel to Peru and find the most incredible ceviche there.

MOST IMPORTANT KITCHEN RULE: Teamwork. One mess-up and the entire service is ruined. And don't try to defend what you did wrong—just fix it and make it better the next time.

MOST BADASS CHEFS WITH WHOM YOU'VE WORKED: There are so many to choose from—can I give you a list? Jon Shook and Vinny Dotolo, Seth Siegel-Gardner and Terrence Gallivan, Linton Hopkins, Jamie Bissonnette, and Ken Oringer.

Marcus Samuelsson

Marcus Samuelsson Group | New York, NY

Born in Ethiopia, Marcus Samuelsson grew up in Sweden, cooking alongside his adoptive grandmother. After graduating from the Culinary Institute in Gothenburg, Samuelsson apprenticed in Switzerland, Austria, and France before finally coming to the United States. In 1995, he was hired as the executive chef of New York's Aquavit, earning three stars from *The New York Times*. Four years later, he was James Beard's "Rising Star Chef," and in 2003 "Best Chef, New York City." The Soul of a New Cuisine: A Discovery of the Foods and Flavors of Africa received a James Beard Award for "Best International Cookbook" in 2007.

PHOTO: MONIKA SZILADI

Since then, Samuelsson co-founded the Marcus Samuelsson Group, now with 10 restaurants in New York, Chicago, Costa Mesa, Bermuda, and Sweden, including Red Rooster Harlem. He has written two more cookbooks, a memoir, founded Food Republic, and even produced an an app: Big Fork Little Fork. He's appeared on both "Top Chef" and as a regular judge on "Chopped." Philanthropist Samuelsson is an ambassador for UNICEF and serves on the board of Careers through Culinary Arts Program and StarChefs.

IF YOU COULD EAT AT ANY RESTAURANT IN THE WORLD TONIGHT, IT WOULD BE: An authentic Persian restaurant in Tehran

WHO YOU LOOK TO FOR INSPIRATION: My husband. He has taken my knowledge in the restaurant industry and focused on the fun and the more lucrative part of the business—liquor and beer distilling.

WHAT YOU'VE LEARNED FROM A MISTAKE YOU'VE MADE: You have to go with your gut instinct. If at any time you feel something isn't right, it's because it's not. I made a mistake of trusting a business associate. The contract was just not solid, and he took advantage of my trust. Unfortunately, I learned that you can't trust everyone. Rookie mistake.

MOST IMPORTANT PLACE TO INVEST MONEY IN YOUR BUSINESS: People. They are what will make or break the business.

Hilda Staples

Bryan Voltaggio Family of Restaurants | Frederick, MD

Hilda Staples arrived in the United States with little more than a suitcase. She was 7, the youngest of three siblings solely in the care of her mother, from whom she inherited an unbreakable work ethic. Growing up in Alexandria, Virginia, offered Staples vastly different opportunities from the ones she left when her family fled Iran.

Staples studied political science, went on to law school (briefly), and eventually embarked on a career in public relations on Capitol Hill, where she met her husband Jonathan Staples. After having twins, Staples found herself at home in Frederick bored, tired, and hungry. Through tenacity, grit,

PHOTO: BRODIE LEDFORD

and gumption, she opened VOLT in 2008 in partnership with Chef Brain Voltaggio, with whom Staples also opened Lunchbox, Family Meal (now with three more locations), and in Washington D.C., RANGE and AGGIO, as well as AGGIO Baltimore. With Chef Mike Isabella, Staples has opened Graffiato in D.C. and in Richmond, where she also manages her husbands restaurant GWAR Bar and his distilleries. A Maestro of everything from sweeping up drywall dust to concept development, investor relations, Staples is the matriarch of an ever-growing family of restaurants.

PHOTO: LACIE GARNES

Evan Sung

Evan Sung Photography | New York, NY

Manhattanites may get a bad rap: stuck to the city, in love with the metropolis, happily captive of the MTA and taxis. But Photographer Evan Sung is a native Manhattanite who's found as much comfort and inspiration abroad as his big (apple) hometown. His travels in the last year alone have taken him to locales from Iceland to Emilia-Romagna and from Senegal back to Seventh Avenue.

A prominent food, lifestyle, and travel photographer now based in Brooklyn, Sung has spent his career expanding his perspective and sharpening his focus. In addition to his long freelance tenure with *The New York Times*, he has traveled and photographed for clients including *Vogue*, *The Wall Street Journal*, *GQ*, *Bon Appétit*, *Food & Wine*, *Gourmet*, *Art Culinaire*, *SKY*, and many others.

Over the course of his career, Sung has developed a natural ability to connect with the spirit of any culinary landscape. A 2015 time-lapse photo project at Atera captured the nuances of prep and service behind some of the city's most exciting cuisine. Sung's work has hit hard cover as well, appearing in several cookbooks with Michelin-starred chefs, including To the Bone with Chef Paul Liebrandt, Classico E Moderno with Chef Michael White, Marc Forgione's eponymous cookbook, and North with Icelandic Chef Gunnar Gíslason. Forthcoming cookbooks include tomes by Masaharu Morimoto and Alex Stupak.

FOOD PHOTOGRAPHY, A JOURNEY

Evan Sung works well with others. He has collaborated on cookbooks with Alex Stupak, Paul Liebrandt, Michael White, and Ruth Reichl. And at this year's International Chefs Congress, he'll shoot dishes from Senagalese Chef Pierre Thiam, his latest partner in the dance of photographer and chef. Bring your iPhone or DSLR to shoot alongside him.

EVANSUNGNYC   ESUNG

MOST INFLUENTIAL COOK WITH WHOM YOU'VE WORKED: Chef Paul Liebrandt is among the most meaningful chef collaborations I've worked on. Chef Liebrandt really introduced me to a whole new level of food and presentation. His precision, expectations from his team and himself, visual sense, and excellent sense of flavor and technique are truly exceptional and unique. It was a marvel to watch him as we worked together on the cookbook.

COOLEST TECHNIQUE YOU'VE LEARNED FROM ANOTHER CHEF: While shooting in Argentina and Uruguay for Greg and Gabrielle Denton's forthcoming cookbook, we had the pleasure of grilling a whole butterflied lamb on the iron cross with a local gaucho outside of Buenos Aires. Just seeing his innate understanding of the flame and heat was incredible.

IF YOU COULD EAT AT ANY RESTAURANT IN THE WORLD TONIGHT, IT WOULD BE: Some old, comfortable, rustic trattoria in Emilia Romagna! I'm a fiend for pasta, and I can't think of anything more reassuring or satisfying!

FAVORITE INDUSTRY INSTAGRAM ACCOUNT: Camille Becerra's moody, quiet, beautiful feed, @camillebecerra. And I enjoy Jeremy Fox's austere shots of his dishes at Rustic Canyon, @chefjeremyfox.

PHOTO: EVAN SUNG

SINGLE ORIGIN GRAND CRU CHOCOLATE

LA QUEMAZÓN

ILLANKA 63%
PERU

Made from Gran Blanco beans, rare white cocoa beans found in the Piura region of Peru, ILLANKA 63% is a distinctive chocolate that delivers exceptional creaminess with a strong tang and complex notes of sun-ripened blackberries, blueberries and black grapes.

Valrhona is working closely with the farmers of Quemazon, Barrios and Ranchos to help reestablish this rare cocoa variety in a sustainable way that benefits the entire community.

ILLANKA 63% is an experience in possibilities, a chocolate that invites the palate on a journey of delicious discoveries.

Discover more on www.valrhonaprofessionals.com

COMPETITIONS

Nicholas Blouin
Rosewood Mansion | Dallas, TX

PHOTO: KEVIN MARPLE

FIRST PASTRY JOB: I began an apprenticeship in a small bakery in my hometown, close to Toulouse, France, when I was 15 years old.

COOLEST TECHNIQUE YOU'VE LEARNED FROM ANOTHER CHEF: Olivier Bajard taught me that every dessert should have three separate textures; should balance sweetness, acidity, and bitterness; and should not be complicated with a variety of flavors.

DESSERT THAT BEST CHARACTERIZES YOUR STYLE: My desserts are appealing to the eye, yet delicious to the tongue. I also enjoy taking an American classic and revamping it to be modern and interesting.

PASTRY CHEF WITH WHOM YOU'D MOST LIKE TO STAGE: After collaborating with Jérôme Chaucesse from the Hôtel de Crillon, I would love to stage with him again to further learn about his technique.

Curtis Cameron
The Little Nell | Aspen, CO

PHOTO: C2 PHOTOGRAPHY

COOLEST TECHNIQUE YOU'VE LEARNED FROM ANOTHER CHEF: The proper way to emulsify. Such a simple thing but so important, especially when working with chocolate.

PASTRY CHEF WITH WHOM YOU'D MOST LIKE TO STAGE: Derek Poirier or Frédéric Bau

FAVORITE VALRHONA CHOCOLATE: Valrhona Araguani 72 percent. The profiles in the chocolate bring me to so many of my favorite flavors in life. The way this chocolate blends the sweet with the intense cocoa flavor, and then has notes of dried fruit, roasted nuts, honey, and a lighter finishing note of anise is like nothing else.

INGREDIENT YOU'RE MOST EXCITED ABOUT PAIRING WITH CHOCOLATE: Greek yogurt, sage, brie, crispy prosciutto, and jalapeño with Valrhona Opalys

PASTRY COMPETITION

Since 2008, Valrhona has celebrated working pastry chefs and their craft with its Chocolate Chef Competition, aka C³. This year, the competition is being held for the first time on American soil at the StarChefs International Chefs Congress with six pastry chefs making their best bonbons and plated desserts with Illanka 63 percent Peruvian chocolate.

Presented by Valrhona

Supported by PROMPerú, Steelite, Fresh Origins, Alto-Shaam, Paderno USA, Stoelting, and J.R. Watkins Co.

PHOTO: ANTOINETTE BRUNO

Erin Kanagy-Loux
Wythe Hotel | Brooklyn, NY

DESSERT THAT BEST CHARACTERIZES YOUR STYLE: Flavorful yet clean, layers of texture, surprising subtleties, adventurous with a strong focus on balance, meticulous command, and appreciation of classic techniques.

PASTRY CHEF WITH WHOM YOU'D MOST LIKE TO STAGE: One of my top choices would be Dana Cree, formerly of Blackbird. I admire her forethought in classical foundations with the effortless use of modern techniques.

FAVORITE VALRHONA CHOCOLATE: Manjari. I really enjoy the depth and richness of the chocolate that is highlighted by the subtle raspberry-esque acidity. I like that the Manjari holds on when used in products but doesn't overpower.

INGREDIENT YOU'RE MOST EXCITED ABOUT PAIRING WITH CHOCOLATE: Kefir! It has a wonderful silky, creamy texture with complex layers of acidity.

Ron Mendoza
Aubergine | Carmel-by-the-Sea, CA

COOLEST TECHNIQUE YOU'VE LEARNED FROM ANOTHER CHEF: Honestly, keeping glucose syrup in the walk-in cooler. BEST TRICK EVER!!!

DESSERT THAT BEST CHARACTERIZES YOUR STYLE: My style seems to continuously evolve, but, overall, my desserts feel balanced in flavor with more savory accents and are organic in presentation.

RESTAURANT WHERE YOU'D MOST LIKE TO STAGE: Relæ because their entire menu reflects simplicity, creativity, an aesthetic appeal, and forward-thinking flavors … or Pierre Hermé because he's Pierre Hermé.

INGREDIENT YOU'RE MOST EXCITED ABOUT PAIRING WITH CHOCOLATE: Sorrel and cucumber. Taking very clean, refreshing flavors and pairing them with Opalys is a great palate cleanser.

Robert Nieto
Kendall Jackson Winery | Fulton, CA

COOLEST TECHNIQUE YOU'VE LEARNED FROM ANOTHER CHEF: I took a chocolate class in Las Vegas and learned a technique on emulsifying ganache. I still use this technique daily.

PASTRY CHEF WITH WHOM YOU'D MOST LIKE TO STAGE: Patrick Roger. The first time I walked into his shop in Paris, I was captivated by the aesthetics of his bonbons and the shop itself.

FAVORITE VALRHONA CHOCOLATE: Caramelia. I like its smooth and creamy texture. It has a wonderful salty, caramel, butter flavor that adds complexity to my desserts.

INGREDIENT YOU'RE MOST EXCITED ABOUT PAIRING WITH CHOCOLATE: I work for Jackson Family Wines and started a chocolate pairing in the last few years. I love pairing chocolate with different wines and complementing the wine with the perfect bonbon creations.

PHOTO: ALAN CAMPBELL PHOTOGRAPHY

Steven Tran
Pacific Institute of Culinary Arts | Vancouver, Canada

FIRST PASTRY JOB: At 15 years old, I worked at a local amusement park, Playland, making elephant ears, churros, and candied caramel apples.

COOLEST TECHNIQUE YOU'VE LEARNED FROM ANOTHER CHEF: Genoise, properly. It's the simplest style of cake, but I was taught to use my judgment and technique and not to cut corners. The ingredients are always the same, but without commitment to proper technique, the results differ vastly.

PASTRY CHEF WITH WHOM YOU'D MOST LIKE TO STAGE: Outside of chocolate work, I love the challenge of constructing sugar pieces. So, my goal is to do a stage with Stéphane Klein of Atelier des Arts du Sucre in France.

FAVORITE VALRHONA CHOCOLATE: Manjari. It was the first Valrohna chocolate I ever tasted, and its distinct flavor taught me that chocolate is much more complex than I thought.

Vincent Attali

Restaurant Joël Robuchon | Las Vegas, NV

FIRST PASTRY JOB: After staging at Fauchon and Mondrian Pâtisserie, I worked my way through all the stations at Financier Pâtisserie. Chef Eric Bedoucha is strict but full of humor.

COOLEST TECHNIQUE YOU'VE LEARNED FROM ANOTHER CHEF: Blowing sugar bubbles into various fruit shapes, passed on by Chef Salvatore Martone.

PASTRY CHEF WITH WHOM YOU'D MOST LIKE TO STAGE: It would be amazing to spend a week in Taipei with Chef Frank Haasnoot.

INGREDIENT YOU'RE MOST EXCITED ABOUT PAIRING WITH CHOCOLATE: Chocolate with lúcuma, the Peruvian fruit. Think of butterscotch notes with chocolate.

PHOTO: MARIA ZAPATA

Baruch Ellsworth

Canlis | Seattle, WA

COOLEST TECHNIQUE YOU'VE LEARNED FROM ANOTHER CHEF: Chocolate tempering. I first learned from Garrett Melkonian how to do it by feeling. Then later I learned to trust a good thermometer from Alex Espiritu. Both sets of knowledge stick with me today.

PASTRY CHEF WITH WHOM YOU'D MOST LIKE TO STAGE: Oriol Balaguer

FAVORITE VALRHONA CHOCOLATE: Opalys. It has a pleasant biscuit-y flavor. It's super white, and, technically, it's excellent.

INGREDIENT YOU'RE MOST EXCITED ABOUT PAIRING WITH CHOCOLATE: Fig leaves. They have a nice banana/walnut flavor to them, which can be infused into dairy pretty easily.

PHOTO: MEGAN SWANN

Peter Scarola

R2L | Philadelphia, PA

COOLEST TECHNIQUE YOU'VE LEARNED FROM ANOTHER CHEF: Baking pastry or tart dough using the Silpain on a perforated sheet pan. It produces the best texture for a pastry crust and gives the pastry a refined appearance. I learned this from a demo by Jerome Landrieu.

DESSERT THAT BEST CHARACTERIZES YOUR STYLE: I like my desserts to have multiple layers of flavor, textures, and clean lines. My desserts have contrast in texture, temperature, and flavor.

PASTRY CHEF WITH WHOM YOU'D MOST LIKE TO STAGE: Christophe Michalak

INGREDIENT YOU'RE MOST EXCITED ABOUT PAIRING WITH CHOCOLATE: Right now it's green cardamom and lemon zest with Taïnori chocolate.

PHOTO: SHANNON STURGIS

EMCEE

Sherry Yard
iPic Theatres & Helms Bakery | Los Angeles, CA

TASTING JUDGES

Elizabeth Falkner
Chef, Author, Competitor | New York, NY

Eric Bertoïa
Paris Gourmet | New York, NY

Johnny Iuzzini
Sugar Fueled Inc. | New York, NY

François Payard
FP Patisserie | New York, NY

William Werner
Craftsman and Wolves | San Francisco, CA

PRESS JURY

Antoinette Bruno
StarChefs | Brooklyn, NY

Kate Krader
Food & Wine | New York, NY

Matthew Stevens
Dessert Professional | New York, NY

FLOOR JUDGES

Stephane Chéramy
JW Marriott Orlando Grande Lakes | Orlando, FL

Adam Thomas
The Broadmoor | Colorado Springs, CO

Jeffrey Barrientos
Westend Bistro at The Ritz-Carlton | Washington, D.C.

WINE REGION YOU MOST WANT TO VISIT: Burgundy

MOST UNDERRATED VARIETAL: Garnacha

ON YOUR NIGHTS OFF YOU DRINK: Champagne, Burgundy, or gin and tonics

Ashley Broshious
Arkenstone Vineyards on Howell Mountain | Napa, CA

WINE REGION YOU MOST WANT TO VISIT: Burgundy or Piedmont

MOST UNDERRATED VARIETAL: Cabernet Franc

ON YOUR NIGHTS OFF YOU DRINK: Something fun from Matthiasson, a Riesling, or a bottle from one of my friends' many new wine projects.

Alexander Carlin
Fourth Wall Restaurants | New York, NY

WINE REGION YOU MOST WANT TO VISIT: Champagne

MOST UNDERRATED VARIETAL: Savagnin

ON YOUR NIGHTS OFF YOU DRINK: Champagne and Chablis

Nicholas Daddona
Boston Harbor Hotel | Boston, MA

WINE REGION YOU MOST WANT TO VISIT: Swartland, South Africa

MOST UNDERRATED VARIETAL: Mourvèdre

ON YOUR NIGHTS OFF YOU DRINK: Rosé!

Only one somm will rise to the top (like a pristine, persistent, tiny bubble in a golden glass of sparkling) to become the Champagne of somms at the 6th Annual Somm Slam—a real-time, mano-a-mano pairing competition led by the Master Sommelier Fred Dexheimer. Ten of the best beverage professionals from across the country will compete in the grape-soaked swirl of the 10th Annual StarChefs International Chefs Congress.

Presented by Uptown Network
Supported by Nespresso, Wines from Spain, Emmi Roth, Le Gruyère AOP, Costières de Nîmes, Ribera y Rueda, Wines of South Africa, Hobart, Packnwood, and Blends

Michael Dolinski
Junoon Restaurant | New York, NY

WINE REGION YOU MOST WANT TO VISIT:
Champagne

MOST UNDERRATED VARIETAL: Riesling

ON YOUR NIGHTS OFF YOU DRINK: Madeira

Jordan Egan
The NoMad | New York, NY

WINE REGION YOU MOST WANT TO VISIT:
Champagne

MOST UNDERRATED VARIETAL: Grüner Veltliner

ON YOUR NIGHTS OFF YOU DRINK: Rosé (Clos Cibonne) or cocktails (usually rum-based)

Todd Lipman
Bistro Du Midi | Boston, MA

WINE REGION YOU MOST WANT TO VISIT:
Piedmont

MOST UNDERRATED VARIETAL: Gamay

ON YOUR NIGHTS OFF YOU DRINK: White or red Burgundy, or cocktails (particularly gin-based)

Steven McDonald
Pappas Bros. Steakhouse | Houston, TX

WINE REGION YOU MOST WANT TO VISIT: Côte-Rôtie

MOST UNDERRATED VARIETAL: Syrah

ON YOUR NIGHTS OFF YOU DRINK: Champagne and beer

Winn Roberton
Bourbon Steak | Washington, D.C.

WINE REGION YOU MOST WANT TO VISIT:
Piedmont

MOST UNDERRATED VARIETAL: Merlot

ON YOUR NIGHTS OFF YOU DRINK: As much as possible

Daniel Toral
50 Eggs | Miami, FL

WINE REGION YOU MOST WANT TO VISIT: Wachau, Austria

MOST UNDERRATED VARIETAL: Furmint

ON YOUR NIGHTS OFF YOU DRINK: White Burgundy!

ALTERNATE

Noah Singerman
Saxon + Parole | New York, NY

WINE REGION YOU MOST WANT TO VISIT: Loire Valley

MOST UNDERRATED VARIETAL: Chenin Blanc

ON YOUR NIGHTS OFF YOU DRINK: It depends on what I'm eating.

JUDGES

Michel Abood | Vinotas Selections
Ryan Arnold | Lettuce Entertain You
Sarah Blau | Aquavit
Camilo Ceballos | Omniwines
Julie Dalton | Wit & Wisdom
Debra Desepoli | Starwood Hotels
Bruno Donaggio | SocialVino
Michael Duffy | Lure Fishbar
Brian Grandison | Hakkasan
Victoria James | Marea
Rita Jammet | La Caravelle
Irene Justiniani | Bar Americain
Gordana Kostovi | Garces Group
Brent Kroll | Neighborhood Restaurant Group
Michael La Vardera | American Estates Wines
Gregory Laketek | West Loop Salumi
Aimée Lasseigne-New | Bottlerocket Wine & Spirit
Nichelina Mavros | Dépanneur and Pier Wines
Brian Mitchell | Max Restaurant Group
Lily Peachin | Dandelion Wine
Ed Peterman | The Quarry Hingham
Jason Prah | Bascule Wine Bar
Martina Priadka | Dakotacooks LLC
Grant Reynolds | Charlie Bird
Tim Riley | Bagby Restaurant Group
Tess Rose Lampert | In Vino
Brooke Sabel | Natirar
Ashley Santoro | The Standard East Village

From interactive recipe books, automated staff training, digital menus and wine lists to driving direct to consumer wine sales — streamline training, cut costs, empower staff and increase revenue with Uptown Network. Here are a few customers who've done that...

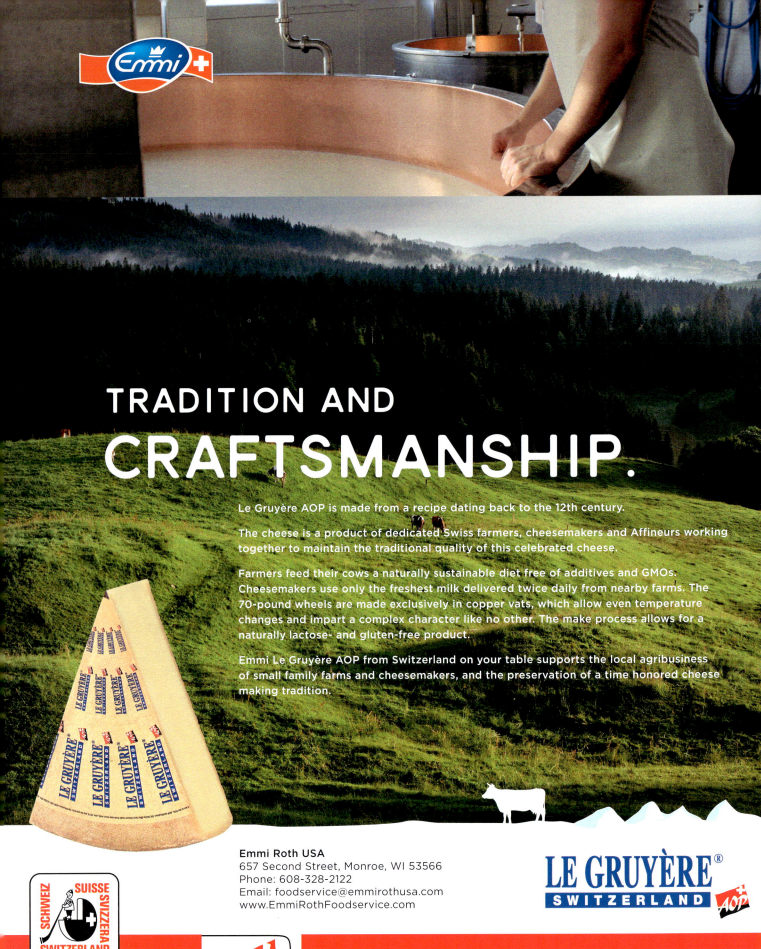

TRADITION AND
CRAFTSMANSHIP.

Le Gruyère AOP is made from a recipe dating back to the 12th century.

The cheese is a product of dedicated Swiss farmers, cheesemakers and Affineurs working together to maintain the traditional quality of this celebrated cheese.

Farmers feed their cows a naturally sustainable diet free of additives and GMOs. Cheesemakers use only the freshest milk delivered twice daily from nearby farms. The 70-pound wheels are made exclusively in copper vats, which allow even temperature changes and impart a complex character like no other. The make process allows for a naturally lactose- and gluten-free product.

Emmi Le Gruyère AOP from Switzerland on your table supports the local agribusiness of small family farms and cheesemakers, and the preservation of a time honored cheese making tradition.

Emmi Roth USA
657 Second Street, Monroe, WI 53566
Phone: 608-328-2122
Email: foodservice@emmirothusa.com
www.EmmiRothFoodservice.com

LE GRUYÈRE®
SWITZERLAND

PHOTO: MEGAN SWANN

☐ CHEF_TEPPY WASSAILNY

MOST INFLUENTIAL MENTOR WITH WHOM YOU'VE WORKED: My grandma. I learned a lot from many other chefs, but my grandma taught me how to cook from my soul.

COOLEST TECHNIQUE YOU'VE LEARNED FROM ANOTHER CHEF: Utilizing food scraps by dehydrating and juicing. For instance, tomatoes: I will dehydrate the skin, and make a powder to season the pulp.

IF YOU COULD EAT AT ANY RESTAURANT IN THE WORLD TONIGHT, IT WOULD BE: Noma

FAVORITE INDUSTRY INSTAGRAM ACCOUNT: @chefbobbyhellen

FAVORITE COOKBOOK: <u>Bar Tartine: Techniques & Recipes</u> by Nicolaus Balla and Cortney Burns, and <u>Life On The Line</u> by Grant Achatz

Joseph Buenconsejo

Wassail | New York, NY

Joseph Buenconsejo was born in the Philippines and aspired to be an engineer—a field he pursued in college until food got in the way. Buenconsejo dropped out and enrolled in culinary school in Manila. After graduation, at the ripe age of 20, he moved to New York City and began a six-month stage at Nobu. A formative experience, Buenconsejo started on the fryer, jumped to grill, then sauté, and even assisted with pastry.

Armed with ambition, a relentless work ethic, and an ever-expanding skillset, Bueconsejo left Nobu to join the opening crew at Jean George Vongerichten's V Steakhouse. There, Chef Ryan Skeen noticed the gleam in Buenconsejo's eyes and approached him with an opportunity to head west: Buenconsejo was game. He moved to Napa Valley, then Carmel where he honed his skills and developed a passion for hyper-local and seasonal ingredients at Domaine Chandon and L'Auberge Carmel.

After a couple of years in California wine country, Buenconsejo continued his tour of Northern California in San Francisco, where he quickly rose through the ranks at Aqua and Masa. Eventually, he heeded the call back East and returned to New York in 2010. Buenconsejo was the opening chef de cuisine of The Lion in the West Village, as well as executive chef of Hotel Americano. In 2015, he took the post as executive chef of Wassail, New York City's first dedicated cider bar. Buenconsejo's soulful, inventive vegetarian menu has earned many notices, including five stars from *The New York Observer*.

PHOTO: MEGAN SWANN

FOREST FLOOR WITH GRUYÈRE TWIGS
Chef Joseph Buenconsejo of Wassail | New York, NY
Adapted by StarChefs
Yield: 15 servings

INGREDIENTS

Gruyère Chips:
400 grams Kaltbach Gruyère, grated on
    microplane
20 grams all-purpose flour

Mushroom Dirt:
1.5 kilograms button mushrooms
15 grams salt
40 grams olive oil
15 grams sesame seeds
15 grams pumpkin seeds
15 grams sunflower seeds
10 grams poppy seeds
8 grams black sesame seeds
3 grams ground urfa biber chile
140 grams day-old sourdough bread
40 grams brown butter

Dehydrated Leaves:
25 grams bean leaves
25 grams parsley leaves
25 grams pea leaves
25 grams Kalettes
25 grams cauliflower leaves
90 grams roasted red bell pepper
140 cashews, soaked in water at least 2
    hours

13 grams lemon juice
1 gram Aleppo pepper
1 gram salt

Gruyère Twigs:
838.5 grams all-purpose flour
407.5 grams 85°F-water
249 grams sourdough starter
42.5 grams honey
39 grams olive oil
250 grams grated Kaltbach Gruyère
34 grams salt
3 grams black pepper

Leek Ash:
500 grams leeks greens

Roasted Vegetables:
180 grams acorn squash flesh
180 grams peeled parsnip
150 grams cored Braeburn or Macoun
    apple
150 grams trimmed and peeled baby
    carrots
100 grams trimmed radish
100 grams peeled celery root
15 grams salt

2 grams black pepper
8 grams finely chopped sage leaves
6 cloves garlic, finely chopped
6 sprigs thyme, picked
100 grams olive oil
20 grams finely chopped chives
12 grams Banyuls vinegar

Smoked Onion Purée:
100 grams pine nuts
10 grams olive oil
40 grams butter
150 grams thinly sliced onion
200 grams thinly sliced sunchoke
200 grams heavy cream
100 grams vegetable stock
Applewood chips
10 grams lemon juice

Gruyère Stock:
500 grams water
500 grams vegetable stock, made with
    brûléed onion
400 grams Gruyère AOP Reserve, grated
    on microplane

Quinoa Porridge:
10 grams olive oil
15 grams butter
100 grams brown quinoa
Salt

To Assemble and Serve:
Butternut squash purée, warmed
Shaved raw horse chestnuts
Crispy fried sunchoke slices
Lemon oil
Seasonal herbs and leaves

METHOD

For the Gruyère Chips:
Heat oven to 350°F. In a bowl, combine Gruyère and flour. Line a sheet tray with a silicone mat. Spread Gruyère mixture onto mat in an even layer, as thinly as possible. Bake until crisp. Break into chips.

For the Mushroom Dirt:
Prepare and heat a hibachi coal grill. In a bowl, season mushrooms with 10 grams salt and all the olive oil. Grill mushrooms until tender, about 8 to 10 minutes. Transfer mushrooms to dehydrator set to 135°F, and dry 2 to 3 days. In a food processor, process mushrooms to consistency of powder; reserve. Heat oven to 350°F. Toast all seeds 8 to 10 minutes. Toast bread until completely dry, and torch one side of the bread pieces. When cooled, transfer seeds and bread to a clean food processor. Pulse mixture a few times but do not completely pulverize (you want to see some larger pieces of the seeds). Add Gruyère Chips and pulse to combine; do not over mix. Drizzle in brown butter, followed by mushroom powder, and pulse until mixture resembles dirt. Season with remaining salt. Transfer to airtight container and refrigerate.

For the Dehydrated Leaves:
Wash all leaves and dry thoroughly with paper towels. To a blender, add bell pepper, drained cashews, lemon juice, and Aleppo; purée. In a bowl, combine pepper-cashew paste and leaves, massaging purée onto leaves. In a dehydrator set to 115°F, dry leaves 10 to 12 hours, until crisp. Season with salt while warm.

For the Gruyère Twigs:
To the bowl of a stand mixer fitted with a hook, add flour, water, starter, and honey. Mix on medium speed for 5 minutes. Grease another bowl with olive oil, transfer dough to bowl, cover with plastic wrap, and let rise for 90 minutes to 2 hours, until doubled in size. Heat oven to 350°F. Punch down dough and portion into lengths about 13 centimeters long and 2 centimeters wide. Arrange on a greased sheet tray and bake twigs until golden brown, about 8 to 10 minutes. Lower oven temperature to 300°F. Sprinkle Gruyère over twigs, followed by Leek Ash. Finish in oven for 2 to 3 minutes. Cool.

For the Leek Ash:
Heat oven to 400°F. Spread leek greens in an even layer on a sheet tray. Roast until greens are fully charred. Let cool completely. Grind into powder.

For the Roasted Vegetables:
Heat oven to 450°F. Cut fruits and vegetables into small pieces, different sizes depending on the produce. Season with salt, pepper, sage, garlic, thyme, and most of the olive oil. Roast produce 6 to 8 minutes, until lightly charred.

Transfer to a bowl and dress with chives and vinegar. Season with salt, pepper, and remaining oil.

For the Smoked Onion Purée:
Heat oven to 350°F. Toast pine nuts 8 to 10 minutes. Heat a sauté pan, add oil and butter and sweat onion and sunchoke until onions are translucent and sunchokes tender. Add toasted pine nuts, heavy cream, and vegetable stock. Bring to a boil, remove from heat, and transfer mixture to blender or food processor; purée. While blending, prepare a smoke gun with applewood chips. Slip end of smoke tube into blender. Smoke the mixture while blending 3 to 5 minutes, depending on depth of smoke flavor desired. Season with lemon juice. Pass mixture through a chinois; chill.

For the Gruyère Stock:
In a pot, bring water and vegetable stock to a boil. Add Gruyère, remove from heat, cover, and set aside for 4 hours. Strain through a chinois. Scale 250 grams Gruyère Stock for Quinoa Porridge.

For the Quinoa Porridge:
In a sauté pan, heat oil and 5 grams butter and toast quinoa. Add Gruyère Stock, bring to a boil, reduce heat, and simmer 15 to 20 minutes. Stir in Smoked Onion Purée, season with salt, and keep warm.

To Assemble and Serve:
Plate elements organically, as the forest floor in autumn. Start with Quinoa Porridge. Top with Roasted Vegetables. Add butternut squash purée around vegetables. Scatter shaved chestnut pieces and fried sunchoke. Cover with Mushroom Dirt, Dehydrated Summer Leaves, and Gruyère Twigs. Finish with seasonal herbs and leaves. Drizzle with lemon oil.

Featured Ingredients: Emmi Roth Kaltbach Gruyère AOP, Kalettes

Rebecca Eichenbaum

Wassail | New York, NY

Rebecca Eichenbaum first began baking in middle school as a sort of rebellion against her nutritionist mother's cooking. But it was an interest in fashion that initially brought her from Miami to New York City in 2007. While pursuing a design degree at the Fashion Institute of Technology, Eichenbaum studied abroad in Milan for a year, a seminal time when she fully realized her passion for food.

After graduating from FIT, Eichenbaum spent three months working in the French Pyrenees and in Corsica, participating in World Wide Opportunities on Organic Farms program (WWOOF). Returning to the United States, Eichenbaum spent time in Savannah, Georgia, working as an amateur pastry chef and baker, while teaching herself new techniques by avidly reading cookbooks. Longing for a mentor, Eichenbaum returned to New York to work at Mas for StarChefs Rising Star Chef Galen Zamarra. In 2013, she joined the opening pastry team at Juni, where she was able to master her skills under the guidance of 2015 StarChefs Rising Star Pastry Chef Mina Pizarro.

As her ideas about food, fermentation, and ingredients began to grow, she found a group of kindred spirits at Wassail, New York's one-and-only cider bar/vegetarian restaurant. Not only have her desserts come into full bloom, but she also has been able to uphold conscious practices in sourcing and technique while letting the seasons guide her creatively.

MOST INFLUENTIAL MENTOR WITH WHOM YOU'VE WORKED: Working for Mina Pizarro at Juni I learned plating techniques and how to construct dishes. As a mentor, she encouraged me to be involved in recipe development and to contribute ideas for new dishes. What really resonates most is not to compromise or settle, and to stay true to your integrity.

COOLEST TECHNIQUE YOU'VE LEARNED FROM ANOTHER CHEF: Using a refractometer. And not just for sorbet bases!

IF YOU COULD EAT AT ANY RESTAURANT IN THE WORLD TONIGHT, IT WOULD BE: Shojin Ryori at a Buddhist Temple, somewhere in Japan.

FAVORITE INDUSTRY INSTAGRAM ACCOUNT: I follow mostly herbalists, foragers, and fermentationists. Jeremy Umansky of Trentinacle, @tmgastronaut, pretty much encompasses it all.

CHEF WITH WHOM YOU'D MOST LIKE TO COLLABORATE: Pam Yung from Semilla

FIG LEAF PARFAIT, CHAGA MUSHROOM, CHOCOLATE, AND FIG CONSOMMÉ

Pastry Chef Rebecca Eichenbaum of Wassail | New York, NY
Adapted by StarChefs
Yield: 16 servings

INGREDIENTS

Fig Leaf Cream:
50 grams fig leaves
150 grams raw sugar
300 grams heavy cream

Fig Leaf Parfait:
100 grams egg whites
2 grams sea salt

Milk Base:
12 grams apple pectin
180 grams raw sugar
1 kilogram milk
100 grams glucose syrup

Fig Leaf Sherbet:
3 grams sea salt, plus additional as
   needed

Fig Consommé, Purée, and Leather:
500 grams black mission figs, halved
200 grams raw sugar
50 grams water
25 grams lemon juice
2 grams salt

Chaga Mushroom Soil:
50 grams raw sugar
50 grams muscovado sugar
100 grams rye flour
125 grams all-purpose flour
15 grams ground chaga mushroom
35 grams cocoa nibs
6 grams sea salt
70 grams Raaka coconut milk chocolate,
   melted
60 grams olive oil

Chaga-Chocolate Milk Foam:
270 grams milk
25 grams ground chaga mushroom
45 grams raw sugar
50 grams cocoa powder
2 grams salt

To Assemble and Serve:
Chervil

METHOD

For the Fig Leaf Cream:
In a food processor, blend fig leaves and sugar. In storage container, combine fig leaf-sugar mixture and cream. Cover and refrigerate 24 hours. Strain through a chinois, reserving drained fig leaves for the sherbet.

For the Fig Leaf Parfait:
To a bowl, add egg whites, salt, and 300 grams Fig Leaf Cream. Whisk to combine. Pour mixture into a siphon and charge twice. Release into quart containers and freeze immediately.

For the Milk Base:
In a small bowl, combine pectin and 30 grams raw sugar. In a pot, combine milk, glucose, and the remaining raw sugar and

bring to simmer. Add pectin mixture to the pot and bring to a boil, whisking to fully dissolve the sugar and hydrate the pectin; boil 1 minute. Strain into a container set over an ice bath to chill.

For the Fig Leaf Sherbet:
To a blender, add 1 kilogram Milk Base, salt, and 125 grams fig leaves reserved from Fig Leaf Cream. Blend on high for about 2 minutes. Strain through a chinois into a canister, season with salt, and freeze overnight.

For the Fig Consommé, Purée, and Leather:
In a bowl, combine figs, sugar, and lemon juice; macerate 1 hour. Transfer bowl to a double boiler and heat mixture until figs release water. Strain liquid through a chinois, reserving figs and liquid separately. Season liquid with salt, and cool over ice bath. In a blender, purée figs. Pass mixture through a fine tamis, and season with salt. Transfer one-third of the purée to a squeeze bottle. Spread the remaining purée onto a dehydrator sheet. In a dehydrator set to 135°F, dry for 1 hour.

For the Chaga Mushroom Soil:
Heat oven to 325°F. In a bowl, combine sugars, flours, chaga, cocoa nibs, and salt. In a separate bowl, combine chocolate and olive oil. Add chocolate mixture to dry ingredients, stirring to combine. Onto a sheet tray lined with a silicone mat, spread mixture in a thin, even layer. Bake 15 minutes. Cool completely.

For the Chaga-Chocolate Milk Foam:
In a pot, bring milk and chaga to a simmer, cover, and remove from heat. Steep 1 hour at room temperature. Chill, cover, and refrigerate mixture overnight. Strain through a chinois into a pot with sugar and cocoa. Over medium heat, cook 5 minutes, whisking constantly. Chill, pour into a siphon, charge twice, and refrigerate.

To Assemble and Serve:
Using a frozen dish, place two pieces of the Fig Leaf Parfait 1 inch apart. Dot Fig Purée around the parfait and place a few loosely rolled pieces of Fig Leather on the parfait. Garnish with chervil. Release Chaga-Chocolate Milk Foam into a pint container and spoon in between the parfait pieces. Sprinkle Chaga Mushroom soil on top of the foam. Place a quenelle of Fig Leaf Sherbet in between the two parfait pieces. Pour in 20 grams Fig Consommé tableside.

René Pernet

Fromagerie du Haut-Jorat | Vaud, Switzerland

Cheese is a family story for René Pernet, Master Cheesemaker at La Fromagerie du Haut-Jorat in Vaud, Switzerland. The devotion to his craft was passed down from his great grandfather, who had an alpage (mountain pasture) dairy, and from his father, also a cheesemaker in Vaud. It is with this legacy and extensive training that Pernet has received such industry accolades as a silver medal at the 2010 International Cheese Awards, a gold medal at the 2012 World Cheese Awards in England, and a silver medal at the 2012 World Champion Cheese Contest in Wisconsin. Pernet and his team are one of the main Le Gruyère AOP providers to Emmi Roth USA, including wheels that have been sent for additional affinage in Switzerland's all-natural aging facilities in Fromco, Moudon, and Emmi Kaltbach Caves. Pernet attributes his success to audacity, hard work, and a little luck, but notes that nothing would be possible without his dedicated team and superior milk providers, who motivate him to face the challenges of each day with a positive spirit.

Pernet will introduce varieties of Emmi Roth Gruyère as challenge ingredients at the 6th Annual Somm Slam.

PHOTO: ANTHONY DEMIERRE

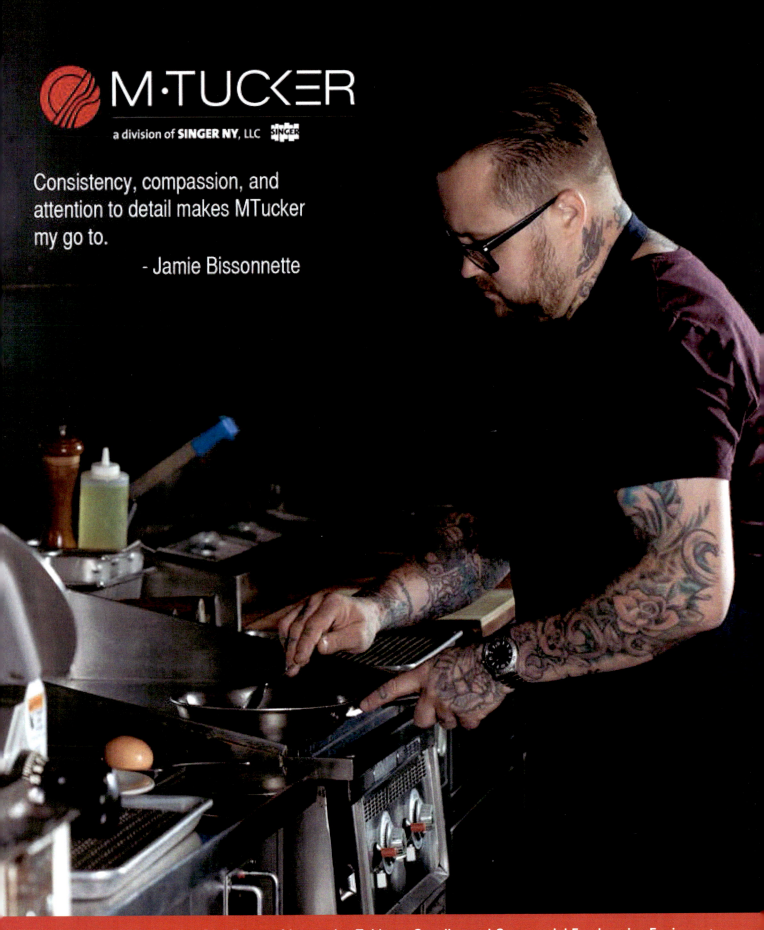

Evan Hennessey

Stages at One Washington | Dover, NH

If the connection between earth, cuisine, and community aren't as apparent in, say, a kitchen decked out with induction burners, NO_2, an array of stabilizers, and immersion circulators, just look closely—because that's where Chef Evan Hennessey works. At Stages at One Washington, he honors New England seafare, foraged treasures, and the culinary community he both leads and depends on.

Before he began melding a passion for product with healthy respect for kitchen gadgetry, Hennessey was a student at Le Cordon Bleu at the Atlantic Culinary Academy, graduating in 2001. He next made his way across the country to work for chefs the likes of Charlie Palmer at Aureole, Grant Achatz at Trio, Andrew Carmellini at Café Boulud, Thomas Rice and Ken Oringer at Clio, and Eli Kaimeh and Thomas Keller at Per Se.

After cooking as executive chef of 43 Degrees North and The Dunaway Restaurant in Portsmouth, New Hampshire, Hennessey opened Stages at One Washington and Flavor Concepts Catering in the neighboring town of Dover, solidifying his place in the community by supporting local farms and maintaining active membership in Chefs Collaborative. His progressive New England cuisine marries Hennessey's classical French training with locally farmed and foraged ingredients. In 2013, Hennessey won the Vitamix Challenge at the StarChefs International Chefs Congress, and in 2014, he was named a StarChefs Coastal New England Rising Star Chef. That same year he was also a semi-finalist for James Beard's "Best Chef, Northeast."

PHOTO: MEGAN SWANN

EVANHENNESSEY

MOST INFLUENTIAL MENTOR WITH WHOM YOU'VE WORKED: Grant Achatz. I learned to analyze flavor, as well as how to simplify what you give the guest in order to focus on the dish at hand without getting too convoluted with techniques. Use complexity to your advantage, create it, but make sure the guest understands it.

COOLEST TECHNIQUE YOU'VE LEARNED FROM ANOTHER CHEF: Open compression. No plastic bag involved or needed.

IF YOU COULD EAT AT ANY RESTAURANT IN THE WORLD TONIGHT, IT WOULD BE: La Petite Maison de Bras

FAVORITE INDUSTRY INSTAGRAM ACCOUNT: Matt Orlando, @amassmo

FAVORITE COOKBOOK: Alinea by Grant Achatz

CHEF WITH WHOM YOU'D MOST LIKE TO COLLABORATE: Dan Barber. Our food philosophies align. Use what's around you, everything that's around you. Nature gives us a bounty of ingredients. We shouldn't have to ship across the country—it's all right here.

OYSTER STEW: GREAT BAY OYSTERS, SEA BLIGHT, SEA ROCKET, SMOKED POLLOCK CRACKERS, AND OYSTER CHIPS

Chef Evan Hennessey of Stages at One Washington | Dover, NH
Adapted by StarChefs
Yield: 6 servings

INGREDIENTS

Broth:
Bones from one 3-pound pollock
1 bulb fennel, diced small
2 small white onions, diced small
2 cloves garlic, smashed
3 fresh bay leaves
2 tablespoons white peppercorns, toasted
2 gallons ice cold water
2 cups whole milk
20 grams thyme sprigs
5 grams Champagne vinegar
Salt
White pepper

Smoked Pollock Crackers:
1 pound skinless pollock fillet
1 pound tapioca starch
Salt
White pepper
Oil for deep frying

Oyster Chips:
24 oysters, shucked, liquor reserved
1 gram rapid set high-methoxyl pectin
1.5 grams agar agar
0.125 gram salt
0.25 gram citric acid
2 sheets gelatin, bloomed

To Assemble and Serve:
18 oysters, shucked, liquor reserved
Sea blight
Sea rocket leaves

METHOD

For the Broth:
In a stock pot, combine bones, fennel, onion, garlic, bay leaves, peppercorns, and water. Bring to a boil, lower heat, and simmer 30 minutes. Remove from heat, cover, and steep 10 minutes. Line a chinois with cheesecloth. Strain stock into a large pot. Simmer until 2 quarts remain. Add milk and return to simmer; reduce by half. Remove from heat, add thyme, cover, and steep 5 minutes. Add vinegar and season with salt and white pepper. Strain through a chinois into a large bowl. Cool over an ice water bath. Cover and refrigerate.

For the Smoked Pollock Crackers:
Prepare and heat smoker. Smoke pollock 20 minutes. Refrigerate 2 hours. In a food processor, process pollock to a smooth paste. Add tapioca starch, salt, and white pepper. Process until mixture comes together in a loose dough. Knead dough until it's no longer sticky. Roll into a 2-inch log. Steam 40 minutes. When cooled to room temperature, refrigerate until chilled. Cut into thin circular slices. Set a dehydrator to 125°F. Arrange slices in a single layer on a dehydrator tray and dry for 24 hours. When crackers are completely dry, transfer to parchment-lined sheet tray. Heat oil in deep fryer to 365°F. Heat oven to 150°F. Bake crackers 10 minutes; cool. Fry crackers until golden, drain on paper towels, and season with salt and pepper.

For the Oyster Chips:
In a Vitamix blender, combine oysters, oyster liquor, pectin, agar agar, salt, and citric acid. Blend on speed 6 until smooth. Increase speed to 10 and blend until mixture reaches 190°F. Add gelatin and blend. Pour into a bowl set over an ice water bath. When chilled and set, return mixture to blender and blend on speed 8. When smooth, spread evenly in a thin layer on a silicone mat. Set a dehydrator to 125°F, and dry mixture 4 hours. Transfer dried oyster sheet to parchment-lined sheet tray. When completely cooled, crack into shards. Set aside Oyster Chips at room temperature, uncovered.

To Assemble and Serve:
To a saucepan with the oysters and their liquor, add 4½ cups Broth. Heat over medium flame until oyster are slightly warm. Working quickly, transfer 3 oysters into each serving bowl. Add ½ cup of warmed Broth to bowls. Finish with Pollock Crackers and Oyster Chips. Garnish with sea blight and rocket. Serve immediately.

Featured Equipment: Vitamix Blender

JUDGES

Sam Mason
OddFellows Ice Cream | Brooklyn, NY

Alexander Smalls
Harlem Jazz Enterprises | New York, NY

Bryan Voltaggio
VOLT | Frederick, MD

Courtney Weyl
Manresa | Los Gatos, CA

Adam Wilson
Vitamix | Cleveland, OH

CHALLENGE

At this year's 6th Annual Vitamix Challenge, six exciting chefs and pastry chefs will flex their blending muscles for a chance to win the Ultimate Vitamix Package in a competition emceed by StarChefs' Managing Editor Will Blunt.

Presented by Vitamix with support from Front of the House and WÜSTHOF

Janine Denetdeel
Talde Miami Beach | Miami, FL

FAVORITE FLAVOR COMBINATION: Agressive salt (from fish sauce, soy sauce, or kombu dashi) and high acid (something simple like lemon juice or using the skin of yuzu)

CREATIVE INSPIRATION: Giving outcast ingredients a chance to reappear on our plates

FAVORITE BLENDING TECHNIQUE: Making a concrete solid or a persistent fiber like lemongrass into a talcum-like powder with liquid nitrogen and the Vitamix

Greg Garrison
Prohibition | Charleston, SC

FAVORITE FLAVOR COMBINATION: Shellfish and smoked fat

CREATIVE INSPIRATION: The seasons

FAVORITE BLENDING TECHNIQUE: Hydrating food additives by boiling them in the Vitamix

Kate Holowchik
Yvonne's | Boston, MA

FAVORITE FLAVOR COMBINATION: Chocolate, cherry, and pistachio. Classic spumoni flavor and any variation on it.

CREATIVE INSPIRATION: Growing up in New Hampshire taught me to be inspired by what grew seasonally, and I like using familiar ingredients and presenting them in a context that takes people out of their comfort zone—without going too crazy.

FAVORITE BLENDING TECHNIQUE: Making and heating custards

Dongchan David Lee
Goggan | New York, NY

FLAVOR COMBINATION: Citrus, saltiness, and richness, such as yuzu juice with wasabi and pine nut; or pork fat with lemon juice and some cayenne pepper kick!

CREATIVE INSPIRATION: My roots and New York City. I'm re-plating and deconstructing classic Korean foods using the best local ingredients.

FAVORITE BLENDING TECHNIQUE: For marinades, purées, vinaigrettes, and coulis. Vitamix blends so evenly and finely.

Giorgio Rapicavoli
Eating House | Miami, FL

FAVORITE FLAVOR COMBINATION: Orange, vanilla, and olive oil

CREATIVE INSPIRATION: The city of Miami. Its cultures and colors play a huge role in my creativity.

FAVORITE BLENDING TECHNIQUE: Using the Vitamix, I always start of on a variable speed of 1 and then slowly intensify to 10. After switching to high speed, I blend until I have the desired consistency.

Linton Romero
Flavor Hook | Dallas, TX

FAVORITE FLAVOR COMBINATION: Earthy and acidic flavor profiles

CREATIVE INSPIRATION: Food and flavor exploration, as well as heightening familiar flavors

FAVORITE BLENDING TECHNIQUE: Purées and fluid gels

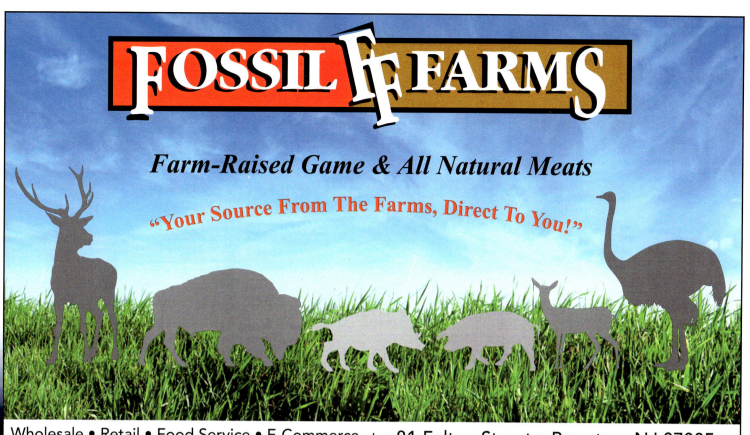

RAMEN

BATTLE

Noodles are going to fly at this year's Ramen Battle led by Competition Executive Chef Katusuya Fukushima. Five of the country's top Ramen Masters will lead a small team of participants in a two-day long workshop that will culminate in an epic ramen-off on the ICC Main Stage. Grab your chopsticks and an ice-cold Asahi. It's time to join the ramen revolution!

Sponsored by Roland, Kikkoman, Sun Noodle, and Asahi with support from Steelite International, Vollrath, Fossil Farms, Packnwood, and Master Purveyors

JUDGES

Tim Cushman
O Ya | New York, NY

Wylie Dufresne
New York, NY

Isao Yamada
Brushstroke | New York, NY

Adam Sachs
Saveur | New York, NY

Katsuya Fukushima

Daikaya | Washington, D.C.

Katsuya Fukushima received a double degree in math and art at the University of Maryland. But throughout college, he skipped classes, preferring to stay home to cook dinner for his roommates and watch the PBS show "Great Chefs." Fukushima took a number of odd jobs to make ends meet, and upon witnessing the kinetic energy of the kitchen, realized he wanted to make cooking his career.

Eager to learn, Fukushima enrolled at L'Academie de Cuisine in Gaithersburg, Maryland. He graduated in 1996 and took a line cook position at Vidalia under Jeffrey Buben. From Vidalia, he began working three jobs simultaneously: at Cashion's Eat Place under Ann Cashion, The National Press Club, and at the Bethesda tapas bar Jaleo. After three years, Fukushima devoted himself solely to Jaleo and followed owner José Andrés to assist with the opening of Café Atlantico.

For the next eight years Fukushima worked with Andrés, who became a mentor and a friend. After a stint at Verbena in New York City and an inspiring season at El Bulli with Ferran Adrià, Fukushima was offered the chef de cuisine position at Café Atlántico and minibar by José Andrés in 2002. With boundless curiosity, Fukushima turned the kitchen at Café Atlantico into one of the most innovative in the country, earning him a 2006 StarChefs Rising Star Chef Award. In a demonstration of his culinary dexterity, Fukushima opened his first restaurant and ramen joint, Daikaya, in Washington, D.C. in 2013.

PHOTO: FARRAH SKEIKY

CHEFKATSUYA

MOST INFLUENTIAL MENTOR WITH WHOM YOU'VE WORKED: José Andrés. When I find myself in a situation, I ask myself, "What would José do?"

COOLEST TECHNIQUE YOU'VE LEARNED FROM ANOTHER CHEF: Reverse cut. Michael Schlow.

A DISH YOU MAKE THAT'S INSPIRED BY ANOTHER CULTURE: Grilled octopus with Robuchan potatoes, inspired by pulpo a la Gallega and Robuchon potatoes. "Chan" at the end of a name is a term of endearment in Japanese.

IF YOU COULD EAT AT ANY RESTAURANT IN THE WORLD TONIGHT, IT WOULD BE: Kitcho in Kyoto

FAVORITE INDUSTRY INSTAGRAM ACCOUNT: Does @karliekloss count?

FAVORITE COOKBOOK: Essential Cuisine by Michel Bras

CHEF WITH WHOM YOU'D MOST LIKE TO COLLABORATE: I dream about cooking with Morimoto-San in Kitchen Stadium against the Ohta Faction.

Jamison Blankenship

Bar Chuko | Brooklyn, NY

PHOTO: MEGAN SWANN

New Orleans native Jamison Blankenship didn't get his start in restaurants until he was 21. But once he got there, he took off, spending just six years in kitchens before he'd be at the helm of a game-changing New York City restaurant.

Before he stepped into the kitchen, Blankenship enlisted in the Air Force. After returning home, he began working front of the house at Emeril Lagasse's original New Orleans restaurant, but the back of the house called. A move to Miami in 1997 helped Blankenship develop his talents, which he then brought to D.C., working at Michel Richard's Citronelle. Next he consulted for restaurants Dish and Nectar, which earned numerous awards and accolades under his leadership.

By 2005, Blankenship had caught the eye of Chef Masaharu Morimoto. And in two short years he rose from line cook to chef de cuisine and became Morimoto's all-around right hand man (leading to repeat appearances alongside Morimoto on "Iron Chef America").

In 2014, Blankenship was ready to move on from right hand man to the chef in charge, and he opened his first solo restaurant, Chuko, a ramen shop. Shortly after, he opened izakaya-style Bar Chuko down the street, which unapologetically revived the "Asian fusion" concept—albeit with highly researched, authentic, beautifully executed dishes.

 BARCHUKO CHUKOBKNY

MOST INFLUENTIAL MENTOR WITH WHOM YOU'VE WORKED: Chef Masaharu Morimoto not only helped launch my career, but he was also very generous with his knowledge and experience. He did not make it easy for me in any way. Being his chef de cuisine was the hardest five years of my life, but, of course, it paid off.

COOLEST TECHNIQUE YOU'VE LEARNED FROM ANOTHER CHEF: Cleaning scallions. A ramen shop uses over a case of scallions a day so it's very important to take care of them from start to finish. This means selecting product, having a sharp knife, proper slicing technique, soaking and rinsing to remove any unpleasantness, squeezing out the excess moisture, and drying. I can look at scallions in a bowl of ramen and know immediately if the kitchen cares.

A DISH YOU MAKE THAT'S INSPIRED BY ANOTHER CULTURE: Our cumin lamb rice bowl is inspired by Halal lamb on rice. It has a bed of steamed Japanese short grain rice topped with a spice mix of cumin, star anise, and Sichuan pepper. It's topped with shaved onion, iceberg lettuce, shiso-ginger-pickled eggplant, and grilled spiced lamb tsukune. This is sauced with our homemade white sauce and hot sauce.

VEGETARIAN MISO RAMEN

Chef Jamison Blankenship of Bar Chuko | Brooklyn, NY
Adapted by StarChefs
Yield: 8 servings

INGREDIENTS

Scallion-Ginger Oil:
1 quart soy oil
1 ounce peeled and coarsely chopped ginger
1 ounce peeled and coarsely chopped garlic
1 ounce coarsely chopped scallion

Broth:
4 ounces kombu, wiped clean with a damp
    towel, soaked in 4 quarts water overnight
2 tablespoons Kikkoman soy sauce
8 ounces white miso

To Assemble and Serve:
8 servings ramen noodles
Seasonal vegetables, blanched accordingly

METHOD

For the Scallion-Ginger Oil:
In a saucepot over high heat, combine all ingredients. Cook until garlic is golden brown. Remove from heat and chill. Refrigerate overnight. Strain through a chinois.

For the Broth:
Drain kombu, straining water into a pot. Cut slits into kombu and return to water. Bring to a boil, remove from heat, and steep until kombu is soft enough to push a finger through the sheet. Remove kombu. Bring liquid back to a boil. Stir in soy sauce, miso, and 2 ounces Scallion-Ginger Oil. Blend with immersion blender until emulsified.

To Assemble and Serve:
In a pot of boiling, salted water, cook noodles to desired doneness. Ladle Broth into bowls, add noodles, and top with vegetables.

Featured Ingredients: Roland white miso, Sun Noodle ramen, Kikkoman soy sauce

PHOTO: MEGAN SWANN

Youji Iwakura

Snappy Ramen | Somerville, MA

Youji Iwakura grew up in Japan and came to the United States to study at Berklee College of Music in Boston. As a singer, Iwakura belted Stevie Wonder tunes, but as a chef, his style veers more towards jazz—improvisational. After graduating from Berklee, Iwakura faced a tough economy and, like many, took a job as a waiter to get by. Iwakura was energized by the restaurant industry and decided to leave his music career behind to learn the sushi trade, starting at Ginza in Brookline, Massachusetts.

After eight years of training, Iwakura moved to the front of the house, which let him focus on an early childhood dream: to become a restaurateur. After working as a bartender at Troquet and as the general manager of several local restaurants, he returned to the kitchen, taking a position at Ken Oringer's Uni sashimi bar. To further hone his skills, Iwakura returned to Japan for two years and worked at an upscale Japanese brasserie. When he came back to Uni, he was named chef de cuisine. In 2010, he helped open Basho Japanese Brasserie as executive chef and created an innovative Japanese-American menu.

With the invaluable skills he learned, Iwakura moved to Oishii Boston. Next he set up his consulting company, Atelierkitchen Zen, in 2012. In 2013, Iwakura joined Snappy Group, first as sake sommelier and then as ramen master at Snappy Ramen in Somerville's Davis Square. Iwakura is working to open his own concept in the Boston area sometime soon.

 YOUJIJS

A DISH YOU MAKE THAT'S INSPIRED BY ANOTHER RESTAURANT: Eggs Benedict Tonkotsu Ramen. I was inspired by memories of local diners in Provincetown, Massachusetts.

IF YOU COULD EAT AT ANY RESTAURANT IN THE WORLD TONIGHT, IT WOULD BE: Michel Bras' restaurant

FAVORITE INDUSTRY INSTAGRAM ACCOUNT: @beautiful.cuisine

FAVORITE COOKBOOK: Nadaman The Japanese

CHEF WITH WHOM YOU'D MOST LIKE TO COLLABORATE: I wouldn't name one, but I like Asian chefs who have a European background for spice, herbs, and other healthy ingredients.

EGGS BENEDICT RAMEN
Chef Youji Iwakura of Snappy Ramen | Somerville, MA
Adapted by StarChefs

INGREDIENTS

Tonkotsu Broth:
(Yield: 4 to 5 servings)
1 kilogram pig femur bones
500 grams pig trotters
½ pig head, skin on
3 liters water
5 grams kombu
1 large onion, skin on, coarsely
    chopped
1 head garlic
1-inch knob ginger, coarsely chopped
10 grams dried shiitake mushrooms
One 750-gram slab pork fatback
½ leek, coarsely chopped
1 teaspoon white peppercorns

To Assemble and Serve:
(Yield: 1 serving)
140 grams ramen noodles
¼ teaspoon bonito powder
⅔ teaspoon grated garlic
⅛ teaspoon aromatic oil
3 tablespoons dried anchovy-infused
    white soy sauce
Four 10-gram slices bacon, cooked
    until crispy
1 Onsen tamago egg
Parmigiano-Reggiano
Wasabi mayonnaise
Shichimi togarashi spice mix
20 grams baby arugula leaves
Seasonal greens
⅛ teaspoon truffle oil
Salt
Black pepper
4 grams fried onions

METHOD

For the Tonkotsu Broth:
Place bones, trotters, and head in
a cambro. Cover with cold water
and store in a cooler overnight.
Drain bones and transfer to a large
pot. Cover bone with fresh water
by 2 inches. Bring to a boil, reduce
heat, and simmer 15 to 30 minutes,
skimming impurities from surface.
Drain bones and scrub clean. To a
separate pot, transfer bones and
cover with 3 liters cold water. Bring
to a boil, skimming impurities every
10 to 20 minutes and wiping scum
from interior of pot. Reduce heat,
stir well, and simmer 1 hour, adding
water as necessary, until liquid is
light and opaque. Float kombu on
surface. After 15 to 20 minutes,
remove kombu, setting it aside
for salad. Bring back to a vigorous
simmer, add onion, garlic, ginger,
and mushrooms. Cook 1 hour. Add
remaining ingredients and simmer 2
to 3 hours, until fatback is tender and
broth is opaque. Remove and reserve
fatback. Simmer 1 hour more, until fat
emulsifies and broth looks like milk.
Stir well, scraping bits from bottom
of the pot.

To Assemble and Serve:
Bring a large pot of water to a boil. In
a saucepot, bring 12 ounces Tonkotsu
Broth to slow simmer. Drop ramen
noodles into boiling water; stir. Drain
when texture is just shy of al dente.
To a warmed ramen bowl, add bonito
powder, garlic, aromatic oil, and soy
sauce. Pour broth into bowl and stir
to combine. Gently place noodles in
bowl with broth. Using chopsticks,
stretch out noodles in the air a couple
of times and lay them back down in
bowl. Place Onsen egg at the center
of noodles and flank it with bacon.
Grate Parmigiano-Reggiano over top.
Cover egg with wasabi mayonnaise.
Sprinkle togarashi in a line across
the egg. Place arugula and greens
on opposing sides and drizzle with
truffle oil. Season with salt and
pepper, and finish with fried onions.

*Featured Ingredients: Sun Noodle ramen,
Roland truffle oil*

PHOTO: HIEN H. NGUYEN

PHOTO: ANTOINETTE B___O

Harold Jurado

TBD | San Francisco, CA

Culinary careers have a good start in Chicago. They have an even better start if you have a mother like Harold Jurado's. Chef of a family-owned Filipino restaurant in the suburbs, Jurado's mother exhibited the kind of passion it takes to cook great food and the discipline necessary to streamline kitchen chaos. Jurado eventually earned his culinary degree from Kendall College, but his earliest teacher was his mother. Together they provided him with both the technical skill and the soul needed to master his culinary craft.

Jurado started at Japonais by Morimoto, moving his way up from intern to sous chef, and he was eventually chosen to help open Japonais in both New York and Las Vegas. While in Vegas, Jurado got wind of Charlie Trotter's plans for a restaurant in the new wing of the Venetian Casino and Hotel. Rolling the dice, Jurado staged at Trotter's eponymous Chicago restaurant and earned the opportunity to join Trotter's opening team back in Vegas. He maintained this momentum with a return to Chicago and work at Sunda, allowing the chef to professionally reconnect with his Asian roots.

Increasingly eager to fill the city's void of Japanese cuisine, Jurado opened the trendsetting Chizakaya in his hometown. The restaurant received local acclaim but shuttered after two years. He then found a new home for his modern-eclectic-comfort food at Matthias Merges's Yusho, where he won a 2015 StarChefs Rising Stars Award. Jurado recently made a jump to the West Coast, and wherever he lands, no doubt he'll make his mom proud.

HSJURADO FOLLOWMECHICITY

MOST INFLUENTIAL MENTOR WITH WHOM YOU'VE WORKED: Matthias Merges at Charlie Trotter's and Yusho. His general knowledge is enough to transform any eager cook into a good cook, but once one starts to understand his philosophies, food and actions just start to make sense.

COOLEST TECHNIQUE YOU'VE LEARNED FROM ANOTHER CHEF: Using scissors, in addition to a knife, to break down a fish.

IF YOU COULD EAT AT ANY RESTAURANT IN THE WORLD TONIGHT, IT WOULD BE: Borg Restaurant in Iceland

FAVORITE CHEF INSTAGRAM ACCOUNT: Art Ledda, @cheftra

FAVORITE COOKBOOK: The Mozza Cookbook by Nancy Silverton

CHEF WITH WHOM YOU'D MOST LIKE TO COLLABORATE: My mom, because I think we could create a great Filipino restaurant in Chicago.

TOMARROW RAMEN

Chef Harold Jurado | San Francisco, CA
Adapted by StarChefs

INGREDIENTS

Bone Marrow Broth: (Yield: 50 servings)
5 pounds ham hocks
1 pound pigs feet
5 pounds chicken bones
1 pound chicken feet
½ onion, charred
4 ounces garlic cloves
¼ cup coarsely chopped ginger
1 pound bacon
½ handful bonito flakes

Rosemary-Yuzukoshō Porchetta:
(Yield: 50 servings)
Salt
1 pork belly
Leaves from 7 sprigs rosemary
1 cup minced garlic
1½ small jars green yuzukoshō

Pickled Hon Shimeji Mushrooms:
(Yield: 16 servings)
2 cups rice wine vinegar
1½ cups sugar
1 pint water
1 teaspoon ground coriander
Peel of 1 orange
1 pound hon shimeji mushrooms, stems
  removed
Olive oil
Salt
Black pepper

Pickled Hijiki: (Yield: 16 servings)
1 cup water
1 cup rice wine vinegar
½ cup sugar
1 tablespoon ground coriander
1 cup cold water
4 ounces dry hijiki

Mayu: (Yield: 4 cups)
2 cups garlic cloves
1 cup blending oil
½ cup sesame oil

Assemble and Serve:
Salt
Ramen noodles
Bean sprouts
Thinly sliced scallions

METHOD

For the Bone Marrow Broth:
In a large pot, combine ham hocks and pigs feet. Cover with water. Bring to boil and cook 30 minutes. Drain and rinse bones and feet; reserve. In separate pot, combine chicken bones and feet, cover with water, and bring to boil. Immediately drain and rinse bones and feet. In a large pot, combine all bones and feet, onion, garlic, and ginger. Cover with water. Simmer at least 12 hours. Add bacon and simmer 3 hours, skimming impurities from surface. Remove bacon, bones, feet, and any marrow from the broth. Remove remaining marrow from bones. In a blender, combine all marrow and bacon; purée. Pour mixture back into broth. Add bonito flakes and steep 45 minutes. Strain and cool. Remove fat from surface, cover, and refrigerate.

For the Rosemary-Yuzukoshō Porchetta:
Lightly salt pork belly and refrigerate overnight. In a blender, combine rosemary, garlic, and yuzukoshō and blend to thick paste. Rub paste into pork belly. Roll and truss pork belly; leave overnight. Heat oven to 325°F. Roast pork belly 2 hours. Let rest at room temperature 30 minutes. Slice porchetta into ¼-inch thick rounds.

For the Pickled Hon Shimeji Mushrooms:
Heat oven to 350°F. In a bowl, combine vinegar, sugar, water, coriander, and orange. Stir until sugar dissolves completely; reserve. In a separate bowl, toss mushrooms with olive oil, salt, and pepper. Roast 5 minutes, until soft and slightly charred. Add mushrooms to pickling liquid. When cooled to room temperature, cover and refrigerate.

For the Pickled Hijiki:
In a saucepan, combine water, vinegar, sugar, and coriander. Heat, stirring until sugar completely dissolves. Remove from heat and transfer 2 cups pickling liquid to bowl with cold water. Stir to combine. Add dry hijiki. Cool to room temperature, cover and refrigerate.

For the Mayu:
In a small stainless steel pot, combine all ingredients. Heat over medium flame until garlic releases juices and mixture begins to sizzle and pop. Reduce heat to medium low. As garlic starts to brown, stir mixture and scrape the bottom of the pot to prevent burning. When garlic is very dark, almost black, remove from heat. Let cool at room temperature for 15 minutes. Transfer mixture to a blender and purée; chill.

To Assemble and Serve:
Prepare and heat grill. In a large pot of boiling salted water, cook ramen noodles until tender and drain. In a pot, warm the Marrow Broth. Grill Rosemary-Yuzukoshō Porchetta. Place noodles in a bowl with Marrow Broth and top with a few slices grilled Porchetta. Garnish with Pickled Honshimeji Mushrooms, Pickled Hijiki, Mayu, sprouts, and scallions.

Featured Ingredients: Roland rice wine vinegar, Sun Noodle ramen

sun
NOODLE BRAND

一生懸命作っています。
Crafting Artisanal Noodles Since 1981

Asian for a New Generation

Sugarcane Pork Pickup Sticks get their lustrous sheen and mouthwatering flavor from our **Kikkoman Sweet Soy Glaze.** It's a one-step wonder that blends the best of sweet, savory, East and West. Want to add a little Asian Cool to your menu? Stick with Kikkoman.

kikkoman®
Asian Cool™

800·944·0600
www.kikkomanusa.com/asiancool

PHOTO: KATHERINE SACKS

Richie Nakano

IDK | San Francisco, CA

Richie Nakano's Japanese-American family often ate big meals together, which helped nudge the budding chef toward a career in food. Working as a waiter and bartender after high school, Nakano started cooking for himself and eventually enrolled in the California Culinary Academy in San Francisco, where he nurtured his culinary foundation.

Nakano started his career cooking Asian food, taking a position at Sushi Ran in Sausalito. He then learned the art of bistro cooking at Va de Vi in Walnut Creek and then Pres a Vi in San Francisco. Looking to expand his repertoire, Nakano took a position at Nopa, where he learned about seasonality, while also mastering the art of layering flavors. Right before working at Nopa, Nakano started his loyally followed Line Cook blog, where he covered everything from culinary school interns to aggressive Yelpers. At the same time, Nakano was eating a lot of ramen in the city and yearned to create a bowl that met his standards.

In 2010, Nakano opened Hapa Ramen as a pop-up food stand at the Ferry Plaza Farmers Market. A few years later, after launching a successful Kickstarter campaign, he opened his first brick-and-mortar ramen noodle shop. His involvement with Hapa ended this year, but Nakano continues to experiment with new recipes and host pop-ups, and he's picked up writing again as a contributor for First We Feast.

 **LINECOOK**

MOST INFLUENTIAL MENTOR WITH WHOM YOU'VE WORKED: Laurence Jossel of Nopa taught me a lot: how to work with farmers, seasonality, and how to cook with the best intentions.

COOLEST TECHNIQUE YOU'VE LEARNED FROM ANOTHER CHEF: Brett Cooper showed me how to make umeboshi stand out. I could never get them right until he showed me the way.

A DISH YOU MAKE THAT'S INSPIRED BY ANOTHER RESTAURANT: A fried chicken steamed bun with bread and butter pickles and hot sauce that's basically a rip off of the spicy crispy chicken sandwich at Jack In The Box.

FAVORITE INDUSTRY INSTAGRAM ACCOUNT @chefjacqueslamerde is always entertaining. It's nice to laugh at ourselves sometimes.

CHEF WITH WHOM YOU'D MOST LIKE TO COLLABORATE: Matt Abergel from Yardbird in Hong Kong

BIG DADDY RAMEN

Chef Richie Nakano of IDK | San Francisco, CA
Adapted by StarChefs
Yield: 4 servings

INGREDIENTS

Dashi:
40 grams kombu
4 liters water
115 grams bonito flakes
10 pounds pork necks
8 onions, coarsely chopped
4 carrots, coarsely chopped
Grapeseed oil
2 chicken carcasses, roasted
2 heads garlic, 1 halved, 1 grated
¼ cup black pepper
2 pods star anise
Salt
Tahini
Miso

Pork Shoulder:
Salt
1 pork shoulder

Fried Chicken:
Rice bran oil
1 boneless chicken thigh, cut into bite-
   size pieces
Salt
Black pepper
¼ cup all-purpose flour
1 egg, beaten
¼ cup panko breadcrumbs

To Assemble and Serve:
Ramen noodles
Salt
Seasonal vegetables
Nori
4 eggs cooked sous vide at 63.5°C

METHOD

For the Dashi:
In a large pot, combine kombu and
water and bring to a simmer. Remove
from heat and discard kombu. Add
bonito flakes and return to a simmer.
Remove from heat, cover, and steep
2 to 3 hours. Strain through a chinois
into a stock pot. In separate pot, cover
pork necks with cold water and bring
to a boil. Discard water and scrub
bones. Heat oven to 400°F. Toss onions
and carrots with grapeseed oil and
lay on a sheet tray. Roast until deeply
caramelized. To the pot with kombu-
bonita broth, add pork necks, onions,
carrots, chicken, garlic, black pepper,
and star anise. Cover with cold water,
place lid on top, and bring to a boil.
Reduce heat and simmer, covered, for
14 hours. Strain through a chinois and
return to the pot, reserving pork scraps
and skin. In a food processor, pulse skin
and meat and return to stock. Season
with grated garlic, salt, tahini, and miso.

For the Pork Shoulder:
Heat the water bath of an immersion
circulator to 80°C. Salt pork shoulder
generously, transfer to a vacuum bag,
and seal under maximum pressure.
Cook sous vide 8 hours. Remove
pork from bag and shred. Cover and
refrigerate.

For the Fried Chicken:
Heat oil in a deep fryer to 350°F. Season
chicken with salt and pepper. Dredge
chicken in flour, followed by beaten
egg, and then panko. Fry until golden
brown. Drain on paper towels.

To Assemble and Serve:
In a large pot of boiling salted water,
cook ramen to desired doneness. Drain
ramen and place in serving bowls.
Garnish with Pork Shoulder, sous vide
egg, Fried Chicken, vegetables, and
nori. Cover with Dashi.

*Featured Ingredients: Roland grapeseed oil and
tahini, Sun Noodle ramen*

PHOTO: THOMAS SPRAVKA

Mihoko Obunai

Mibo Ramen | Atlanta, GA

Born in Japan, Mihoko Obunai inherited a passion for cooking from her mother, who regularly cooked 10-course meals for the entire family. Eager, passionate, and full of wanderlust at a young age, Obunai left Tokyo for New York to attend New York University. When not studying, Obunai was working at a small Japanese restaurant called Zutto.

After college, Obunai joined the Peace Corps in Peru. While there, she picked up Spanish and befriended several chefs, all of whom encouraged her to follow her true passion: cooking. Returning to New York, Obunai attended The French Culinary Institute (now the International Culinary Center), and began packing her résumé with restaurants like La Caravelle, L'Absinthe, Bayard's, and Guastavino's, where she worked with mentor Daniel Orr.

By 2005, Obunai was once more ready to move. She opened Repast in Atlanta, Georgia, with husband and co-executive chef, Joe Truex. The project blended the couples' two philosophies into the restaurant's menu and earned them both a 2007 StarChefs Rising Stars Award. Still looking to expand her reach, Obunai taught at Le Cordon Bleu College in Atlanta, and participated in the "Atlanta-to-Antigua Culinary Tour" in 2015, uniting two distant, but vibrant, culinary cultures. Since the closing of Repast, Obunai has pursued a series of wildly successful ramen pop-ups nationwide (called Mibo Ramen), the most recent being the ramen-izakaya "Ramen Freak" at The Sound Table in Atlanta.

 **CHEFMIHOKOOBUNAI** **CHEF_MIHOKO**

MOST INFLUENTIAL MENTOR WITH WHOM YOU'VE WORKED: Chef Daniel Orr. He was the chef who respected me as a woman in a kitchen.

COOLEST TECHNIQUE YOU'VE LEARNED FROM ANOTHER CHEF: I can break down whole pigs, cows, goats, rabbits, you name it. I learned a lot about butchering while cooking under French chefs—how to make head cheese, charcuterie, chicharrones, stock, broth, and sauces. Now I create my own ramen broth.

IF YOU COULD EAT AT ANY RESTAURANT IN THE WORLD TONIGHT, IT WOULD BE: Central in Lima, Peru

FAVORITE INDUSTRY INSTAGRAM ACCOUNT: @jamieoliver

FAVORITE COOKBOOK: Peru: The Cookbook by Gastón Acurio

CHEF WITH WHOM YOU'D MOST LIKE TO COLLABORATE: Chef Alejandro Ruiz of Casa Oaxaca. I had the best gastronomic dining experience in Mexico. I would love to combine my Japanese cuisine and his Oaxacan cuisine, including pairings with sake and mezcal.

MISO-CHEESE-CORN-BUTTER RAMEN

Chef Mihoko Obunai of Mibo Ramen | Atlanta, GA
Adapted by StarChefs
Yield: 4 servings

INGREDIENTS

2 teaspoons olive oil
1 clove garlic, finely chopped
1 teaspoon fresh ginger, finely
  chopped
4 ounces ground pork
5 ounces bean sprouts, rinsed
2 tablespoons sweet corn kernels
2 tablespoons green onion, finely
  chopped
1 quart chicken stock
2 teaspoons Kikkoman light soy sauce
¼ cup miso paste
1 teaspoon sesame oil
Salt
6 ounces ramen noodles
2 tablespoons pickled ginger
1 ounce butter, diced small
2 tablespoons grated Pecorino
Black pepper

METHOD

To a wok over medium heat, add olive oil and cook garlic, ginger, and pork until pork is no longer pink. Add bean sprouts, corn, and green onion and cook a few minutes. Add chicken stock and soy sauce and bring to a boil. Reduce heat and stir in miso paste. Add sesame oil and remove broth from heat. In a large pot of boiling salted water, cook ramen 2 minutes; drain. Ladle broth into serving bowls and add noodles. Garnish with pickled ginger, butter, and cheese. Season with salt and pepper.

Featured Ingredients: Roland miso paste and sesame oil, Sun Noodle ramen, Kikkoman soy sauce

Careers through Culinary Arts Program
C·CAP

Careers through Culinary Arts Program (C-CAP) prepares underserved teens for college and careers in the restaurant and hospitality industry. Headquartered in NYC, C-CAP also operates in Arizona (statewide), the Los Angeles, Philadelphia, and Washington, D.C. regions, Chicago and Hampton Roads, VA. C-CAP was founded in 1990 by Richard Grausman, renowned cookbook author and culinary educator. The Board of Directors is co-chaired by Chef Marcus Samuelsson and Mark Weiss. C-CAP's programs include job training and internships, scholarships through cooking competitions, college advising, lifetime career support, teacher training and curriculum enrichment.

Who does C-CAP serve?

16,000+ students
250 public high school teachers
178 schools
600 industry professionals support C-CAP

How can I get involved?

Mentor a Student
Donate Products or Equipment
Support our Programs and Scholarships
Host a Fundraising Event

@CCAPINC

For information or to get involved:
contact us at info@ccapinc.org, 212-974-7111, or visit www.ccapinc.org

EAT@ICC

ART OF PRESENTATION POP-UP

Presented by Steelite International, with support from Uptown Network and Careers through Culinary Arts Program

John daSilva

Spoke | Somerville, MA

Even as a teenager, John daSilva knew he wanted to cook professionally. After graduating from high school in Gloucester, Massachusetts, he went straight to the New England Culinary Institute in Burlington, Vermont, to study cooking techniques and tradition. DaSilva continued his training at The Boarding House Restaurant on Nantucket Island, spending the next four years as sous chef with Chef Erin Zircher—a defining period that opened his eyes to all corners of the Mediterranean, and taught him how to lead a kitchen.

It was a lesson that would serve him well when he moved back to Boston, where he worked his way up the ranks to executive sous chef of Barbara Lynch's flagship No. 9 Park. In the meantime, he was named one of Zagat's "30 Under 30" for Boston. The real chance to lead came after daSilva spent six months working on a friend's 10-acre farm in Concord. The immediacy of contact with local product inspired a fresh passion in him, a passion daSilva brings daily to the kitchen of Spoke Wine Bar, where he earned a 2015 StarChefs Rising Stars Award.

PHOTO: ALIZA ELIAZAROV

CHEFJOHNDASILVA SPOKEWINEBAR

MOST INFLUENTIAL MENTOR WITH WHOM YOU'VE WORKED: Erin Zircher at the Boarding House in Nantucket. She challenged me to work smarter and harder than the next cook. She showed me how to use the weather and seasons as a means of inspiration, and a guide for how to construct a cohesive, thoughtful menu. Erin taught me to be a fair and loyal leader in the kitchen, and she even taught me my mean face.

COOLEST TECHNIQUE YOU'VE LEARNED FROM ANOTHER CHEF: On a recent trip to Manhattan, I discovered how April Bloomfield and her team produce their famous melt-in-your-mouth ricotta gnudi. Game changer!

IF YOU COULD EAT AT ANY RESTAURANT IN THE WORLD TONIGHT, IT WOULD BE: Relæ in Copenhagen. I love Christian Puglisi's philosophies and vision.

FAVORITE INDUSTRY INSTAGRAM ACCOUNT: @aprilbloomfield

CHEF WITH WHOM YOU'D MOST LIKE TO COLLABORATE: Mourad Lahlou. His modern interpretation of classic Moroccan food is thoughtful and beautiful, and doesn't lose sight of its roots. From what I'm told, he's a kind, strong, and patient leader in the kitchen.

ROASTED BRANZINO, CAULIFLOWER, HAZELNUTS, VADOUVAN, AND ROASTED GRAPES

Chef John daSilva of Spoke | Somerville, MA
Adapted by StarChefs
Yield: 4 servings

INGREDIENTS

Pickled Cauliflower and Hazelnuts:
½ head orange cauliflower, separated
 into small florets
1 cup hazelnuts, coarsely chopped
1 quart rice wine vinegar
2 cups water
1½ cups sugar
¼ cup salt
1 tablespoon mustard seeds
1 tablespoon coriander seeds
1 tablespoon black peppercorns
4 bay leaves

Roasted Grapes:
1 pound seedless red grapes
1 tablespoon extra virgin olive oil
Salt
Black pepper

Vadouvan Brown Butter:
4 shallots, peeled, dehydrated, and
 ground
1 tablespoon finely chopped
 curry leaves
1 tablespoon ground cumin
1 tablespoon ground turmeric
½ tablespoon ground fenugreek
½ teaspoon ground cardamom
½ teaspoon ground nutmeg
½ teaspoon ground clove
½ tablespoon ground mustard seeds
½ teaspoon red chile flakes
½ pound butter, browned and strained

Brown Butter Cauliflower Purée:
½ head orange cauliflower, coarsely
 chopped
2 shallots, minced
1 cup milk
1 stick butter, browned
 and strained
Salt

Roasted Branzino:
Fillets from 2 branzini, halved
½ cup grapeseed oil

To Assemble and Serve:
Fresh herbs

METHOD

For the Pickled Cauliflower and Hazelnuts:
In a bowl, combine cauliflower and hazelnuts. In a medium saucepan, combine vinegar, water, sugar, salt, and spices. Bring to a boil, reduce to a simmer, and cook 10 minutes. Strain and pour over cauliflower and hazelnuts. Cool to room temperature.

For the Roasted Grapes:
Heat oven to 250˚F. Toss grapes with oil and season with salt and pepper. Place grapes on a parchment-lined sheet tray and roast until grapes are slightly shriveled and light golden brown, about 1 hour.

For the Vadouvan Brown Butter:
In a saucepan, combine all ingredients. Warm over low heat until aromatic. Remove from heat and reserve warm.

For the Brown Butter Cauliflower Purée:
In a medium saucepan, combine cauliflower, shallot, and milk. Cover with a piece of parchment paper. Cook over medium heat until cauliflower is tender and most of the liquid has evaporated, about 20 minutes. Place the cauliflower mixture and brown butter in a blender and purée. Season with salt. Cover and reserve warm.

For the Roasted Branzino:
Heat oven to 450˚F. Season fish on both sides with salt and place on paper towels, skin side down. Heat 2 large skillets over medium-high flame. Divide oil evenly between the 2 skillets. When oil begins to smoke, add fish, skin side down, pressing gently on the flesh for an even sear. When skin starts to turn golden on the edges (after about 2 to 3 minutes), transfer skillets to oven. When fish is cooked to medium, remove from oven. Keep fish warm, skin side up.

To Assemble and Serve:
Place a spoonful of Cauliflower Brown Butter Purée in the bottom of a serving bowl or plate. In a pan, warm the Pickled Cauliflower and Hazelnuts and Roasted Grapes with a small amount of Vadouvan Brown Butter. Spoon over the purée. Top with 2 pieces of Roasted Branzino and garnish with herbs and more Vadouvan Brown Butter.

PHOTO: ANTOINETTE BRUNO

Mattie McGhee

RANGE | Washington, D.C.

Originally from New Jersey, Mattie McGhee's path to the kitchen began as a simple paying gig during his studies at community college. He picked up some shifts at the local Hilton hotel cafeteria and quickly realized his interests lay far more in food than collegiate endeavors. Wanting to expand his culinary skills, McGhee headed to New York and the Culinary Institute of America. McGhee furthered his education by completing the prestigious apprenticeship program at The Greenbrier Resort in West Virginia under Chefs Richard Rosendale and Michael Voltaggio.

McGhee then moved to New York City, where he worked at the Waldorf Astoria's Peacock Alley, and he completed stages at several Michelin-starred restaurants. In 2008, McGhee was invited to return to The Greenbrier as sous chef of the Main Dining Room and was quickly promoted to chef de cuisine.

In 2011, McGhee moved south to become chef de cuisine of Angle at the five-star, five-diamond Ritz Carlton Palm Beach. There, he furthered his interest in partnering with local farms, finding the freshest possible ingredients while supporting area suppliers. In 2013, he joined Bryan Voltaggio to helm RANGE in Washington, D.C., where he showcases his refined yet whimsical style of modern American cuisine. In 2014, he was named a StarChefs Rising Star Chef for the Washington, D.C. area.

 **MATTIEMCGHEE**

MOST INFLUENTIAL MENTOR WITH WHOM YOU'VE WORKED: Chef Richard Rosendale. Rich has ever evolving talent that is instilled in everyone he mentors.

COOLEST TECHNIQUE YOU'VE LEARNED FROM ANOTHER CHEF: Gelatin clarification

A DISH YOU MAKE THAT'S INSPIRED BY ANOTHER CULTURE: Thai curry braised lamb neck

IF YOU COULD EAT AT ANY RESTAURANT IN THE WORLD TONIGHT, IT WOULD BE: Ryugin in Tokyo, Japan

FAVORITE INDUSTRY INSTAGRAM ACCOUNT: Chris Ford, @butterloveandhardwork

FAVORITE COOKBOOK: The Epicurean by Charles Ranhofer

OCTOPUS, LENTILS, SPROUTED WHEATBERRIES, AND PISTACHIOS

Chef Mattie McGhee of Range | Washington, D.C.
Adapted by StarChefs
Yield: 8 servings

INGREDIENTS

Octopus:
One 4- to 6-pound octopus
2 quarts olive oil
Peel of 1 lemon
2 teaspoons black peppercorns, toasted
2 sprigs tarragon
4 sprigs thyme

Grape-Olive Relish:
900 grams red grapes
230 grams simple syrup
Olive oil
125 grams shallot brunoise
125 grams sliced Kalamata olives
125 grams sliced Castelvetrano olives
50 grams Banyuls vinegar
130 grams sorghum syrup
3 grams salt
2 grams Dijon mustard

Lentils:
Olive oil
¼ cup small diced carrot
¼ cup small diced onion
¼ cup Le Puy lentils
1 quart vegetable stock
2 bay leaves

To Assemble and Serve:
Sprouted wheatberries
Pistachios, coarsely chopped
Fennel fronds

METHOD

For the Octopus:
Heat water bath of an immersion circulator to 77°C. In a vacuum bag, combine all ingredients and seal at 98 percent. Cook octopus sous vide for 7 hours. Remove from water bath and let octopus cool in bag. Remove from bag and portion each tentacle into 2-ounce pieces.

For the Grape-Olive Relish:
Toss grapes in simple syrup. In a dehydrator set to 140°F, dry for 2 hours. In a large sauté pan over high flame, heat olive oil and sweat shallots and olives 2 minutes. Remove from heat and gently fold in vinegar, sorghum, salt, and mustard. Cool at room temperature for 1 hour. Fold in dried grapes.

For the Lentils:
In a medium pot, heat olive oil and sweat carrots and onions. When onions are translucent, add lentils, stock, and bay leaves and simmer 20 minutes, until lentils are tender. Pour off excess liquid and reserve, keeping warm.

To Assemble and Serve:
Prepare and heat grill with white oak wood. In a bowl, combine equal parts wheatberries, Grape-Olive Relish, and Lentils. Spoon mixture onto center of serving plate. Lightly char octopus on grill and heat through. Toss octopus with pistachios to lightly coat, and arrange 3 portions on top of lentil mixture. Garnish with fennel fronds.

Featured Ingredient: Roland le puy lentils
Featured Plate: Steelite International

TE BRUNO

PHOTO: ANTOINETTE BRUNO

Daniela Soto-Innes

Cosme | New York, NY

Daniela Soto-Innes comes from a long line of women who love food and cooking. Visiting the food markets and restaurants of Mexico City as a child only stoked her curiosity further. By the time she was 14, Soto-Innes was ready to work. She started as an intern with Marriott Hotels, a position that turned into a job that landed her near Houston at The Woodlands Waterway Marriott. Soto-Innes stayed there for three years, building up a skill set in the context of a professional restaurant. Looking for some serious training, Soto-Innes moved to Austin, Texas, where she graduated from Le Cordon Bleu College of Culinary Arts.

From there, Soto-Innes traveled and staged at restaurants in Texas, New York, and Europe, finally returning to Texas to stage at Mark's American Cuisine with Chef Mark Cox. Eventually she joined the opening crew of Brennan's of Houston under Chef Danny Trace. Two years later, Soto-Innes continued exploring at progressive American restaurant Triniti and charcuterie-driven Underbelly with StarChefs Rising Star Chef Chris Shepherd.

A stage at Pujol found Soto-Innes back in Mexico. When that ended, she worked under Gerardo Vazques Lugo, owner of Nicos in Mexico City. Lugo helped Sotto-Innes figure out her own path and plan. That led her back to Pujol for full-time work with icon Enrique Olvera. When Olvera was looking to bring his operation to New York City, he tapped Soto-Innes as opening chef de cuisine. Now at the helm of Olvera's Cosme, Soto-Innes has earned three stars from *The New York Times* and a 2015 StarChefs Rising Stars Award.

 DANIELASOTOINNES DANISOTOINNES

MOST INFLUENTIAL MENTOR WITH WHOM YOU'VE WORKED: By far, Enrique Olvera. Working with him is not only a lot of fun, but he makes me think outside the box at all times. He makes everything look so easy and smooth. He sets goals for me, and gives me timelines (and a lot of pressure), which I really like. He is always asking if I am happy with what I am doing and keeps my feet on the ground.

COOLEST TECHNIQUE YOU'VE LEARNED FROM ANOTHER CHEF: Nixtamalization. It's a preparation of grains, fruits, or vegetables, in which they are soaked in an alkaline (usually limestone and water) solution or ash, and hulled; or in fresh fruits and vegetables it creates an outer skin.

IF YOU COULD EAT AT ANY RESTAURANT IN THE WORLD TONIGHT, IT WOULD BE: Pascal Barbot's L'Astrance

FAVORITE COOKBOOK Las Primeras Palabras de la Cocina by Andoni Luis Aduriz, Dani Lasa, and Unai Ugalde

CHEF WITH WHOM YOU'D MOST LIKE TO COLLABORATE Pamela Yung from Semilla. I admire her a lot! She is not only a great chef, but a wonderful person.

VEAL TONGUE, PUMPKIN SEED SALSA, AND BRUSSELS SPROUTS PICO DE GALLO

Chef Daniela Soto-Innes of Cosme | New York, NY
Adapted by StarChefs
Yield: 6 servings

INGREDIENTS

Veal Tongue:
4 liters water
175 grams kosher salt
2 grams pink salt
75 grams brown sugar
½ teaspoon ground allspice
3 cloves garlic, peeled
2 bay leaves
2 veal tongues
50 grams olive oil

Brussels Sprouts:
Grapeseed oil
20 purple Brussels sprouts, trimmed and halved
Salt
15 grams minced white onion
10 grams lime juice
5 grams minced Serrano chile
10 grams cilantro chiffonade

Pumpkin Seed Salsa:
6 Brunetta tomatoes
30 grams pumpkin seeds, roasted
3 cloves garlic, peeled
30 grams coarsely chopped white onion
5 grams Key lime juice
10 grams cilantro leaves
5 grams hoja santa leaves
3 grams epazote
1 habanero, charred and deveined

To Assemble and Serve:
Olive oil
Sea salt

METHOD

For the Veal Tongue:
To a pot, add water, salts, sugar, allspice, garlic, and bay leaves; bring to a boil. Remove from heat and steep 10 minutes. Strain and cool completely. Place tongues in brine, making sure brine covers tongues completely, and refrigerate 5 days. Drain tongues, transfer to vacuum bag with olive oil, and seal. Heat the water bath of an immersion circulator to 70°C and cook tongues sous vide for 24 hours. Cool tongues, peel outer membranes, and cut into 4-ounce portions.

For the Pumpkin Seed Salsa:
In a food processor, combine all ingredients and pulse until a coarse paste forms. Taste and season with salt, if necessary.

For the Brussels Sprouts:
Pan fry Brussels sprouts until crisp, drain on paper towels, and season with salt. In a bowl, combine onion, lime, and chile with Brussels sprouts. Fold in cilantro and season with salt.

To Assemble and Serve:
Coat a cast iron skillet with olive oil and sear Veal Tongue until golden brown on all sides. Cut each portion into six slices and place on right side of serving plate. Put a tablespoon of Pumpkin Seed Salsa next to Veal Tongue. Top with Brussels Sprouts. Finish with sea salt.

Featured Plateware: Steelite Anfora

PHOTO: ANTOINETTE BRUNO

PHOTO: MEGAN SWANN

Lee Wolen

Boka | Chicago, IL

Cleveland native Lee Wolen knew he'd be a chef as a teen, a calling spurred by time spent at a local vocational culinary school. Immersing himself in modernist cuisine early in his career, Wolen worked as sous chef at Moto in Chicago, and then went on to another sous position at Butter in NYC. He also spent time overseas at Le Manoir aux Quat'Saisons in England and at El Bulli. The most influential kitchen for Wolen was Eleven Madison Park, where he was sous chef for three years, helping Daniel Humm earn four stars from *The New York Times*, three Michelin stars, and a top 10 ranking on San Pellegrino's "World's 50 Best Restaurants" list.

Wolen joined The Lobby at The Peninsula Chicago in 2012 as chef de cuisine, earning the restaurant its first five-star rating in eight years from *Time Out Chicago*. His next undertaking came after a serendipitous meeting with Rob Katz and Kevin Boehm of Boka Restaurant Group. Now chef and a partner at Boka, Wolen is working passionately to bring fine dining to a larger audience, making the polish of great cuisine accessible and even fun, while maintaining Boka's Michelin star status and working with charitable initiatives like the Academy for Global Citizenship. Wolen was named a StarChefs Rising Star Chef and the *Chicago Tribune* Dining Awards "Chef of the Year" in 2015.

 LEEWOLEN BOKACHICAGO

MOST INFLUENTIAL MENTOR WITH WHOM YOU'VE WORKED: Daniel Humm. His vision of food is unlike any other chef I've met.

COOLEST TECHNIQUE YOU'VE LEARNED FROM ANOTHER CHEF: Roasting strawberries on the Binchōtan grill at El Bulli

A DISH YOU MAKE THAT'S INSPIRED BY ANOTHER RESTAURANT: I used to have a chicken dish on my menu that was inspired by the roasted chicken at The NoMad in NYC.

IF YOU COULD EAT AT ANY RESTAURANT IN THE WORLD TONIGHT, IT WOULD BE: Paul Bocuse's l'Auberge du Pont de Collonges

FAVORITE INDUSTRY INSTAGRAM ACCOUNT: Andrew Zimmern, @chefaz

CHEF WITH WHOM YOU'D MOST LIKE TO COLLABORATE: Michael Anthony. I think we share a similar vision for food and I've always respected his work.

SMOKED FOIE GRAS, TÊTE DE COCHON, DILL EMULSION, RADISH, ONIONS, AND BITTER GREENS

Chef Lee Wolen of Boka | Chicago, IL
Adapted by StarChefs
Yield: 15 Servings

INGREDIENTS

Tête de Cochon:
40 liters water
1.6 kilograms salt, plus additional as needed
One 7-pound hog head, cut in half vertically (brain discarded)
200 grams white wine
30 grams pink salt
5 sprigs thyme
1 bay leaf
8 black peppercorns
Ground black pepper
Sherry vinegar

Smoked Foie Gras:
2 quarts salt
1 tablespoon pink salt
1 lobe grade-A foie gras, deveined

Baby Onions:
5 small white onions, peeled and halved
Olive oil
Salt
Blended oil

Dill Emulsion:
3 eggs, boiled 3 minutes and chilled
1 cup grapeseed oil
Juice of 1 lemon
1 tablespoon Dijon mustard
1 cup dill fronds
Salt
Sugar

Black Onion Powder:
4 onions, thinly sliced
1 tablespoon squid ink

To Assemble and Serve:
Pickled pearl onions
Pickled mustard seeds
Shaved radish
Dill sprigs

METHOD

For the Tête de Cochon:
In a large pot, bring half the water to a boil and add salt. Remove from heat when salt dissolves; chill. When cold, place hog head in brine and refrigerate 12 hours. Heat oven to 225°F. Rinse hog head thoroughly and pat dry. In a large container, combine white wine, pink salt, thyme, bay leaf, peppercorns, and remaining water. Place head halves in 6-inch hotel pans and cover with seasoned liquid. Securely cover hotel pans with lids or foil. Cook in oven 7 hours or until jowl separates easily from skull. Pull meat off bones and cool in cooking liquid. Pick all lean meat, separating it from fat. Cut fat into small dice and reserve. Scale lean meat and record weight. Scale 10 percent of recorded weight in fat. To a large mixing bowl, combine the scaled fat and the lean meat. Season with cooking liquid, salt, pepper, and Sherry vinegar. Scale 1 kilogram of meat mixture, and roll into a very tight torchon wrapped in cheesecloth; tie securely. Repeat process for every 1 kilogram meat. Strain cooking liquid, discard the solids, and season with salt and Sherry vinegar. Place the torchons in the liquid and set overnight in refrigerator.

For the Smoked Foie Gras:
In a deep half hotel pan, combine salts. Cover foie gras in salt mix and let sit overnight in a refrigerator, about 12 hours. Remove and rinse foie gras. Place on a sheet tray and let dry overnight in refrigerator. Prepare and heat a smoker to 200°F. Smoke foie gras 15 minutes; let cool. Wrap in plastic wrap and store in freezer.

For the Baby Onions:
Bring a pot of water to a boil. Place onions in a vacuum bag with olive oil and salt. Cook onions in boiling water until just under tender. Chill. To a sauté pan over medium heat, add blended oil and sear onions, cut side down, until they begin to char. Remove and separate onions into individual petals.

For the Dill Emulsion:
In a blender, blend all ingredients until emulsified. Cover and refrigerate.

For the Black Onion Powder:
In a dry sauté pan over medium-low heat, sweat onions until tender. Add squid ink and cook another 3 to 4 minutes. Lay onions on a silicone mat. In an oven with a pilot light on, dry overnight. Pulverize in a spice grinder.

To Assemble and Serve:
Medium dice Tête de Cochon. Using a slicer, shave Smoked Foie Gras into very thin slices. On a serving plate, sparsely arrange 5 Tête de Cochon pieces. Place 2 slices of Smoked Foie Gras on top and adjacent to tête. Garnish with Dill Emulsion, Baby Onions, pickled pearl onions, pickled mustard seeds, radish, and dill sprigs. Finish with Black Onion Powder.

HOBART
Legacy® Mixers

BE INSPIRED. CREATE INSPIRED. HOBART INSPIRED.

Hobart has been the mixer of choice for culinary artists for more than a century. With its exclusive swing-out-bowl and Shift-on-the-Fly™ capability, the Legacy enables you to mix ingredients with ease – for the ideal balance of creative expression and consistent control.

Visit Hobartcorp.com/GetInspired for ideas and inspiration.

HOBART
Proud supporter of you.®

THE TASTE OF MENORCA

QUESO Mahón MENORCA

Our cows graze freely in the island. + Milk flavoured with the pastures of Menorca. + Ancient methods of elaboration and maduration. + Humidity. + The light of Menorca. + The salt breeze permeates the pasture.

D.O.P. MAHON

A UNIQUE PRODUCT

These factors coupled with its unique square shape with rounded edges and characteristic orange color, make the Mahon-Menorca cheese has its own personality.

Enjoy all its varieties:
tender: soft, *semi-cured:* characteristic and unmistakable and *cured:* a treat for cheese lovers.

P.D.O. stamp guarantee of quality and authenticity.
The Regulating Council for Mahón-Menorca Protected Designation of Origin (P.D.O) certifies our cheeses and endorses their origin, Menorca.

Easy shopping:
For internet or in shop in every country.

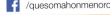 /quesomahonmenorca   @quesomahon

www.quesomahonmenorca.com

 MENORCA TALAYÓTICA
Candidata Patrimonio Mundial

 CONSELL INSULAR DE MENORCA

www.cime.es

HOT DIGGITY DOG

WITH SUPPORT FROM SERVEWISE

 **CHEZPASCAL**

A DISH YOU MAKE THAT'S INSPIRED BY ANOTHER CHEF: Cassoulet. I learned this way of making the dish from Gordon Hamersley. We have a rule that the dish doesn't come on the menu until all the leaves fall off of the two trees in front of our restaurant. If they look like they might come off too early in the season, I secretly duct tape a few on to prolong the season.

IF YOU COULD EAT AT ANY RESTAURANT IN THE WORLD TONIGHT, IT WOULD BE: Quince. I worked for Mike Tusk at Oliveto, and I have the most respect for how and what he cooks.

FAVORITE COOKBOOK: Cooking by Hand by Paul Bertolli

CHEF WITH WHOM YOU'D MOST LIKE TO COLLABORATE: Chef Kees Elfring of Marius in Amsterdam. I did my internship with him when he had a different restaurant in Holland, and I learned so much about food and culture (and marijuana) there.

Matt Gennuso

Wurst Kitchen | Providence, RI

Rhode Island native Matt Gennuso traveled far and wide to learn all he could about food, so that in the end he could return home to share his cuisine with Providence. Gennuso's journey began at the Culinary Institute of America. He spent one year in Holland honing his skills and then worked under notable chefs such as Paul Bertolli of Oliveto in Oakland, California, and Tom Colicchio during his time at Gramercy Tavern in New York. In Boston, Gennuso worked at Hamersley's Bistro where he mastered his butchery skills.

PHOTO: ALIZA ELIAZAROV

In 2003, back in his home state, Gennuso opened Chez Pascal, where he features Rhody produce on his French-inspired seasonal menu. In 2009, he started selling his sausages from a truck, which eventually turned into a walk-up window and casual eatery called Wurst Kitchen that specializes in outstanding Rhode Island "saugies."

Phillip Gilmour

Hi Hello | Brooklyn, NY

PHOTO: MEGAN SWANN

Kansas native Phillip Gilmour's love of food started at an early age, largely influenced by his Auntie Mame-esque grandmother, Dr. Marilou Morris. Having traveled the world twice over, she cooked everything from Persian and French to Thai and Midwestern comfort food. That exposure to international cuisine, his working class background, and having to fend for himself led to a passion for food. Gilmour started working in restaurants at 14. From 18 to 28, he traveled the world, using restaurant jobs to fund his travels.

He moved to New York in 2000 and started bartending at Diner in Williamsburg, Brooklyn. While working at the Japanese restaurant Bozu, Gilmour helped his friends open Roberta's pizzeria in Bushwick. Seeing their success inspired him to open his first restaurant, Momo Sushi Shack, followed by his cafe Hi Hello, the Yakitori restaurant Moku Moku, and Momo Sushi Shack in Miami at the Mondrian Hotel.

 **PHILL_GIL HIHELLOBK**

COOLEST TECHNIQUE YOU'VE LEARNED FROM ANOTHER CHEF: My business partner, Makoto Suzuki, uses salmon roe instead of chicken eggs for mayo. Kinda changed my life eight years ago.

A DISH YOU MAKE THAT'S INSPIRED BY ANOTHER CULTURE: At Momo Sushi Shack, we periodically do a lamb offal gyoza with brain, tongue, kidney, liver, penis, and testicles of a lamb ground with a little pork belly fat. My inspiration was trying to do a Japanese version of haggis. I have Scottish roots so I secretly think I'm genetically predisposed to crave organ meats.

CHEF WITH WHOM YOU'D MOST LIKE TO COLLABORATE: Mark "the Gooch" Noguchi. He has been my biggest supporter. Also, he's an angel that walks among men, so it would be dream to work with someone like that instead of the pirates and carnies I've surrounded myself with for the last 28 years.

Bill Kim

Belly Shack | Chicago, IL

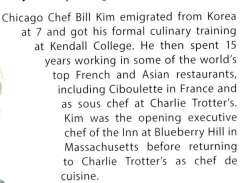

PHOTO: ANTOINETTE BRUNO

Chicago Chef Bill Kim emigrated from Korea at 7 and got his formal culinary training at Kendall College. He then spent 15 years working in some of the world's top French and Asian restaurants, including Ciboulette in France and as sous chef at Charlie Trotter's. Kim was the opening executive chef of the Inn at Blueberry Hill in Massachusetts before returning to Charlie Trotter's as chef de cuisine.

But it was as executive chef of Le Lan that Kim crystallized both his cultural and culinary experiences with the restaurant's progressive Asia-inspired menu, earning him a 2008 StarChefs Rising Stars Award. That same year Kim opened his fast casual fantasy, Urbanbelly, a modern noodle and dumpling house that brought his imagination and internationalism to the fore. A second concept, Belly Shack, followed, highlighting pan-Asian cuisine with Latin notes and characteristic "Kim" creativity. In 2012, he opened Asian Barbecue spot BellyQ.

 BELLYSHACKCHI **BELLYSHACK**

MOST INFLUENTIAL MENTOR WITH WHOM YOU'VE WORKED: Charlie Trotter

COOLEST TECHNIQUE YOU'VE LEARNED FROM ANOTHER CHEF: Nobu Masaharu taught me how to peel a quail egg by shaking it in a coffee cup. He showed me this in England when we were doing an event there, and I still use it today.

A DISH YOU MAKE THAT'S INSPIRED BY ANOTHER CULTURE: My wife is Puerto Rican, so I'm inspired by Latin cuisine. Belly Shack is a love story told through food: it's Asian and Latin together.

IF YOU COULD EAT AT ANY RESTAURANT IN THE WORLD TONIGHT, IT WOULD BE: Frédy Giradet in Switzerland, before it closed.

FAVORITE INDUSTRY INSTAGRAM ACCOUNT: @chefdlefevre

FAVORITE COOKBOOK: Asian Noodles by Nina Simonds

MOST INFLUENTIAL MENTOR WITH WHOM YOU'VE WORKED: Mike Lata taught us what it is to be proper cooks at all phases of cooking. He is an example of how to lead, mentor, and what it means to be chef-owners.

A DISH YOU MAKE THAT'S INSPIRED BY ANOTHER CHEF: We do a late night ramen dish at Hog & Hominy inspired by and paying homage to Tien Ho, who walked us through the proper way to make a ramen broth after a late night pop-up at the restaurant. We also have a boudin pizza named The Prewitt after Ryan Prewitt, who, on a trip to Memphis just before we opened, brought us this really amazing boudin.

IF YOU COULD EAT AT ANY RESTAURANT IN THE WORLD TONIGHT, IT WOULD BE: Asador Etxebarri

FAVORITE COOKBOOK: <u>Mastering Pasta</u> by Marc Vetri

Andrew Ticer

Porcellino's | Memphis, TN

There just so happen to be a few nonnas south of the Mason Dixon line. Chef Andrew Ticer grew up with one such Italian-Tennessee family. And when he met Michael Hudman, who had a similar upbringing, great plans began to hatch. Ticer left Memphis after college to attend Johnson & Wales in South Carolina. He then returned to apprentice under Jose Guitierrez at Chez Philippe. Eventually Ticer's Italian heritage came calling, setting the young chef on a sojourn to The Italian Culinary Institute in Calabria.

PHOTO: CAROLINE HATCHETT

Back in the States inspired and ready to work, Ticer cooked while refining a business plan and scouring for real estate. Today, Ticer and Hudman are at the fore of Memphis's food scene with restaurants Andrew Michael Italian Kitchen, Hog & Hominy, and Porcellino's, a craft butcher shop. In 2014, they won a StarChefs Rising Stars Award and have been finalists for James Beard's "Best Chef, Southeast."

MOST INFLUENTIAL MENTOR WITH WHOM YOU'VE WORKED: Donald Link taught us to work hard, be responsible, seek perfection, and never settle. We also really appreciate how he structures his business and how he mentors those he works with.

COOLEST TECHNIQUE YOU'VE LEARNED FROM ANOTHER CHEF: The onion caramel from Erik Anderson

A DISH YOU MAKE THAT'S INSPIRED BY ANOTHER CULTURE: John T. Edge, whose book <u>Hamburger and Fries</u> has a wealth of information, turned us onto the Oklahoma-style onion burger that came up during the Great Depression. People needed to stretch their beef, so they would add onions. We really dug the story: people wanting burgers but not being able to afford enough meat. Ours is an authentic version. We use some different techniques, but the outcome is the same. It's so simple and so good.

Michael Hudman

Porcellino's | Memphis, TN

Memphis might not have as much Italian street cred as Boston's North End or Arthur Avenue in the Bronx, but that doesn't mean Italian cuisine doesn't thrive there. Home-grown Chef Michael Hudman came from a large Italian family and grew up watching his "maw maw" prepare ravioli and meatballs for Sunday suppers. When he found a culinary kindred spirit in Andrew Ticer, the duo struck out on a path bound by a sense of tradition.

PHOTO: CAROLINE HATCHETT

Making his way to Johnson & Wales in South Carolina after college in Memphis, Hudman apprenticed under Jose Guitierrez at Chez Philippe. Heeding the call of his heritage, Hudman then enrolled at The Italian Culinary Institute in Calabria. Back stateside, he cooked while collaborating with Ticer on a business plan. Andrew Michael Italian Kitchen opened once the duo finally found the right space. Hog & Hominy and butcher shop Porcellino's quickly following. Along with Ticer, Hudman won a 2014 StarChefs Rising Stars Award and has been twice nominated for James Beard's "Best Chef, Southeast."

PHOTO: WILL BLUNT

Ben Thompson

The Rock Barn | Arrington, VA

🐦 **THEROCKBARN**

COOLEST TECHNIQUE YOU'VE LEARNED FROM ANOTHER CHEF: When it comes to butchering, there is always something to learn from another person. I always appreciate that three different butchers can come up with three different approaches to the same cut.

A DISH YOU MAKE THAT'S INSPIRED BY ANOTHER CULTURE: At The Rock Barn, we make a mortadella inspired product called "Daisy Della." We use Virginia peanuts and smoked jowl bacon to garnish. The spices we use are American South in flavor profile, and then we smoke it.

IF YOU COULD EAT AT ANY RESTAURANT IN THE WORLD TONIGHT, IT WOULD BE: Wherever Francis Mallmann is cooking tonight

FAVORITE INDUSTRY INSTAGRAM ACCOUNT: @farmert

FAVORITE COOKBOOK: Lately, I have been inspired by The River Cottage Meat Book by Hugh Fearnley-Whittingstall and Zingerman's Guide to Giving Great Service by Ari Weinzweig.

Benjamin Thompson grew up in Colorado Springs and joined the United States Navy in 2000 to become a ship's cook aboard the USS Hampton. After five years of service, Thompson married Reagan Holland, and began working in Charlottesville, Virginia, at Oxo Restaurant. The two eventually left for New York, where Thompson attended the Culinary Institute of America, an experience that helped Thompson to secure an externship at Per Se in New York City and then a position at The French Laundry in Napa Valley.

In 2009, he and Holland moved to Nelson County, Virginia, where they founded The Rock Barn. There, they work with a farm co-op to raise hogs exclusively for their business. Rock Barn charcuterie goes to local restaurants, farmers markets, and The Rock Barn retail shop, as well as their pork share program—a CSA for pig meat. For this work, Thompson was earned a 2014 StarChef Rising Star Artisan Award.

SPICY OKRA DOG

Chef Benjamin Thompson of The Rock Barn | Arrington, VA
Adapted by StarChefs
Yield: 50 to 60 links

INGREDIENTS

1.6 pounds lean beef
6 pounds lean pork
2.4 pounds pork fat
1 pound water
2.8 ounces salt
3.6 ounces sugar
3.2 ounces dry mustard
0.5 ounce dextrose
0.5 ounce finely ground coriander
0.4 ounce ground white pepper
0.2 ounce granulated garlic
0.1 ounce ground nutmeg
0.4 ounce curing salt #813 (6.25 percent)
0.2 ounce paprika, 120 ASTA
0.8 ounce chili flakes
3.2 ounces nonfat dry milk
1 pound pickled okra, rinsed and sliced into ¼-inch rings
26- to 28-millimeter sheep casings

METHOD

Through a meat grinder fitted with a ⅜-inch die, grind beef, pork, and pork fat. Remove die and fit with ³⁄₁₆-inch die; grind meat. Remove die and fit with ³⁄₃₂-inch die; grind meat. Transfer meat to a large mixing bowl. Mix in half the water followed by salt, sugar, mustard, dextrose, coriander, white pepper, garlic, nutmeg, curing salt, paprika, and chili flakes. Thoroughly mix in dry milk, making sure all ingredients are combined. Add remaining water and mix well. Fold in okra. Using a sausage stuffer, stuff sheep casings with meat mixture, making 7-inch links. Prepare and heat a smoker with hickory wood chips. Smoke sausages until internal temperature reaches 150°F and is sustained for 2 minutes.

HEY, ASIA!

WITH SUPPORT FROM SERVEWISE

Angus An

Maenam | Vancouver, Canada

PHOTO: HAMID ATTIE

After studying fine arts at the University of British Columbia in Canada, Angus An enrolled at New York's French Culinary Institute, studying under legends Jacques Pépin, Alain Sailhac, and André Soltner. Moving to Montreal, he worked with Chef Normand Laprise at Toqué before making Michelin-starred rounds in London at The Ledbury, The Fat Duck, and Le Manoir aux Qaut'Saisons. An then traveled to Bangkok to work for his mentor-in-the-making, David Thompson, who gave An a serious education in Thai cooking.

An also met his business partner and wife, Kate, in Bangkok. The duo soon returned to Vancouver and opened the celebrated Gastropod. Upon the late economic crisis, the couple saw their chance to rebrand, and Maenam was born. An continues to serve homey and stylized Thai cuisine reflective of his childhood and culinary training. In spring 2015, he opened Fat Mao Noodle Bar in Vancouver's Chinatown.

 CHEFANGUSAN

MOST INFLUENTIAL MENTOR WITH WHOM YOU'VE WORKED: Normand Laprise and David Thompson. Normand showed me simplicity and the importance of starting with the best ingredients. David showed me flavors no one else could. He introduced me to Thai flavors, and to the notion of balance and layering flavors.

A DISH YOU MAKE THAT'S INSPIRED BY ANOTHER CULTURE: Black pepper crab. It started with one of our best customers who is from Singapore, and was craving this dish from his homeland. I did some research, and knew that there was a similar Thai version. It's such a popular item that it requires pre-booking.

FAVORITE INDUSTRY INSTAGRAM ACCOUNT: @mariobatali

CHEF WITH WHOM YOU'D MOST LIKE TO COLLABORATE: Earl Ninsom from Langbaan and PaaDee. He's doing killer Thai food just down the coast, and he's a good friend.

MOST INFLUENTIAL MENTOR WITH WHOM YOU'VE WORKED: Chef John Besh. Not only did I learn about the ebb and flow of the industry, but also how to approach each side of that coin dynamically. I was challenged to learn the history behind the food we served and make sure that there was always a story and purpose behind our preparations.

A DISH YOU MAKE THAT'S INSPIRED BY ANOTHER CULTURE: Cast iron pan "paella" with black sticky rice, coconut milk, squid ink, andouille, Louisiana shrimp and crab, Florida clams, and charred octopus. It is reminiscent of so many cultures to me: jambalaya, risotto nero, paella, and Vietnamese coconut sticky rice.

IF YOU COULD EAT AT ANY RESTAURANT IN THE WORLD TONIGHT, IT WOULD BE: Osteria Francescana [in Modena, Italy] or Red Lantern on Riley [in Darlinghurst, Australia]

Michael Gulotta

MoPho | New Orleans, LA

Born and raised in New Orleans, Michael Gulotta began cooking in local restaurants at age 17. After graduating from the Chef John Folse Culinary Institute, he joined the newly opened Restaurant August under Chef John Besh. Gulotta then took leave to train in the Italian Riviera and Germany's Black Forest. When Hurricane Katrina hit, Gulotta returned home to help rebuild and assist with August's re-opening. He was named chef de cuisine in 2007 and led the award-winning kitchen for six years, while establishing relationships with local farmers and purveyors.

PHOTO: WILL BLUNT

Gulotta opened his first restaurant, MoPho, in January 2014. Located in New Orleans' Mid City, MoPho connects the flavors of Southeast Asia with the Louisiana pantry that's in Gulotta's bones. In its first year MoPho was nominated for "America's Best New Restaurant" by *Bon Appétit* and named "Restaurant of the Year" by *New Orleans Magazine*.

COOLEST TECHNIQUE YOU'VE LEARNED FROM ANOTHER CHEF: My son Bobby just graduated from the Culinary Institute of America. He started working at minibar, and he's helped me hone a number of Western skills that I didn't grow up with. He also taught me the most incredible curing and pickling techniques.

IF YOU COULD EAT AT ANY RESTAURANT IN THE WORLD TONIGHT, IT WOULD BE: The Fat Duck in England. The idea of using the entire animal is very much in keeping with the Lao tradition.

FAVORITE COOKBOOK: Phia Sing was the royal chef and master of ceremonies at the Royal Palace in Luang Prabang. His cookbooks are important not just because they offer great recipes, but they are a record of our culture and people.

Seng Luangrath

Thip Khao | Washington, D.C.

Fleeing Laos and living in various refugee camps, Seng Luangrath became her family's de facto cook, honing her skills from the women in the camp. Arriving in the United States in 1983, Luangrath spent a few years in California before moving to Northern Virginia in 1989.

Luangrath took over Bangkok Golden in 2010, initially cooking traditional Thai food but soon shifting her focus to Laotian cuisine. In December 2014, Luangrath opened Thip Khao, in Washington, D.C., and immediately received praise from top critics. In June 2015, Luangrath was one of nine chefs to cook at a James Beard benefit for Women in Culinary Leadership Program. In July, Luangrath launched Khao Poon, a Lao noodle pop-up (soon-to-be noodle shop). In August, Thip Khao was named one of the "America's 50 Best New Restaurants" by *Bon Appétit*.

PHOTO: GENA ROMA PHOTOGRAPHY

Phuket Thongsodchareondee

Cake Thai Kitchen | Miami, FL

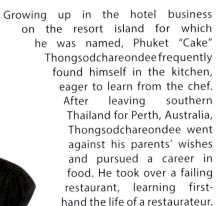

PHOTO: CAROLINE HATCHETT

Growing up in the hotel business on the resort island for which he was named, Phuket "Cake" Thongsodchareondee frequently found himself in the kitchen, eager to learn from the chef. After leaving southern Thailand for Perth, Australia, Thongsodchareondee went against his parents' wishes and pursued a career in food. He took over a failing restaurant, learning first-hand the life of a restaurateur.

In 2008, Thongsodchareondee moved to Miami and started out as many immigrants do: cooking here and there for a living. When he was introduced to Japanese cuisine, Thongsodchareondee found direction and landed a position under StarChefs Rising Star Chef Makoto Okuwa. He worked at Makoto for four years, with a year-long interlude in San Francisco at Amphawa and Full Moon Thai. In 2014, Thongsodcharoendee ventured out on his own, opening Cake Thai Kitchen. Drawing from his varied experiences and using both experimentation and his immaculate palate, he's recreating Thai street food for his Miami 'hood.

 KZCAKE

MOST INFLUENTIAL MENTORS WITH WHOM YOU'VE WORKED: Carlos Ohata at Kone Sushi taught me all the basics of sushi. Kob Varaphol at Amphawa in San Francisco mentored me about kitchen organization. Makoto Okuwa taught me about the different fish handling preparations. Also at Makoto, Yoshi Migita, a sushi master, showed me many elaborate techniques.

COOLEST TECHNIQUE YOU'VE LEARNED FROM ANOTHER CHEF: Controlling the temperature of a hot wok. It's more than knowing the right amount of flame. You have to adjust your tossing rhythm, and you shouldn't dump all ingredients into a wok at once.

IF YOU COULD EAT AT ANY RESTAURANT IN THE WORLD TONIGHT, IT WOULD BE: Noma. I am inspired and amazed by how they forage for daily ingredients and cook with the ebbs and flows of seasons.

Gabe Rosen

Biwa and Noraneko | Portland, OR

PHOTO: ANTOINETTE BRUNO

In 1995, Iowa native and University of Iowa student Gabe Rosen quit his telemarketing job and took a gig as a dishwasher at Linn Street Café. Two years later, he left school and the Midwest entirely for Portland, Oregon, and The Western Culinary Institute. After graduating, Rosen interned at Michael Mina's Aqua in San Francisco and then returned to Portland to work at Couvron. A year later, he went back to school to complete his degree in Japanese Language at Portland State University. For his final year, he studied in Japan at Hokkaido University in Sapporo.

Once again returning to Portland, Rosen partnered with Kina Voelz and opened Biwa in 2007. Izakaya restaurants in Portland have since exploded—a trend largely due to Biwa's success. Presently, Rosen has teamed up with long-time colleague Ed Ross to open Noraneko, a traditional ramen shop with the addition of a cocktail bar, late night menu, and DJ that plays until 2am.

BIWAPDX

MOST INFLUENTIAL MENTOR WITH WHOM YOU'VE WORKED: John Gorham was the first chef that I worked with who was SO delighted by the act of cooking. I had never liked cooking with other people before.

A DISH YOU MAKE THAT'S INSPIRED BY ANOTHER CULTURE: Our restaurants are more-or-less Japanese, but we try and keep them lighthearted by mixing in dishes from our various experiences—for example, we are serving Wisconsin-style brats at our ramen shop right now.

FAVORITE COOKBOOK: Gaku Homma's The Folk Art of Japanese Country Cooking. I was also profoundly influenced as a young cook by Jean-Georges Vongerichten's Cooking at Home with a Four Star Chef.

KARAAGE

Chef Gabe Rosen of Biwa and Noraneko | Portland, OR
Adapted by StarChefs
Yield: 20 servings

INGREDIENTS

Chicken:
10 pounds bone-in, skin-on chicken
    thighs
3 quarts water
3 cups sake
1½ cups tamari
1½ cups shio koji
¾ cup kosher salt
½ cup plus 4 teaspoons minced
    ginger
1 pint chopped scallions

To Assemble and Serve:
5 quarts rice bran oil
2 cups schmaltz
3 cups potato starch
1 cup cornstarch

METHOD

For the Chicken:
Debone chicken and cut into 4 pieces, leaving the skin attached. In a large bowl, combine water, sake, tamari, shio koji, salt, and ⅓ cup ginger. Add chicken and marinate 90 minutes. Drain and mix with scallions and remaining ¼ cup ginger.

To Assemble and Serve:
In a deep fryer, heat rice bran oil and schmaltz to 330°F. In a bowl, whisk together potato starch and cornstarch. Coat chicken pieces in starch mixture, shaking off excess. In batches, fry chicken for 4 minutes and 20 seconds, or until cooked through.

FERMENTATION
FUNK

WITH SUPPORT FROM SERVEWISE

Jessica Koslow

Sqirl | Los Angeles, CA

In 2005, after finishing a graduate degree, Jessica Koslow moved from California to Atlanta with her career in flux. But soon she had a revelatory meal at Anne Quatrano's Bacchanalia and Star Provisions. Koslow inquired, and Quatrano hired. For a year, she learned how to cook in one of the South's most esteemed kitchens.

Still, Koslow felt the pull to make her degree work, and moved to New York to become a television producer. Unable to shake food, she moved to Los Angeles and took an office job, moonlighting at Village Bakery. In 2010, the office closed and Koslow took off for Dench Bakers in Melbourne, Australia. Returning to Los Angeles a year later, with a brief stop to work at Quatrano's Abattoir, Koslow opened Sqirl restaurant and market, where she won a 2014 StarChefs Rising Stars Award. She has become an integral part of the East Hollywood community and is active in Edible School Yard, Bakers Will Bake, Farm On Wheels, and Sustainable Kitchen.

PHOTO: ANTOINETTE BRUNO

SQIRL_CONFITURES SQIRLLA

MOST INFLUENTIAL MENTOR WITH WHOM YOU'VE WORKED: Anne Quantrano. She gave a hungry girl a chance, and she runs her restaurants with soul and a perspective all her own.

COOLEST TECHNIQUE YOU'VE LEARNED FROM ANOTHER CHEF: Taking a pickling liquid (vinegar or lacto), reducing it and using it in dressings. It separates the kids from the adults.

IF YOU COULD EAT AT ANY RESTAURANT IN THE WORLD TONIGHT, IT WOULD BE: Fäviken. I was supposed to be there this time last year and a matter at home stopped my trip.

FAVORITE COOKBOOK: The Good Cook, a Time-Life series by Richard Olney

CHEF WITH WHOM YOU'D MOST LIKE TO COLLABORATE: Michel Bras. When I started cooking in 2005, The Gargouillou of Young Vegetables was the mantra of Bacchanalia's kitchen, and it flows at Sqirl, as well.

CELLARDOORPROVISIONS

QUICHENCOUNTRY

COOLEST TECHNIQUE YOU'VE LEARNED FROM ANOTHER CHEF: Beurre monté

A DISH YOU MAKE THAT'S INSPIRED BY ANOTHER RESTAURANT, CHEF, OR CULTURE: Naturally leavened bread and kefir butter from Bar Tartine

IF YOU COULD EAT AT ANY RESTAURANT IN THE WORLD TONIGHT, IT WOULD BE: Fäviken

FAVORITE INDUSTRY INSTAGRAM ACCOUNT: Elmore Mountain Bread, @elmoremountainbread

FAVORITE COOKBOOK: Tartine Bread by Chad Robertson. It is responsible for me becoming a professional cook.

CHEF WITH WHOM YOU'D MOST LIKE TO COLLABORATE: Cortney Burns and Nick Balla of Bar Tartine

Tony Bezsylko

Cellar Door Provisions | Chicago, IL

When Baker Tony Bezsylko lived in San Francisco, finding great bread was easy. But upon moving to Chicago, Bezsylko found that great bread was hard to find. The struggle to find that perfect loaf was so distressing that he stopped eating it altogether. This abstention, however, inspired Bezsylko to take matters into his own hands. After buying a copy of Tartine Bread, baking bread turned into an obsession. He eventually began sharing his creations with friends, who enjoyed the bread so much that they began paying him for weekly loaves.

PHOTO: MEGAN SWANN

Bezsylko teamed up with Chefs Ethan Pikas and Justin Behlke to open pop-up restaurant Thurk. The concept turned into Cellar Door Provisions, where the team aims to keep themselves and their community in touch with the multitude of ways people can celebrate and exalt ingredients that are naturally perfect.

CELLARDOORPROVISIONS

QUICHENCOUNTRY

MOST INFLUENTIAL MENTOR WITH WHOM YOU'VE WORKED: Kevin Binkley from Binkley's in Phoenix, without a doubt. He is such a talented craftsman and strong force in the kitchen and is so exacting in his standards, that you cannot help but become a better cook.

A DISH YOU MAKE THAT'S INSPIRED BY ANOTHER RESTAURANT: Smoked potatoes in any fashion by Bar Tartine

IF YOU COULD EAT AT ANY RESTAURANT IN THE WORLD TONIGHT, IT WOULD BE: Relæ

FAVORITE CHEF INSTAGRAM ACCOUNT: Ayako Kurokawa, @burr0w

FAVORITE COOKBOOK: Tartine Bread by Chad Robertson

CHEF WITH WHOM YOU'D MOST LIKE TO COLLABORATE: David Kinch

Ethan Pikas

Cellar Door Provisions | Chicago, IL

Chef Ethan Pikas is co-owner of Chicago's Cellar Door Provisions, where there's a commitment to sourcing from the bottom up—from the salt and flour to the proteins served and the relationships that such sourcing fosters. Much like his restaurant, Pikas also started from humble beginnings. He was introduced to the industry as a dishwasher, making ends meet as he pursued a degree in creative writing. Struggling to find a place in the world of the written word, and in need of an outlet for his creative yearnings, Pikas started to get serious about cooking.

PHOTO: MEGAN SWANN

He enrolled in culinary school, eager to develop technique in both savory and pastry skill sets with which he is still constantly progressing and experimenting. Along with partners Tony Bezsylko and Justin Behlke, Pikas launched Cellar Door in 2014, striving to create a personal and exceptional take on Midwestern cuisine that is simultaneously inventive, warm, and familiar.

Jeff Vance

Spur Gastropub | Seattle, WA

PHOTO: ANTOINETTE BRUNO

Jeff Vance grew up in a small town in British Columbia with a thriving Italian community. His best friend's family made its own wine and salami—a hands-on culinary connection that stayed with Vance even as his family moved to Calgary, Southern California, and finally Spokane, Washington.

Vance spent seven years working the lines of low-key restaurants for cash to support his leisure activities: music and skateboarding. At 23, he wanted to study architecture. The creativity appealed to him, but being desk-bound didn't, so Vance turned to cooking. He worked first at an Italian restaurant and then found a pivotal gig under Jeremy Hansen at Santé, where he was promoted to sous chef in six months. Looking for new territory, Vance moved to Seattle and discovered Spur, where he was hired a day after arriving and worked his way from garde manger to chef de cuisine in less than six months.

COOLEST TECHNIQUE YOU'VE LEARNED FROM ANOTHER CHEF: Dana Tough and Brian McCracken at Spur taught me how to make a quick cheese with carrageenan to set the curd. It gives you the power to control the consistency of cheese without all of the variables that come with traditional cheesemaking.

IF YOU COULD EAT AT ANY RESTAURANT IN THE WORLD TONIGHT, IT WOULD BE: Atelier Crenn. I admire the way that Dominique Crenn defies convention and explores her own path through experimentation and progression.

FAVORITE COOKBOOK: Relæ: A Book of Ideas by Christian Puglisi

CHEF WITH WHOM YOU'D MOST LIKE TO COLLABORATE: Aitor Zabala, the creative director for Think Food Group.

Seth Sempere

Spur Gastropub | Seattle, WA

PHOTO: ANTOINETTE BRUNO

Seth Sempere had a classical introduction to the industry: pizza delivery. Expanding his repertoire to bartending gave Sempere a glimpse into his future, especially when Fireworks—the Italian restaurant in Vermont that gave him his start—added a lounge. Before Sempere left Vermont on a road trip, he earned a B.A. in literature and nonfiction writing. But landing in Seattle by fall 2011, it was the pour, not the pen, that pulled Sempere in.

At Suite 410, Sempere was part of the team that made the bar's reputation as a cocktail den. He then entered the world of Dana Tough and Brian McCracken restaurants, first bartending at Coterie Room, and by 2013 managing the bar at Spur, where he showcases his preternatural ability to pair cocktails with the fun and refined gastropub menu. He also lends his talents to rum bar Rhumba, and in 2014 won the Bombay Sapphire Most Imaginative Bartender competition. Sempere is the Vice President of the Washington State Bartenders Guild.

MOST INFLUENTIAL BARTENDERS WITH WHOM YOU'VE WORKED: Gina Richard of Select Oyster Bar in Boston and Tommy Stearns of Canon in Seattle. The sincere combination of hospitality and creativity that we achieved together sets the standard for what I do.

IF YOU COULD SIT AT ANY BAR IN THE WORLD TONIGHT, IT WOULD BE: Kipling's, a tiny pub in Brattleboro, Vermont. I learned more than I can remember about how to work hard, manage a crowd, respect a guest, and make people happy from Jill and Kip Record.

SPIRIT YOU'RE MOST EXCITED ABOUT: Rum! It offers a greater breadth than any other spirit. Rhums Agricole are dry, earthy, and floral. Many other rums could be mistaken for sexy outliers of bourbon or Scotch. And then there are the rums that replace dessert.

MOST INFLUENTIAL MENTOR WITH WHOM YOU'VE WORKED: Chef Richard Capizzi. Our time together at Per Se is something really unforgettable. Dedication was the message that resonated in me through example. His drive and passion to the craft is something that evokes a question that you ask yourself: Are you 100 percent committed? It's really that general truth. The more you give, the more you receive.

FAVORITE INDUSTRY INSTAGRAM ACCOUNT: I'm digging Instagram feeds from farmers these days. Tucker Taylor, @farmert.

FAVORITE COOKBOOK: Essential Cuisine by Michel Bras

CHEF WITH WHOM YOU'D MOST LIKE TO COLLABORATE: Chef Dominique Crenn. Beyond her achievements as a female chef, reading her professional philosophies, mainly on vulnerability, struck a chord with me.

Mina Pizarro

Juni | New York, NY

Philippines-born Pastry Chef Mina Pizarro moved to New Jersey at the age of 12, aspiring at a young age to graduate college and become a TV personality. Pizarro pursued advertising—a position that flipped the switch on her creative drive and ultimately helped push her into the kitchen.

Pizarro found a work-study position at the Institute for Culinary Education in New York City, which allowed her to test the waters before committing to full tuition. Falling for pastry, Pizarro committed first to nine months, then a career.

PHOTO: MEGAN SWANN

An internship at Daniel Boulud's DB Bistro Moderne led to a job offer, from which Pizarro went on to work in some of the best fine-dining kitchens in New York, including DB, Le Cirque, Per Se, Veritas, and SHO Shaun Hergatt before decamping to California. Returning to the city with a West Coast perspective, Pizarro worked first for Cesare Casella at Il Ristorante, then took the helm at Shaun Hergatt's Juni, where she won a 2015 StarChefs Rising Stars Award.

MOST INFLUENTIAL MENTOR WITH WHOM YOU'VE WORKED: Ken Oringer. His knowledge of different cuisines and ingredients has really inspired me to never stop learning.

COOLEST TECHNIQUE YOU'VE LEARNED FROM ANOTHER CHEF: Making bread from Chefs Jonny Black and Brad McDonald. The conditions for making bread change every day, so you really have to feel the dough and tweak it daily. This soulful type of cooking has spilled over into other aspects of my kitchen.

FAVORITE INDUSTRY INSTAGRAM ACCOUNT: Shola Olunloyo, @StudioKitchen1

FAVORITE COOKBOOK: The Art of Fermentation by Sandor Katz

CHEF WITH WHOM YOU'D MOST LIKE TO COLLABORATE: Chef Magnus Nilsson of Fäviken. The idea of creativity through necessity and tradition is something that has always fascinated me.

Andrew Whitcomb

Colonie | Brooklyn, NY

Nestled between the sweeping coastlines and snow-topped mountains of his Maine home, Andrew Whitcomb was keenly aware of nature at a young age. From adjacent farmlands and farmers markets to his parents' garden, local and sustainable produce played an important role early in Whitcomb's life.

When it came time for college, however, Whitcomb studied engineering. But after a fortuitous visit to the Culinary Institute of America, Whitcomb dropped out of the University of Southern Maine and made his way to Hyde Park. After graduation, he cooked at

PHOTO: MEGAN SWANN

Deuxave in Boston and then Ken Oringer's Earth back in Maine. Whitcomb eventually moved to New York City, rapidly moving up the ranks from line cook to executive chef at Colonie, where he earned a 2015 StarChefs Rising Star Sustainability Award. At Colonie, Whitcomb has eliminated 95 percent of the restaurant's waste and continues to develop meaningful relationships with suppliers.

PHOTO: MEGAN SWANN

APPLEWOOD-SMOKED FRIED CHICKEN, FERMENTED HONEY, AND ITALIAN LONG PEPPER HOT SAUCE

Chef Andrew Whitcomb of Colonie | Brooklyn, NY
Adapted by StarChefs
Yield: 8 to 10 servings

INGREDIENTS

Fermented Honey:
1 pound raw honey
3 ounces warm water

Italian Long Pepper Hot Sauce:
2½ pounds ramps
10 percent brine
5 pounds Italian long peppers
Apple vinegar

Smoked Chicken:
2 chickens, broken down, extra fat
   and skin removed
Rice koji
Applewood chips

Fried Chicken:
Oil for frying
500 grams all-purpose flour
500 grams red cornmeal
25 grams black pepper
20 grams togarashi
20 grams salt
Buttermilk

METHOD

For the Fermented Honey:
Combine honey and warm water and pour into a large, wide-mouth canning jar. Cover with cheese cloth and secure with a rubber band. Store in a warm, dry place. After six weeks, check the mixture and continue testing weekly until desired level of fermentation has been achieved.

For the Italian Long Pepper Hot Sauce:
Clean ramps with cool water, making sure all dirt and debris are removed. Place in a large canning jar. Pour brine over top, making sure all ramps are submerged, using a weight if needed. Ferment for 1 month. At the end of the month, wash Italian long hot peppers and remove stems. Add peppers to ramps in brine. Submerge completely. Ferment 2 months more, then test for maturity. Continue checking week by week until desired level of fermentation is reached. When ready, strain vegetables, reserving brine. Place vegetables in a blender and blend until smooth, using brine, as needed. Scale the mixture and add its weight in vinegar. Store in a cooler until ready to use. Flavor will continue to develop over time.

For the Smoked Chicken:
With a pastry brush, coat chicken on all sides with a small amount of rice koji. Place on a sheet tray set with a wire rack and rest overnight in front of a fan. on the next, day heat oven to 250˚F. Set up a stove-top smoker. Heat applewood chips until they combust, then extinguish. Repeat. Put chips inside the smoker and place a perforated tray on top. Add chicken and immediately cover. Transfer to oven and smoke 3 hours. Repeat the process, then let stand at room temperature for an hour before cooling in the refrigerator.

For the Fried Chicken:
In a deep fryer, heat oil to 375˚F. In a large bowl, whisk together flour, red cornmeal, pepper, togarashi, and salt. In a separate bowl, pour in buttermilk. Individually dredge each piece of Smoked Chicken: first in buttermilk, then in flour mixture. Place chicken onto a parchment-lined sheet tray and rest at room temperature 1 hour. Once rested, lightly dust each piece in the flour mixture again, shaking off any excess. In different baskets, fry legs, thighs, breasts, and chicken wings separately. Remove from oil when pieces are golden brown and the internal temperature reaches 165˚F.

To Assemble and Serve:
Serve Fried Chicken with Fermented Honey and Italian Long Pepper Hot Sauce drizzled on top.

FOODS&WINES *from* **SPAIN** · *Madrid*

www.spain.info

* *Tapas; don't try to say it with your mouth full!*

I need Spain

HOSTS

PHOTO: SCOTT SUCHMAN

Derek Brown

Drink Company | Washington, D.C.

Derek Brown has one of those dream jobs that your high school counselor never tells you about. He drinks for a living. Brown is a cocktail and spirits writer, spirits judge, and owner of award-winning bars Mockingbird Hill, Southern Efficiency, Eat the Rich, and The Passenger. Brown is almost single-handedly shaping the cocktail scene in Washington, D.C., a feat for which he was named a StarChefs Rising Star Restaurateur in 2014. He also travels around the globe, teaching (and still learning) about how drinking is an integral part of our culture and values.

Brown landed his very first bartending gig with exactly zero prior experience, bluffing his way through a rum punch by creating an elaborate concoction of nearly every bottle on the bar. Moving on from that early fluster, he has since developed celebrated beverage programs as a bartender, sommelier, and consultant for some of D.C.'s and the country's finest restaurants and bars. Brown has received numerous accolades for his bartending, teaching, and wine stewardship, including being named one of "Five Top New Sommeliers" in the country by *Wine & Spirits* in 2007, "Sommelier of the Year" by *DC Modern Luxury* in 2008, "Bartender of the Year" by *Washington City Paper* in 2009, and has made drinks at the White House. In 2015, *Imbibe* lauded Brown as "Bartender of the Year," and he was a semifinalists for James Beard's "Outstanding Wine & Spirits Professional" Award.

BETTERDRINKING DRINKMORESHERRY

MOST INFLUENTIAL BARTENDER WITH WHOM YOU'VE WORKED: Dale Degroff. He's the real deal and, to be fair, he inspired just about everyone who's picked up a shaker in the last 20 years. He's really moved the craft forward with his books, classes, BAR Program, and so on. But he's also built institutions like the Museum of the American Cocktail that will carry on long after the present resurgence.

COCKTAIL LISTS YOU REFERENCE FOR INSPIRATION: Dead Rabbit for sure. Anything Jackson Cannon does. Or Alex Day. Also Trick Dog. Man, there's a lot of inspiration out there, and incredible bartending.

IF YOU COULD SIT AT ANY BAR IN THE WORLD TONIGHT, IT WOULD BE: Walker Inn. Cozy and the cocktails are spot on.

FAVORITE INDUSTRY INSTAGRAM ACCOUNT: I love following @Sherryfest. Beautiful pictures and all the wines and cocktails I want to drink.

WINE YOU'RE MOST EXCITED ABOUT: It's always Sherry, especially Manzanilla. It's an endless source of inspiration for me.

THE DOUBTING DUCK

Bartender Derek Brown of Drink Company | Washington, D.C.
Adapted by StarChefs
Yield: 1 cocktail

INGREDIENTS

1½ ounces Manzanilla Sherry
1 ounce dry vermouth
½ ounce yellow Chartreuse
1 dash celery shrub
1 dash orange bitters
Lemon peel
Olive

METHOD

In a mixing glass, combine all ingredients; add ice. Stir and strain into a chilled coupe. Garnish with lemon peel and olive.

Featured Ingredient: Spanish Manzanilla Sherry

PHOTO: EVAN SUNG

PJ Calapa

Ai Fiori | New York, NY

Having grown up in the Mexican border town of Brownsville, Texas, PJ Calapa was exposed to a range of cuisines and flavors at an early age. As a child, he began working in his grandmother's kitchen and later in his grandfather's wholesale fish business. Calapa continued to nurture his culinary passion during his undergraduate studies at Texas A&M University, when he worked on the hot line at Christopher's World Grille.

After graduation, Calapa moved to New York and enrolled at the Culinary Institute of America in Hyde Park, where his passion and tireless efforts catapulted him to the top of his class. Since then, he has continued to pursue excellence, sharpening his culinary skills and incorporating early food memories with his own gastronomic intuition.

As a CIA graduate, Calapa worked at Bouley in Tribeca, Eleven Madison Park, and Nobu 57, where he started as a line cook and quickly rose through the ranks to become executive sous chef. It was at Nobu 57 that Calapa learned about the delicate art of Japanese cuisine, which still informs his vision for fine dining. In 2010, Calapa joined Chef Michael White's Altamarea Group to help launch Ai Fiori, which earned three stars from *The New York Times*, a Michelin star, and Calapa a 2013 StarChefs Rising Star Chef Award. Calapa continues to oversee Ai Fiori's kitchen, along with Costata and Campagna and the Barn at the Bedford Post Inn.

TEXCHEF AIFIORI

MOST INFLUENTIAL MENTORS WITH WHOM YOU'VE WORKED: David Bouley/Cesar Ramirez for setting the highest standard for execution and creativity. Matt Hoyle for teaching me how to handle volume at the highest of levels while staying very organized, and Michael White for bringing it all back to cooking from the heart.

COOLEST TECHNIQUE YOU'VE LEARNED FROM ANOTHER CHEF: Slicing fish, letting the knife do the work: "No chop, sliiiice!!" – Nobu Matsuhisa

A DISH YOU MAKE THAT'S INSPIRED BY ANOTHER RESTAURANT: Insalata di Astice from Ai Fiori. It's a Nova Scotia lobster terrine inspired by my first job in New York City, garde manger at Bouley in 2004, return from Chiang Mai.

IF YOU COULD EAT AT ANY RESTAURANT IN THE WORLD TONIGHT, IT WOULD BE: Degustation in 2007, when Chef Wes [Genovert] was still behind the stove.

CHEF WITH WHOM YOU'D MOST LIKE TO COLLABORATE: Massimo Bottura or Francis Mallman

PHOTO: MEGAN SWANN

NAVAJAS CRUDAS

Chef PJ Calapa of Ai Fiori | New York, NY
Adapted by StarChefs
Yield: 7 servings

INGREDIENTS

100 grams Spanish extra virgin
   olive oil
30 grams thinly sliced garlic
60 grams shallot, 50 grams thinly
   sliced and 10 grams brunoise
3 fresh bay leaves
30 grams thyme
250 grams Manila clams, rinsed and
   scrubbed
250 grams dry white wine
15 grams thinly sliced chives
15 grams lemon juice
100 grams fennel brunoise
100 grams Jamón Ibérico de Bellota
   brunoise
2 kilograms razor clams, cleaned and
   thinly sliced, shells reserved
Grated lemon zest
6 fennel fronds
Fleur de sel

METHOD

In a large sauté pan, heat half the olive oil and sweat garlic and shallot. Add bay leaves and thyme, followed by Manila clams spread in an even layer. Deglaze with wine and quickly cover. Steam clams until they just open, and then remove from pan. Strain cooking liquid and chill. Shuck clams and reserve shells. Chop clams and combine in a bowl with remaining olive oil, shallot brunoise, chives, lemon juice, fennel, Jamón Ibérico, razor clams, and 30 grams chilled cooking liquid from Manila clams. Plate mixture in cleaned razor clam shells. Garnish with lemon zest and fennel fronds. Finish with fleur de sel.

Featured Ingredients: Spanish olive oil, Fossil Farms Jamón Ibérico de Bellota

PHOTO: SHANNON STURGIS

Bob Truitt

Altamarea Group | New York, NY

Bob Truitt has made quite the journey since starting on his path to pastry in 2000. In his hometown of Philadelphia, after his first gig apprenticing for James Beard Award-winning Chef Guillermo Pernot at ¡Pasión!, Truitt joined Restaurateur Stephen Starr's Buddakan as assistant pastry chef, working with Chef Masaharu Morimoto on the opening of his stateside debut in Philadelphia. Truitt eventually went on to partner with friend and mentor Will Goldfarb in 2005 as chef de cuisine of his experimental Room 4 Dessert in New York. In 2007, Truitt made his way to Catalonia to stage at the legendary El Bulli. Under the mentorship of Albert Adrià, he learned how to look at ingredients and traditional techniques through a different lens.

Back in New York, Truitt's next move brought him to Chef Paul Liebrandt and his Tribeca restaurant Corton, where he won a StarChefs Rising Stars Award. Truitt complemented Liebrandt's modern French cuisine with whimsical, texturally engaging creations, including the Caramel Brioche, which was selected as one of *The New York Times* "Best New Restaurant Dishes of 2008." Corton received three stars from *The New York Times*, five stars from *Time Out New York*, and four stars from *New York Magazine* through the course of Truitt's tenure. Corton also was nominated for "Best New Restaurant" by the James Beard Foundation.

In 2010, Truitt was named executive pastry chef of The Altamarea Group, where he oversees pastry for the group's 12 outlets including Ai Fiori, Marea, Costata, and Ristorante Morini. In 2013, he was named one of *Food & Wine*'s "Best New Pastry Chefs."

🅞 🅥 **ALTAMAREAGROUP**

MOST INFLUENTIAL MENTOR WITH WHOM YOU'VE WORKED: Will Goldfarb—not only for his incredible creativity and mentoring me through my younger career, but also for his persistence and dedication. No matter how much got in his way, he was still able to open Room 4 Dessert, again, on the other side of the world.

COOLEST TECHNIQUE YOU'VE LEARNED FROM ANOTHER RESTAURANT: Balinese meringue from Will Goldfarb and vacuum form molding from Brian Sullivan at Food 360.

A DISH YOU MAKE THAT'S INSPIRED BY ANOTHER CHEF: Tart Vaucluse, inspired by the iconic chocolate dessert Louis XV by Alain Ducasse in Monaco

IF YOU COULD EAT AT ANY RESTAURANT IN THE WORLD TONIGHT, IT WOULD BE: La Teca in Oaxaca

FAVORITE INDUSTRY INSTAGRAM ACCOUNT: Antonio Bachour, @bachour1234, and Hija de Sanchez, @hijadesanchez

FAVORITE COOKBOOK: Diccionario Enciclopédico de la Gastronomía Mexicana by Ricardo Muñoz Zurita, a gift from my wife's parents

OLIVE OIL BONBONS

Pastry Chef Bob Truitt of Altamarea Group | New York, NY
Adapted by StarChefs
Yield: 145 bonbons

INGREDIENTS

Olive Oil Ganache:
900 grams Valrhona 35% Ivoire white chocolate, coarsely chopped
40 grams cocoa butter
390 grams whole milk
100 grams glucose syrup
4 grams salt
320 grams Arbequina extra virgin olive oil

Guanaja Shells:
Tempered cocoa butter
Tempered green-colored cocoa butter
2 kilograms Valrhona Guanaja 70% dark chocolate, tempered to 32°C

METHOD

Olive Oil Ganache:
In a double boiler, combine white chocolate and cocoa butter; melt. In a saucepan, bring milk, glucose, and salt to a boil. Pour milk mixture into chocolate mixture. Stir to combine. Remove from heat, cool to 40°C, add olive oil, and emulsify with an immersion blender. Cool to between 30°C and 32°C.

For the Guanaja Shells:
Using a toothbrush to create a splattering affect, decorate the interior of bonbon molds with cocoa butters. When the cocoa butter has crystallized, use a large ladle to fill molds with tempered chocolate. When filled, immediately invert molds and tap out excess chocolate, scraping as you go to clean out any extra chocolate. Stand mold on its side, rotating after 2 minutes to ensure even thickness. Scrape clean any excess, and let crystallize. Fill molds with Olive Oil Ganache. When ganache crystalizes, cap with tempered chocolate. Scrape clean, and let crystallize.

To Assemble and Serve:
Unmold and serve bonbons.

Featured Ingredient: Spanish Arbequina extra virgin olive oil, Valrhona chocolate

PHOTO: NOAH FECKS

Ken Oringer

Toro | New York, NY

As a kid, Ken Oringer knew he wanted to be a chef. He set about making that happen once he headed to Bryant College, where he earned a degree in hotel and restaurant management. He then went on to graduate from The Culinary Institute of America.

Oringer's first kitchen job was at Brooklyn's famed River Café, working with Chef David Burke. He then moved to the incubator of great chefs, Al Forno, in Providence, Rhode Island, where he befriended a Cambodian cook who gave him an insider's tour of the flavors of Southeast Asia. Oringer continued to learn how to adapt Asian ingredients at Jean-Georges Vongerichten's Le Marquis de Lafayette in Boston and as chef de cuisine at Silks at the Mandarin Oriental in San Francisco. After five years, and trips abroad to Singapore, Vietnam, Hong Kong, Spain, and Argentina, Oringer decided the time was right to open a restaurant.

In 1997, Oringer opened Clio in Boston to rave reviews. In 2001, he took home James Beard's "Best Chef, Northeast." He expanded Clio in 2002 to include Uni, a sashimi bar offering the freshest seafood. Next came Barcelona-style tapas bar Toro, the Mexican restaurant La Verdad, and KO Prime in Hotel Nine Zero. In 2009, Oringer and Chef Jamie Bissonette opened Coppa, an Italian style enoteca. In 2013, Oringer opened a New York-outpost of Toro, which earned two stars from *The New York Times*.

 **KENORINGER**

MOST INFLUENTIAL MENTOR WITH WHOM YOU'VE WORKED: Jean Georges. He thinks about food on a truly global platform and really understands nuances of different spices and flavors.

A DISH YOU MAKE THAT'S INSPIRED BY ANOTHER CULTURE: At Toro, the blowfish tails are inspired by blowfish served all over Japan (but not the poisonous variety!). Because I love street food, we treat them like chicken wings. They're coated with a heavy Moroccan spice blend, blackened on the plancha, and served with lemon. It's like a fish chicken wing.

IF YOU COULD EAT AT ANY RESTAURANT IN THE WORLD TONIGHT, IT WOULD BE: Sushi Seki in Tokyo. They're pure technique, and have a legendary touch with fish and rice. The best of the best.

FAVORITE INDUSTRY INSTAGRAM ACCOUNT: Ivan Ramen, @ramenjunkie

FAVORITE COOKBOOK: La Technique by Jacques Pépin

CHEF WITH WHOM YOU'D MOST LIKE TO COLLABORATE: Morimoto. He's so talented and so creative, not to mention right across the street from Toro!

RADISH Á LA PLANCHA, CUTTLEFISH, IBÉRICO XO, AND MOJAMA

Chefs Jamie Bissonnette and Ken Oringer of Toro | New York, NY
Adapted by StarChefs

PHOTO: MEGAN SWANN

INGREDIENTS

Ibérico XO: (Yield: 4 quarts)
2 quarts Ibérico ham trimmings, ground
3 cups finely diced ginger
3 cups finely diced garlic
10 dried Thai chiles
6 fresh Thai chiles
¾ cup Cognac
2 orange peels
3 ounces dried shrimp, pulverized
1 pound dried scallops, simmered in water
    until soft, shredded, cooking liquid reserved
1 gallon chicken stock
1 quart oyster sauce
Oil

To Assemble and Serve:
(Yield: 4 to 6 servings)
1 pound radishes, cut into bite-sized pieces
Salt
Black pepper
4 ounces cuttlefish, thinly sliced
2 tablespoons Spanish extra virgin olive oil
⅓ cup coarsely chopped Thai basil leaves
⅓ cup coarsely chopped mint leaves
⅓ cup coarsely chopped cilantro leaves
Fried garlic chips
6 ounces mojama (Spanish salt-cured tuna),
    thinly sliced
Fleur de sel

METHOD

For the Ibérico XO Sauce:
In a large sauté pan over medium heat, render fat from ham. With a slotted spoon, remove ham from heat and reserve. In the same pan, sweat ginger, garlic, and chiles until soft and aromatic. Deglaze with Cognac. Add orange peels, shrimp, and scallops; sauté. Add stock, oyster sauce, water reserved from scallops, and rendered ham. Bring to a boil and cook until liquid has reduced and solids are tender. Transfer to a storage container and top with enough oil to cover. Sauce should hold for 6 to 8 weeks.

To Assemble and Serve:
Prepare and heat plancha. Season radish with salt and pepper. Cook on plancha for 4 to 5 minutes, making sure to caramelize evenly on all sides. Transfer to a bowl and toss with cuttlefish, half the herbs, and ¼ cup Ibérico XO. Place into a serving bowl and garnish with fried garlic and remaining herbs. Finish with mojama and fleur de sel.

Featured Ingredients: Fermin Ibérico ham, Spanish olive oil

Jesse Schenker

The Gander | New York, NY

For Chef Jesse Schenker, childhood's major focus wasn't found in the toy store, school yard, or even in the deep recesses of his own fantastical imagination. His focus was on the kitchen. He requested menus from his parents' dinners out, and unlike other kids his age, Schenker collected cookbooks. His collection—like his culinary skills—has grown (to around 350 books).

Schenker's first food job was at McDonald's, but he then went on to stage at some of New York's most illustrious restaurants, including Le Bernardin, Per Se, and Jean Georges. Schenker went on to work at Gordon Ramsay at the London before finally opening the temple to his own gastronomical dreams, Recette in Manhattan's West Village.

With Recette, which opened in 2010 when the chef was just 27 years old, Schenker had a forum for his own unmitigated creativity. A contemporary urban restaurant, Recette is the kind of place where comfort meets attitude and indulgence meets sophistication. Just months after its opening, Recette received glowing two-star reviews from *The New York Times* and *New York Magazine*.

In 2014, Schenker opened The Gander in the Flatiron District, where he serves a menu of sophisticated, yet casual, American dishes complimented by a deep international wine list. Over the years, Schenker has received a number of awards and accolades, including a spot on *Forbes'* "30 Under 30" list and 2011 StarChefs Rising Stars Award. He also was victorious in his battle on Food Network's "Iron Chef America." Most recently, Schenker wrote his first book, <u>All or Nothing: One Chef's Appetite for the Extreme</u>, a memoir.

 JBSCHEF THEGANDERNYC

MOST INFLUENTIAL MENTOR WITH WHOM YOU'VE WORKED: Gordon Ramsay

A DISH YOU MAKE THAT'S INSPIRED BY ANOTHER CULTURE: The Gander's spaghetti and clams is inspired by the Italian classic, spaghette alle vongole. Our version is a refined take on the dish, using the lobster bisque as the sauce, three different varieties of clams, guanciale, and fennel marmalade.

IF YOU COULD EAT AT ANY RESTAURANT IN THE WORLD TONIGHT, IT WOULD BE: Tickets in Barcelona, Spain

FAVORITE COOKBOOK: My go-to is <u>Culinary Artistry</u> by Andrew Dornenburg.

CHEF WITH WHOM YOU'D MOST LIKE TO COLLABORATE: I'm learning every day from cooks and chefs all over the world. I would love to collaborate with so many people, but Chan Yan-tak would be great.

PHOTO: BILL MILNE

SPAGHETTI AND CLAMS

Chef Jesse Schenker of The Gander | New York, NY
Adapted by StarChefs
Yield: 4 servings

INGREDIENTS

2 cups clam juice, reduced by half
1 cup heavy cream
1 tablespoon olive oil
½ ounce finely chopped leek
½ finely chopped onion
1 clove finely chopped
20 littleneck clams
1½ cups dry white wine
1 ounce butter
2 fennel bulbs, diced small
2 cups dry vermouth
1 pinch fennel seed
1 pound spaghetti

METHOD

In a pan over medium flame, heat clam juice, add cream, and simmer for 10 to 15 minutes, until viscous. In a separate pan over high flame, heat oil, and add leek, onion, garlic, and clam. Add wine and cover. Cook for 8 minutes. Using a slotted spoon, remove leek, onion, garlic, and clams, setting aside in a bowl and reserving cooking liquid in another bowl. Add butter to same pan, followed by fennel, vermouth, and fennel seeds. Cook over low heat, stirring occasionally, until sticky, about 40 minutes. In a pot of salted, boiling water, cook pasta to al dente and drain. Add pasta to the pan, and return clams and cooking liquid to the pan. Toss and serve hot.

PHOTO: MEGAN SWANN

 RICHARD.PIETROMONACO 🐦 CHEFCASTER

MOST INFLUENTIAL MENTOR WITH WHOM YOU'VE WORKED: Larry Forgione. He was one of the first American chefs to develop and source products with local farmers in the early 80s.

COOLEST TECHNIQUE YOU'VE LEARNED FROM ANOTHER CHEF: How to open a beer bottle with a chef knife, during my CIA externship in 1984.

A DISH YOU MAKE THAT'S INSPIRED BY CULTURE: Spicy tuna taco with sriracha and wasabi cream—a cool blend of Asian and Mexican flavors, textures, and influences.

FAVORITE CHEF INSTAGRAM ACCOUNT: Jeff Schwarz, @c_h_e_f. He is also a chef yogi.

FAVORITE COOKBOOK: Going old school here. The Joy of Cooking is still the best culinary reference recipe book.

CHEF WITH WHOM YOU'D MOST LIKE TO COLLABORATE: Andrew Chase of Café Katja NYC. He cooks Bavarian food like no other, and you can still find him behind the stove each night!

Rich Pietromonaco

Houston Hall | New York, NY

A New York City native, Richard Pietromonaco has been surrounded by food his entire life. Growing up on the east coast gave him the opportunity to scoop up softshell crabs from the docks in Staten Island, reel in striped bass from the Jersey shore, shuck Wellfleet oysters fresh from Cape Cod, and catch flounder off Long Island. Pietromonaco's father was an avid gardener, giving his son the opportunity to harvest fruits and vegetables from his backyard.

As a teenager Pietromonaco started working in a fine Italian Restaurant, and began to realize that he wanted to pursue cooking as a career. He enrolled at the Culinary Institute of America and graduated in 1985. Since then, Pietromonaco has worked for iconic American chefs such as Larry Forgione of An American Place and Bradley Ogden of Campton Place. In 1989, Pietromonaco was hired to be the corporate chef for Sfuzzi, Inc., which has 20 outposts of Italian-inspired restaurants throughout the United States. In 1995, Pietromonaco was hired to serve as chef de cuisine at Drew Nieporent's acclaimed Tribeca Grill.

He joined Heartland Brewery Inc. in 1997 as corporate chef and partner and has been with the company ever since, playing a vital role in building 12 restaurants around Manhattan, including Houston Hall. He travels extensively and summers in Montauk, where he stills fishes for flounder.

GIANT BAVARIAN PRETZELS WITH ALE-CHEESE SAUCE

Chef Richard Pietromonaco of Heartland Brewery Inc. | New York, NY
Adapted by StarChefs
Yield: 128 dips of giant pretzel pieces (or 2 quarts)

INGREDIENTS

3 ounces butter
2 ounces finely chopped shallot
1 ounce finely chopped garlic
3 ounces all-purpose flour
One 12-ounce bottle ale, reduced by half
1 quart heavy cream
4 ounces cream cheese
6 ounces grated yellow cheddar
4 ounces grated aged cheddar
4 ounces grated Parmesan
¼ ounce cayenne
Salt
Black pepper
Giant Bavarian pretzels, warmed

METHOD

In a pan over low heat, melt butter and sweat shallots and garlic. Add flour, stirring often with a wooden spoon, until flour is golden brown, about 10 minutes. Stir in ale reduction followed by heavy cream. While stirring vigorously with a whisk, slowly add all cheeses. When thoroughly combined, season with cayenne, salt, and pepper. Pour cheese sauce into a ramekin and serve with pretzel.

PHOTO: MEGAN SWANN

PHOTO: DORON GILD

Claire Bertin-Lang
CBL Consulting | New York, NY

Claire Bertin-Lang has nearly a decade's worth of experience buttressing her as director of Mix@ICC. A native New Yorker, she began tending bar at one of New York's classic dives at just 19 years of age. After graduating from Georgetown University, Bertin-Lang worked both on the brand side and for consultants, executing major projects, beverage programs, and trade and consumer events. Bertin-Lang started her own event consulting company, CBL Liquid Consulting, in 2011. Recent projects include Eat Drink SF, Road Soda, the Tales of the Cocktail Spirited Awards, and *Wine Enthusiast*'s Red & White Bash. This is Bertin-Lang's fourth ICC.

PHOTO: SHANNON STURGIS

Phil Bey
The Blue Point | Duck, NC

Phil Bey began his career in Delaware at 15. But it was while attending Johnson & Wales University in Charleston, South Carolina, that he fell in love with the foodways and heritage of the South. Bey spent the next seven years in the city, cooking in many of its fine-dining restaurants. He expanded his culinary horizons at Todd Jurich's Bistro in Norfolk and later as sous chef at Anne Quatrano's Baccanalia in Atlanta. Bey then brought his passion to the Big Island of Hawaii, where he consulted for Holuakoa Café and Garden. Bey moved back across the country to join the team at The Blue Point on the Outer Banks of North Carolina. This is his seventh year running the ICC Main Stage Kitchen.

Adrien Henriet
StarChefs | Brooklyn, NY

Medicine was *the* profession in Adrien Henriet's family, but cuisine was the passion. (He was practically force-fed rosette saucisson as a child.) Growing up in Bretagne, France, Henriet watched his family navigate the kitchen and French markets with nimbleness and intuition. That he fell into food was inevitable—but only after earning degrees from La Sorbonne in law and philosophy and a master's in public affairs from Sciences Po Paris, for good measure.

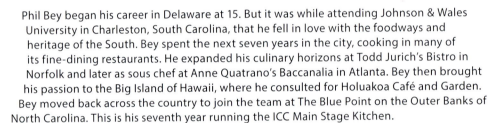

PHOTO: ALIZA ELIAZAROV

As a student, Henriet was a marketing intern for Petrossian Caviar, a stepping stone that took him to Brooklyn and an internship at StarChefs, for whom he's gone on to plan the 2015 New York Rising Stars Gala and the Valrhona C³ Pastry Competition at the 10th Annual International Chefs Congress. Henriet spends evenings working in the kitchens of Pearl & Ash and Rebelle.

PHOTO: LINDSEY CACIOPPO

Sara Moll
Vin Social | Brooklyn, NY

Sara Moll, a Certified Sommelier through the Court of Master Sommeliers, is events director for Xavier Wine Co., a boutique wine shop and cellar in Manhattan's Meatpacking District with a focus on sustainable, organic, and biodynamic producers. She is also founder of Vin Social, the mission of which is to make wine accessible through highly curated events. Moll is an advocate for honest, sustainably produced wines made by passionate, authentic people, and she thrives on enhancing her guest's appreciation for the world of wine and the hard-working people who put it in the bottle. As wine director of ICC, Moll helps curate wines for the annual congress, including the Somm Slam and wine workshops.

PHOTO: DARREN SAMUELSON

Susanna Ok
The Battery | San Francisco, CA

Susanna Ok was born and raised in Hawaii, and received a dual bachelors degree in psychology and Hispanic gender studies from Kenyon College in Ohio. Upon graduation, Ok joined the Peace Corps and was sent to Nicaragua, where she was assigned to a two-and-a-half-year tenure in the Sustainable Agriculture and Food Security program, and developed a comprehensive bilingual manual detailing the practices of sustainable food security in rural communities. Currently residing in San Francisco, Ok works for the private events department at The Battery. Before relocating to San Francisco, she was chef de cuisine of Downtown@theHiSAM on Oahu, one of Hawaii's leading sustainable restaurant and catering programs. OK returns to ICC (and its special back-of-house madness) as Catering Kitchen Manager.

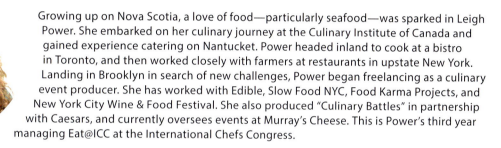

PHOTO: MEGAN SWANN

Leigh Michelle Power
Murray's Cheese | New York, NY

Growing up on Nova Scotia, a love of food—particularly seafood—was sparked in Leigh Power. She embarked on her culinary journey at the Culinary Institute of Canada and gained experience catering on Nantucket. Power headed inland to cook at a bistro in Toronto, and then worked closely with farmers at restaurants in upstate New York. Landing in Brooklyn in search of new challenges, Power began freelancing as a culinary event producer. She has worked with Edible, Slow Food NYC, Food Karma Projects, and New York City Wine & Food Festival. She also produced "Culinary Battles" in partnership with Caesars, and currently oversees events at Murray's Cheese. This is Power's third year managing Eat@ICC at the International Chefs Congress.

Paul Repetti
David Ellis Events | Cedar Knolls, NJ

A fourth generation chef with more than 20 years of experience, Paul Repetti started out as a dishwasher and prep cook in his father's restaurants. His creative vision evolved while staying at a small vineyard in Champagne, France, where he absorbed the connection between land, food, farmers, and restaurants. Back stateside in the late 1990s, after working in a series of farm-to-table restaurants, Repetti worked for some of the largest hotels and resorts in the Northeast. Now, he's seven years in as a chef with New Jersey-based David Ellis Events. Along with his wife, Repetti owns a farm and heirloom orchard, producing vegetables, herbs, and maple syrup; raising heritage chickens; and keeping honeybees. He's a member of Slow Food USA, The Livestock Conservancy, and the Northeast Organic Farming Association of New Jersey. Repetti joins StarChefs as ICC's executive chef.

PHOTO: MEGAN SWANN

PHOTO: AMELIA + DAN PHOTOGRAPHY

Jessica Wurst
New York, NY

Jessica Wurst attended the University of Arkansas and has forged her career as an events producer in New York City. From 2012 to 2014, she worked as an events specialist for Bamboo London in Brooklyn, a creative strategy agency for the beverage industry. Since 2014, Wurst has struck out on her own, producing specialty food and cocktail events. Her projects have included work with the Manhattan Cocktail Classic, the New York City Wine & Food Festival, and the Chivas Masters Competition. Since 2013, Wurst has coordinated the evening events at the StarChefs International Chefs Congress, seamlessly ensuring memorable experiences for all attendees and presenters.

INDEX

INDEX

RENE OZORIO
WABI SABI

A concept, an aesthetic &
a world view. Simply, an intuitive way
of living that emphasizes finding
beauty in imperfection.

rustic yet sophisticated